T0208201

THE ART OF PERCEPTION

A Formidable Guide to
Understanding Yourself and Others

JARROD WILSON

THE ART OF PERCEPTION
A FORMIDABLE GUIDE TO UNDERSTANDING YOURSELF AND OTHER

iUniverse books may be ordered through booksellers or by contacting:

iUniverse
1663 Liberty Drive
Bloomington, IN 47403
www.iuniverse.com
1-800-Authors (1-800-288-4677)

ISBN: 978-1-5320-9250-3 (sc)
ISBN: 978-1-5320-9251-0 (e)

Library of Congress Control Number: 2020906178

Print information available on the last page.

iUniverse rev. date: 03/31/2020

CONTENTS

INTRODUCTION

There's something truly magnificent and fascinating about being a human being. We all have our own unique outlook of everything around us. The power of perception is so significant it motivated me to write a book emphasizing the influence it has in many instances. Your life can be changed by simply shifting the perception of your life. It's not always easy. It can be tough. Like weight lifting, we can gain more and more power through consistency. When you open your mind to possibility, you'll see the many ways your mind can direct you to prosperity.

This isn't a book that's going to mislead you on how to attain wealth, peace, or happiness; it is a book with genuine hopes of depicting what it all truly means. Some concepts we've grown to accept have created illusions that separate us from the authentic self, which explains why many people feel out of touch within, discouraged, depressed, etc. This is a book that is guaranteed to increase your level of awareness, resulting in a better, more consistent, positive flow of thoughts to help guide you in getting in touch with the true you.

The introduction of this book has been purposely

extended so that there is critical information available as soon as you start reading. I encourage you to read the introduction as well as other chapters consistently. This will make a difference in your life that you will see.

The only difference in our consistent or inconsistent attitudes on a day to day basis is our state of mind. By retaining this information consistently, you'll begin to keep the right thoughts in mind unconsciously. This will create more peace in your life, peace with yourself, peace with your circumstances, and peace with any challenges you may face.

Most of us understand what perception is and how it differs from person to person, but do we really? The consistent fear, anger, depression, conflicts, dysfunction, miscommunications, and misconceptions that the human race fails to overcome says otherwise. If we truly understood, the way we handle our emotions and others would be a lot different.

Our approach to life is all under the basis of our awareness and understanding of it. The more we seek ways to create, express, and find peace, the more we can inspire others to do the same. To imbue mankind with sincerity, boldness, sensible, and even flawed ways of thinking will hopefully help alter the approach to our misjudgments that usually cause conflict.

We must learn to rediscover ourselves and the things we were initially programmed to see. That consistent programming starting from birth is what makes us inevitably become swayed by our subjective attitudes. It's a gift and a curse. We want to use this as the gift it was meant for. If you take heed to some of these examples throughout this book, you will have enough awareness to think twice about the way you choose to see situations. It makes the difference in everything we do or believe, which can be life-changing.

These new neuron connections gained from reading will give you the same paradigm-altering, psychological influences I used to create this very book. Through repetition, I begin to realize the control I had as a conscious being. Now, in times where I may have impulsively reacted with constant fear, embarrassment, anger, or even addictively, I've managed to change the way I see.

You have the power to see your way to calmness, acceptance, success, courage, happiness, and many other things. We don't entertain these thoughts as much as we do the bad. We've misconceived where the real source of our reality stems. It is in our ways of thinking and the things we give attention to.

If there may be an error somewhere in the way we have programmed ourselves to think, it can happen without us consciously noticing sometimes. To change this, we must focus on how we feel and the way we see, interchanging vastly until we find the perception that brings us peacefulness. Focus on that feeling, let it uplift you, believe in it. Trust me; this isn't easy. For example, when you're mad (or in any emotional state), it seems impossible to control how you feel, but every time you attempt that simple step, your brain begins to change.

If you want to learn the skill of managing your emotions and state of mind, then this is the book for you. Throughout my entire life, I never had this particular skill. Now I marvel at the beauty in all the time I've spent forming this mentality. I've been writing this book on and off for about four years. A year before I even knew I wanted to write a book, I had a burning desire to learn about the mind and emotions.

There I was, standing in the middle of my room, my eyes would begin to water, I felt like punching the wall, I could've used that energy and did something I'd regret, then I made the best decision of my life. I don't know what was different about the pain I experienced that day compared to any other time throughout my life, but it may have just been a breaking point. I was tired of suffering emotionally. It's not to say I was always emotional, depressed, or had the worst upbringing. Many people have been through a lot more than me. Generally speaking, life has its ups and downs that we all experience. It was as if yea, life was kicking me while I was already down, but what about my faults and lack of awareness that put me in those situations? The feeling I had at that moment made me never want to be controlled by anyone or anything emotionally ever again.

You obviously can't escape feelings and emotions, but if I learned a lot about them, I could become skilled enough to direct this energy to my advantage. Looking back at that moment now I didn't know exactly what it was that I was in search of, but it always felt like then and even now something was guiding me in ways beyond my ability to articulate. The life-changing thing I did at that moment which is key here is I gave myself direction. This was something I had never truly done before, which is why I was always felt out of tune with the universe. So at that moment I went and read. I would learn so much over this time. It was like the desire increased my production to where I read book after book. I watched video after video. I created a website. I made connections to things from different authors and subjects, which eventually became the inspiration behind my idea to write. I started to realize how everything is connected.

I had sensed a link to what many speakers, authors, pastors, and even scientists were essentially expressing spiritually and objectively. I had sensed something consistent about the repeated destruction throughout history. One day it hit me as I was in bed, PERCEPTION. That is where it all starts. It made me realize I was still learning new things and growing every day, and that is what was creating different reactions from me. With each new day, new information, and my thoughts, I may have felt great and others not so great, but why? It felt as if it was the outer world doing things to me until I looked at it differently and realized it was me. Little did I know I was actually already strengthening my consciousness in ways that would change my life. I know this information is valuable and methods work because I've done it to myself.

My goal now is to help you discover the real power of yourself and begin to direct your life in a different direction as the driver, not someone just in the backseat. When I say driver, I don't mean that everything will always go your way, and this doesn't necessarily mean my life is perfect or that I've achieved the materials or mastery of what this universe provides. Life will always provide us with challenges. For that reason, we never quite master life. So how do we cope with or fight these endless challenges in life? Interestingly, we can master our perceptions, even if we may initially react too quickly.

It is the conscious effort you put into establishing a different way of thinking that will overcome any adversities life may throw at you. It would be unrealistic to think it is possible to be positive 24/7. The pain we endure is sometimes needed to transition into the person you've always wanted to be. Yet, when we attempt to master perception, we must realize how peace and positivity are a result of how we see situations, even adverse circumstances. So it is you that is always in control.

The most important thing to realize is that the perceptions that create motivation, peacefulness inspiration, courage, and gratification all create actions reflecting that state of mind. To cleverly and reasonably form more uplifting speculations of life's challenges while consciously understanding the feelings that come as a result of each reflection is masterful. Not only will you begin to use this to your advantage, but you will be unconsciously training your stress response to simmer down. You will learn the methods necessary for real success and happiness.

I've unlocked the key to the source of what makes us feel as if materials and mastery are everything, or even attainable. The perfect life would be idealistic, but too robust since life is full of endless growth. It's easy to symbolically attach the ideal experience to the money, fame, traveling, love, etc. Truth is there is always something testing our emotions in some way amid any success or failures throughout life. So this particular subject goes beyond even what you may ideally perceive as success. What matters in life is how we feel and perception is a direct reflection of that at any given moment. If you don't do anything else, take note of how to skillfully transcend your conclusions to ones that always make you productive and peaceful. We all have different things that motivate us, stimulate us, or even make us angry. Understand these feelings and think about them cleverly when needed to fuel you, remember it is all energy. This is something personal, a battle with yourself. A battle that you can win. If practiced by enough people, it can change our whole perception of one another.

It is the awareness of the synchronicities life provides no matter your circumstances that depict what I mean by power and direction. It is the way we maneuver through life in a way that is of a higher stature mentally that does wonders for your soul. I would argue that it is our perceptions of certain things that cause our suffering, and even our bliss, rich or poor. When I speak of power, expand from what you may symbolically or typically align your perceptions with. The real power is all in our mind and how we've become conditioned to value certain things over others.

What means everything to one person might not hold the same value to someone else. What man sees based on his perception of its value doesn't solidify its fate. Depending on his goals, ignorance, situation, and understanding will determine the things he wisely values and the things he neglects, only to potentially wish he hadn't. We all can get caught up losing sight of things we should value. We may become so comfortable we forget some people would do anything to have what we have. No matter if it is a job, house, clothes, a spouse, food, privilege, money, etc. Taking time to value things is essential. We may naturally get so caught up chasing and wanting more we never become content with anything. This means we're never truly happy.

I theorize the nature of wanting more is associated with the thrill and stimulation we get from new experiences. It makes us have to think, it can be exciting and can make us feel a bit uncomfortable depending on your attitude toward life. When things have been experienced over and over again, it sinks to a deeper part of our brain that allows us to think of other things we may want. This is a process that allows your brain to operate more efficiently but also is the source of your consciousness. This means the information you program to a deeper part of your brain will define who you are and how you perceive life mostly without your realization. These particular instinctive attitudes are extremely hard to override but with consistency, you can literally train yourself to operate based on different principles.

The important thing to do in life is to apply the principles and perceptions needed in order to create the feelings necessary to act in alignment with what you want. That is the beginning of it becoming a physical manifestation. Our ability to reflect is what separates man from animals. Man has yet to truly understand the power he possesses with consciousness because he fails to understand that there's something more powerful that goes beyond it. Our values at times can become backed by some view of life associated with the moment because when the circumstances change, our values can easily change with it.

You may never find a billionaire with his/her last words gasp for air to say anything about money. They may provide some valuable information, or they more than likely would have a wish for a desirable moment with another human being. They may end up expressing feelings they should've shown a long time ago at that moment.

After writing this book and spending years studying all of this information, I've realized how important it is to know how and when to tune into the moment. It becomes useful in critical situations. For example, it is generally known that many people overthink. When we stop overthinking by learning the concept of what I call "mind bait," we can analyze everything for what it is at that moment.

I created this name to describe how our thoughts are doing something similar to what we do to catch fish. The fishermen want the fish to believe the particular food is real. This is comparable to how your mind wants you to think specific thoughts are real. Your brain wants you to entertain it in some way (potentially negatively) by throwing random thoughts in your head to hook you in. It happens in a flash. It's quite amazing how quickly and efficiently our minds can construct imaginative short films in less than a second. If you fall for the bait, you become the victim, unfortunately. The skill comes in overtime with patience, desire, consistent studying, mental effort, and, most importantly, experience.

It starts when you begin to catch yourself thinking negatively at a quicker time than you usually would. Remember, it doesn't take long to sink into an emotion resulting in anxiety, fear, depression, anger, etc. Not only that, the more you entertain those thoughts, the more powerful, dominant, and controlling they become. So at that moment, it becomes a game of bait. Most fish give in to the bait, some know better, but still risk nibbling around it, and some are "aware" enough to avoid it.

Building upon this skill will lead to you having an ability to immediately counter any beliefs you don't want interfering with your peace, or in the fishes case its life. The ability to tune into the moment is simply learning how to feel good. This doesn't mean you don't allow yourself to feel bad. Even in those cases, you'll begin using those feelings to your conscious advantage. I'll talk more about directing energy later on in the book. It can be the start of a new life for you when you've gained a higher level of awareness. This is because you make your best decisions when you're feeling good, so work on making this consistent, and you will see change.

It shows the power of gratitude. It's essential to have this because as much as we think about the past and future, the real control lies within your very next breath. The things you do and say right now quickly become a thing of the past. Right before our eyes, we create memories and circumstances we'll later look back on and appreciate or regret even more. Yet, the only thing that matters despite those things is what you do next.

The information and opportunities available to us is something we use to help us make rational decisions. The fact that many of our imaginary thoughts feel so real can confuse our observations of the world, and even ourselves. This is why I feel inspired to use this information to live mentally predominate and efficiently. Some may get the sense of me having a desire to change the world rooted in idealism, and you'd be right in some aspects, but concerning realism, neither seem to be possible without the other. This realization increased as I took heed to my spirituality as well as the conceptual scientific understandings of life objectively. It ultimately brought me to my own conclusions of the bigger picture of it all.

When I metaphorically used the driver/backseat analogy earlier, it was a representation of the things we lack awareness of. For so many years, I was in the backseat. I read tons of books and watched tons of videos trying to understand how to tap into my mind. I studied subjects about affirmations, the law of attraction, neuroplasticity, the subconscious mind, energy, vibrations, frequencies, spirituality, etc. While this did play a part in me ultimately reprogramming myself, I did it all looking for a never-ending answer that was always left up to my subjective interpretation. In other words, the answer was always within me.

The process involved with me becoming the person

I am today was through pain, which created a forceful desire that still drives me today. The method of learning is a beautiful thing and shouldn't be instinctively causing feelings of failure. Embrace the process of how you change or become great in life. It was through experience and consistent research that often was repetitive that made it over time, become a part of me genuinely. No certification, awards, or diplomas came out of this. It was an authentic desire and personal experience. It made me ponder on what exactly makes me qualified enough to elaborate on this subject. While there are many books and tons of information out there to learn continually, it isn't about knowing it all, but what you've come to realize.

I'll always look to learn more. The fact that knowledge is endless makes it critical to understand some grounded principles in life. This means no matter what you may learn, there's always some connection to those powerful principles. The beauty is in connection with the many different ways people show the essence of all of our abilities. It made me realize it goes beyond what a diploma can show. This isn't to take away from the self-discipline and effort it takes to attain a degree. It's to help you see the skills in others and how everyone is valuable in some way. I'll get more in detail with the symbolic things that make us appear intellectual and ignorant later on in the book. It's essential to grasp the understanding of how to distinguish and analyze people in a way beyond through materials, awards and diplomas. As I look back on my own life, I learned why this is so vital.

I remember taking a psychology course in college. It

was pretty straightforward material. The concepts weren't complicated. I ended up making an A in this course despite paying more attention to women and my phone during the lectures. I'd show up only half the time and almost couldn't take my final because I missed a class which she gave specific instructions and location. After making up an excuse, my considerate psychology teacher gave me another opportunity to take it. I remember sitting outside the building ten minutes before it was time to go in. In my hand, I had a study guide that I had looked at for the first time at that moment. My eyes quickly shifted on each page. I'd mumble answers in my head repetitively. It was like speed studying. I would eventually go in and do well on the test. I had done this before in other classes, and it worked. While this may seem like a brag, it isn't, and this is why. I never remembered that material afterward. I had made an A in a course that didn't leave me with an ability to help others or even myself potentially. It wasn't the teacher's fault. It was mine. Where did my intentions lie? It was in passing the class because that's what I needed for a diploma that made potential employers feel like I was qualified. Despite obviously needing something symbolic to help evaluate peoples ability to provide certain services, it creates flawed outlooks and potentially vile or egotistical intentions.

It wasn't until I created a real passion for it that the material stuck with me. It made me realize we may rely too heavily on these things to determine someone's worth, not taking into account their experiences and personal passions. In most cases, people are attempting to look appealing, knowledgeable, and qualified in whatever ways that are aligned with the cues associated with intelligence. Even if we achieve it in an inauthentic way, it is powerful because it is needed to change most people's perception generally.

So while I can elaborate on the college courses, the classes on Harvard's edX site I've taken, the amount of people I've helped through the app I created, or the lectures I've given, it doesn't give you the right insight needed to understand the real me. I'm simply saying you should allow people to show you who they are before judging. Learn how to feel and make sense of people's energy they give to you. As you continue to read, you'll start to realize how the more skillful you become at your analyzations, the better you feel and handle life.

Figuratively speaking, if I entertained the thought of corrupt governments, wars, murders, taxes, debt, and any other evildoings, then surely I'd feel like I was in hell. If I focused on the beautiful scenery, the beautiful people, and the sensation of just taking a deep breath, I'd be sure to feel like I was in heaven. Being able to think positively and be happy is a learned skill. Many people are way more negative than positive, so it makes them hateful to others, and even themselves. Then you have those people who are always positive, but it's just the way they naturally think.

We don't always choose to see life from the right perspectives. Imagine if we gained enough awareness to instinctively stop ourselves in time to channel those negative thoughts into positive energy. If I tell myself I can't do something, there will be a feeling that leads to discouragement. If I tell myself I can, there will be a feeling of certainty and energy that creates the likelihood of me accomplishing whatever I want. Master your mind, and you will master your emotions that are always a reflection of what we first think.

If you were to take a minute to ponder about feelings and the cause of them for a moment, you'd see how possible it can be to direct them. Anything that you've ever gotten mad, sad, happy, disappointed, or fearful about is a direct reflection of your thoughts and perception of the situation. Even in dangerous, intimidating, or uncomfortable situations, the calmer you are, the better. Typically fight or flight kicks in which causes you to become extremely instinctive; it can be hard to fault people for their reactions in this mental state. After all, sometimes the action is warranted.

In a lot of cases, it was a scenario created in your head that you reacted to. Or it could be a cue picked up by your subconscious mind sensing danger from previous experiences that could date back thousands of years. Your ancestors may have picked up certain instinctive behaviors needed to survive during that time. It makes me realize how humans are still to this day, consciously trying to understand themselves. Overcoming embedded behaviors is difficult, but only when we aren't attempting to construct and empower different brain neurons to counter the ones that are already naturally strong.

Remember that you can change the physical makeup of your brain when you change your thoughts. There are things about you that you may blame on genetics, but it may be more critical to focus on the genes you have activated. Your thoughts may not be able to change your genes, but they can activate certain ones and neglect others. For example, you could still pass on a family gene to your kids even if you didn't end up with lousy eyesight, although it runs in your family.

When you think of genes, you may strictly perceive the physical aspect of it. You know genes are a result of things like similar face structure, eyes, hair, height, etc. Rarely do we think of genes and how they're actively playing roles in our everyday life. We have 20,000 genes, and most of the activity from them is in our brain. It influences our behavior, emotions, and actions in different ways. It's what makes us unique individuals.

Genes are an extension of DNA; they are used for making protein as well as regulating amounts distributed throughout the body. Our body needs proteins to produce hair, nails, eye color, etc. Protein is what also helps our muscles, enzymes, neurons, and many other bodily chemicals operate efficiently and can fight potential threats to the body.

Your body copies coding from your DNA with genes. The particular coding it uses from the nucleotides determines the type of gene expression. Sometimes our body operates dysfunctionally, which can result in sicknesses or mental illnesses if we produce too much or too little protein in certain areas in the body. It can create life-changing results because your body has the code to produce things that can cure you as well. This is why, periodically, you may hear about miracle recovery stories.

Genes must be activated to produce protein. This is why epigenetics has become a fascinating subject. We may be wired to act specific ways from birth, but it can be changed. So you do not have to stay the same. Life and experiences may change you in ways, but you can consciously do this yourself. It's important to note how your environment plays a big role in what influences specific genes to be activated. This explains why animals overtime can adapt and withstand things that may have killed them in the past.

There have even been studies conducted with mice that are shown cues that make them triggered or fearful. These traits were passed down to their offspring without the baby mice experiencing this firsthand. The fear of this particular cue was already embedded in them. It is all amazing to think we can potentially tap into these codings to do great things. This is what it takes to overcome generational curses and trauma that creates the same approach by us. We don't have all the answers, but taking control of your thinking and environment will have drastic impacts on your reality and body. Realize what is at stake with every thought you have and how it is creating you.

Anxiety can be a typical result of not knowing how to deal with your thoughts. Statistically, it's said to affect about 40 million Americans. It gets even more profound when we analyze the experiences that may have caused schizophrenia in many people. Mental health is real, and becoming aware of how our brain naturally operates is critical. It should amaze you that anything you want in life is yours if you gain the right perception of how to get it. Life is meant for us to embrace our imagination and manifest anything we'd like. With a lack of awareness, we quickly may become the victim of our thoughts. This can impact our self-esteem or confidence in ways that keep us from being an elevated version of ourselves.

You'd be surprised how many people hold back on doing what makes them happy for the sake of no criticism. The feeling of being out of place among peers or at odds with people is discomforting. As a result, we can subconsciously conform to many aspects of life. This can be detrimental to us in many ways. It reminds me of the famous quote by Malcolm X, "If you have no critics, you'll likely have no success." This isn't strictly limited to the typical idea of success. There is a possibility of success spiritually, and mentally as well.

The avoidance of criticism can make you hold back from being your authentic self. You could be waking up and doing the same things as everyone else and never questioning why. You just know everyone else does it. It's the American way. Many popular beliefs (while not always logical) firmly hold a general outlook by many people without much critical analysis. Why? It is assumed because of the ratio of opinion matched with the traditionalized consensus that one is correct and the other isn't. The average person likely doesn't want to be that one person that makes things complicated, so they follow suit. Those people who you wouldn't consider the average person (in terms of their flaunted conclusions) may be more bold with their opinions or have gained a habit of always being that one person who disagrees. In both cases, their approach to the situation is backed by a more in-depth reference of one's thoughts and perceptions.

To an extent, we all have to discipline ourselves even at times when we don't want to. It reminds me of the workforce and how your boss has a boss and so on. The point is to come to your right senses about everything, even the things that tamper with the ego. Even the things that make you uncomfortable. It's amazing to become so in tune with the universe that you find comfort in the unknown. As much as we enjoy being comfortable it won't last. Life at some point will creatively bring some sort of test our way that can easily cause frustration, fear, or anxiety. Life pushed me to do something inspirational that used to make me uncomfortable until it overpowered my fears, worries, or doubts. Look at these times as an opportunity to test your ability and the universes laws. They work in your favor according to how you decide to see. The interesting thing about perception is that even attempting to "blend in" in a sense can bring criticism. So you might as well express your natural aura.

It seems like many of us entertain the thoughts that keep us from reaching our potential, or don't think enough for ourselves. Be confident, value your opinions, and never be afraid to express who you are. Instead of allowing your thoughts to control your feelings, begin taking conscious control, and directing your thoughts to how you desire to feel. Never be afraid to be different. This is the gift you have as a unique individual on this earth.

Stray away from people who discourage you from

growing and being yourself. We must seek people who bring the best out of us. Hanging with positive or negative people can have a drastic impact on our lifestyle and the things we accomplish over time. If you discuss your dreams with someone and they debunk them as if they're not reachable with that "come back to reality" mindset, it's like saying come back to the programming that keeps you at the same vibration leading to no results.

Don't worry about what others may say about you, nobody else has to understand it, because no matter how vividly or fluently you may portray your experiences, people still can't see it precisely from your point of view. We all don't experience life the same way, although there are relatable childhood memories we can all recall.

There are billions of people in the world, but you'll never find a matching fingerprint like yours. You'll never find somebody who has experienced life quite as you have. The only person that's always around you is you. I'm assuming you, too, feel as if no human could ever truly, understand you. There would be too many indescribable feelings and moments to illustrate. Take this into consideration towards everyone else as well.

If we all could show a movie depicting our life thus far, I'm sure it would be very intriguing. More importantly, the viewers would undoubtedly understand you a lot more. Everything you've been through gives you a good reason to act the way that you do. We all don't have a camera around 24/7 to show others our life, (which is probably a good thing), but we do have forms of expressions that can still create a thought-provoking connection.

There's exquisiteness in everything that forms your perception of the world, and you should embrace that. We must align ourselves with our imagination and the things we love to do long enough to see it begin to form in our reality because it is already there. It can be a little uneasy at first, but staying in our comfort zone isn't always a good thing. It can hold you back if you allow it. What are some things you love to do that make you feel blissful? Express it to the world! There are ways to express what we've all been through. That's where writing comes in for me.

Expression of self is something done in a variety of forms from dancing, music, drawings, groups, spirituality, ideas, sports, education, and many other ways. Expressions and ideas all stimulate for different reasons and intentions. The concept of the periodic table, capitalism, racism, religion, science, evolution, space, and whatever else you can think of are all expressions based on studies, speculations, theories, events, and, of course, perceptions. It's to make sense of the world. Someone brainstormed and concluded of this in their head before we witnessed it becoming a reality or an indirect expression.

Even when there were flaws in particular concepts, the belief in them is all that matters. It's the repetition and art of suggestion that paints an inevitable reality for the perceiver. Once it's firmly accepted, it becomes hard for them to see the world any differently, which only illustrates the power in the way we choose to see.

We all can see a tree, people, or a building and see the same thing objectively, but it gets more profound than that. What is our perception of these things that makes them good or bad? A rainstorm can be a blessing for a town that's been in a drought and a nightmare for a family caught at sea. A tree provides oxygen, but people cut down entire forests for something they perceive as more valuable like paper.

The tragic occurrence on September 11th could have left many with an embedded perceptual fear of buildings, planes, or heights. Beyond the vague and shallow ends of logical assessments, deeper, at the core, we find the empirical propositions that create a beautiful, consequential, inconsistent, imbalance in the ways we choose to see. That's why art and poetry are so fascinating, so deep, and appreciated. It's because of the distinctive view and expression of another human being.

A picture of art has so much meaning and vision all in one drawing. Poetry can describe someone's view and experience of life so exclusive that it becomes well respected. At the same time, we can relate. It goes way deeper when we add our imagination, experiences, feelings, matchless personalities, culture, and energy into the equation. There's this connection to everything from multiple ways, known and unknown, but always in existence. There are laws that this universe operates around. If everything is vibrating, then the things we may manifest are intertwined with the way we see, since the way we feel or vibrate is a result of how we think.

Perspective is everything. Perspective is why you can go to google to search anything you'd like, only to find someone agreeing or objecting. It doesn't matter how many facts are presented in any debate, music, or book; someone will always be around exaggerating its insignificance. They may have had this attitude towards any premise or theory they were about to encounter before they even gave it a chance.

Find someone you think is attractive, and it won't take long before you find someone who finds no interest in them at all. They'll have a hard time seeing what you see in them. Knowing this only illustrates how important being yourself is. The more you embrace who you are, the happier you are. That is because we are vibrating higher when we are doing the things we love to do. This doesn't mean you should ignore constructive criticism or think the nature of humans would ever love to do downright vile things. That'll never be ok. If you aren't harming yourself, the world, or other people, by all means, create and express. Not everyone will be acceptant of who you are or what you do, simply because of their idea of what is most important or meaningful in life. These can be things driven by ego or symbolically associated with manhood or womanhood.

Success and happiness are no longer a measure of society's materialistic and flawed principles. It is only from the fulfilling sensation of whatever it is that makes you feel content and free. When you observe people who are always playing their favorite sport, working out, in the studio, or writing, etc. They feel free whenever they are participating in these activities. They've become drawn more and more to it like a drug in a sense because it takes their mind off of any problems they may have. Many would argue living your dream isn't always easy. Often it involves more work and dedication. It made me realize not to become too consumed in your talents. Create when you feel like it. You're not in any rush or competition with anyone. Balance your life and make time to just enjoy it. I'm more than just a writer, and many times I've taken time away.

The feeling goes beyond money. It's what gives us life when we need to express. When we hold back fulfilling expressions or fail to discover who we are, it can make you feel dead spiritually. We all have a desire to feel free, we have to figure out what expressions bring these sensations out of us.

Many people desire riches and materials, they wish and pray for this. What we wish for is not in the materials, but in the way that the materials will make us feel. We have the power to control how we feel, so we already have everything we can imagine. We want to see this in our physical reality before we've sustained a feeling long enough to allow these things to gravitate to us naturally. It always starts within.

It's typical to strive to make money any way we can, and we all have to put food on the table. It is also important not to suppress your natural urge to discover, grow, dream, inspire, and become truly in touch with who you are in life. These things go beyond money but if you need it to help achieve certain goals, allow those jobs to fund them. As a result, there will be a different bodily response that comes from you working because, ultimately, you have a plan, a goal. After all, trillions of dollars are circulating the world continuously.

There are millions of transactions happening at any given moment from people using different products and services. With excellent service, a marketing plan, and dedication, it is possible to do whatever you want. The question is, what do you want? That is the root of success and happiness. That can be a tough question to answer for many reasons, which I'll talk about later in chapter 1. Hopefully, the insight will give you better methods to help you learn more about yourself. We have been taught to think out of fear and material, neglecting the true self. Which is why there are confusion and misconceptions with the actual steps it takes to achieve this particular emotion.

Action is all based on desire, which is a feeling. All of which becomes physical first starts from the nonphysical, a thought. By taking advantage of this, surely, wealth can be attained, but the feeling of being wealthy was already enriched in our attitude before we had it physically. What else would give us enough stimulation to move and act in such a way that demands the confidence of someone worthy?

Many wise people know that there's a difference in being broke and being broken. You can be broke and still be mentally or spiritually rich. When you have no more hope or faith, it is then when you become your circumstances. Being broke is temporary when you have a fertile mind and spirit. Still, life won't guarantee you physical wealth; we have to give a portion of that to chance not only from birth but to the decisions we make after that. Money doesn't make you real, but neither does being poor. Ultimately the concept speaks toward a more grounded principle that prioritizes the inner before the outer. That way no matter what position you're in, the sense of gratification and self worth are never wavered.

Someone's perception of things goes beyond the facts and reality of what's there. At least until we expand our ability to see. *Saper Vedere*, this means "knowing how to see." The more perspectives you see subjects, the deeper you broaden your understanding of them. This was a practiced concept by a man named Leonardo da Vinci.

It is impossible to assume two people will agree on anything with two different fixed views, that's impractical. He was once quoted saying, "There are three classes of people: Those who see. Those who see when they are shown. Those who do not see." One of you would have to consider their premise or perspective genuinely. Then you may start getting to the root of the conflict.

Even when people do consider other perspectives if it ultimately doesn't align with what they may want, it can create damaged relationships or even violence. This isn't true enlightenment, and it's why humans still haven't learned how to live amongst each other gracefully. It would be easy to create a theory centered around how pride is overpowering more sensible steps to conflict resolution, despite (most times) humans knowingly being able to embrace things beyond their desires. I'll discuss this more in chapter 1.

If you're unthinkably defensive occasionally like me, you may react too quickly to consider things. Especially if it's something you believe strongly. Your perspective becomes a threat to mine. And if I do consider this thought, it may potentially change my perception. The way we perceive something creates our opinion about it. We can all recall things we've done in the past that make us instantly say, "What was I thinking?" Why is that? It's because of your perspective at that moment is different compared to now. It's also easy to question why we did something when the outcome wasn't something desired or capable of being predicted.

The point is we always think our present moment perception is right. Later on, we may end up questioning ourselves about why we saw things that way. During heated exchanges, anything is liable to be said out of anger or spite, things that are once said can't be taken back. We all must realize that when we're emotional, we aren't thinking logically. The areas of the brain that are in control of thinking clearly shut down. Being emotional isn't necessarily a bad thing. After all, it's inevitable and a part of life, it's how your body communicates with you. What's most important is how you form emotions that leave you prosperous mentally. So it's ok to feel, but it's essential to realize the source to why, and how you can consciously direct it.

It may bruise our ego when we aren't right, get criticized, or don't receive what we want, but nobody should want a bunch of yes-men around them. There are things that you may hear that make you feel uncomfortable but know when to embrace that constructive criticism. It only ends up helping you. When you become truly comfortable with who you are, you're less likely to become defensive instinctively. To be able to laugh, or never forget what truly matters in life will change your reactions to so many things.

Every so often, I come across a particular person who's demeanor is programmed to embrace things at a high level. They can take a joke, (they may even make jokes about themselves), acknowledge their flaws, talk about their ideas, and may even dance by themselves completely out of tune with the public eye and are just having a good time. Their energy feels so comforting and so free it's as if they've mastered themselves in a sense. At least that's what my aspirations would be, to be. To stop thinking so much about how to live or what to have before you can live and act a certain way, do it now. These types of people don't worry about how weird they sound, look, or appear.

Our flawed perceptions can come from a lack of information, biases, hunger, traumatizing experiences, anger, sadness, rumors, assumptions, expectations, and programming that dates back to the moment we were born. We're always battling some feeling that dictates our attitude. To be more efficient, we must take care of ourselves. Whether it's eating right, sleeping, meditating, learning, acknowledging our mistakes, drinking water, dismissing negativity, gaining acceptance, healing, or taking mental health breaks.

You know your body better than anyone else would. You know when something isn't right or is bothering you. Take control of it the best way your know how. You'll start realizing how much of your view of the world and yourself at any given moment is directly associated with how you feel mentally or physically. The awareness can help you stop yourself from doing or thinking in impulsive ways until you're feeling better.

There are specific areas of the brain that cause this natural phenomenon. Your prefrontal cortex, parietal lobes, anterior cingulate cortex, and amygdala all constantly shape our perception. There is still much unknown and even being discovered about the brain and mind. The duality is the ultimate manifestation at its highest, no matter your philosophical observation on the subject. The brain and mind together are undeniably prevailing.

Many of the influences of these areas of the brain happen mostly outside of our awareness. I could go on and on about these areas of the brain and give you informative, straightforward, scientific explanations as to why they're significant. I could present examples of studies or even conduct my own to help support my theories. Then I begin to look at it in another way. We study people, and even animals to give us a better understanding of ourselves all the time. Yet, I don't think it truly means we're right; it just gives us a perceived logical approach or guideline to explain things.

Say an entrepreneur uses 100 women between the ages 21-35 for a particular study dealing with a trio of colognes. He's trying to collect information to help give better insight into what type of colognes attract women the most. If he finds something significant, his next product sales could go through the roof. The women are given a choice of which colognes smell the best to them.

At the end of the study, he discovers that 80% of these women all liked the cologne "Lava" the best. So, in theory, there's an 80% chance that if you wear his product, the woman you're mingling with may love the way you smell. He digs deeper, trying to figure out why this rate was so high and noticed something interesting. The cologne "lava" had a sweet smell to it as if it was a mixture of honey, caramel, or coffee.

The entrepreneur conducted this study in the morning, and none of the women were given any breakfast beforehand. He pitched them all a full breakfast, but only after the experiment was complete. It turns out the results of this study were subliminally caused by the fact that everyone was probably a bit hungry, or in need of some coffee. By the time he realized this, it was too late. His product didn't blow up as he had hoped. Still, had a man decided to wear that cologne and a woman happened to like it, the chances of her agreeing to go out for food or drinks drastically increased.

The point is we look at percentages and stats and think it conveys accuracy when it's the way we perceive how to use this information. Had the entrepreneur decided to conduct the same study with 100 different women, or even at a different time of day, the results may have been entirely different. So while I do generally enjoy and believe gathering data is beneficial, the conclusions we come to, or the approach based on this information are more relevant.

Think about even today how particular statistics and studies are constructed to bring about a specific perception. These statistics could make people feel inferior, unsafe, or powerful. It's not to say numbers don't help us with making better decisions; it's the perceptions gained from these statistics that can still result in a wrong approach, or consequently, no actions being taken at all.

It's as if now that the possibilities have been set, we know what type of expectations to have. Even today, many people have become analytical freaks, but the numbers don't always show the essence of life and possibilities. A part of why we still take chances even when the odds are stacked against us, or when the statistics don't match our desire is because the brain is also a romance. Those stories or times where there's an underdog can make you root for them. It also constructs an influential theory around willpower and perception; if we're able to mentally practice methods influencing creative conclusions, the results would be astonishing and conducive.

I've read books that we're incredibly informative but lacked that energy, subjectivity, or even emotion that captures me as a reader. In this book, I aim to give you a favorable balance of them both with my own experiences, philosophies, and research. We can all read useful information, but what is it that genuinely affects us? It's the emotion, inspiration, repetition, and examples you may relate to that go beyond objectivity or scientific conclusions.

Despite the brain and its many ways of functioning, it's much easier to relate to this experience when real-world examples and visuals are given. Hopefully, I can show you the marvelous things your mind can do in a way you may have never realized. We react to events and things that happen in our life in milliseconds a lot of times. When you begin to acknowledge how we as humans operate consciously, your whole life will start to be centered around how you can direct this power.

When psychologists say, "95% of the day we are operating subconsciously and 5% of the day we are operating consciously," what does that mean to you? It feels like we are always 100% in control of what's happening, yet, there's something else controlling your breathing, heart rate, body temperature, digestive system, and many more things at any given moment.

When you're able to acknowledge how most of the things you did today like walk, talk, drive, and cook are all learned behaviors, you'll start realizing the dynamics of that statement. With repetition, we can begin doing these things instantly without thinking. You must feed your mind healthy thoughts even when you consciously don't feel like it's working.

There's something more potent than your consciousness that you don't give enough credit to. That's the complications and challenges that come with trying to not only explain the essence of your existence but to enforce methods that create the most optimal mental attitude. The knowledge of what's happening keeps you mindful of where your brain can mislead you. Reading is a great way to feed your brain with new information. You could read a book once and gain a 10% level of awareness from it. Let's say you read it again. Your awareness may jump to 15%. The more you consistently study this information, the more of an impact it will have on your thoughts, thus your life.

The interesting thing about the many books I've read is that none of them were ever quite explained in the same way. Even if it's on the same topic. A book is someone's perspective. What makes you so unique is that nobody can do it, quite like you. The beauty behind that causes more conflict than embracement in our world, a world where we spend a lifetime looking for everything within us.

It's hard to look at life differently outside what we've always known, but that's not our fault. From a child, you've been taught and told what "life" is before you were truly conscious enough to make your own decisions. So the basis of your choices is from what you were repeatedly told before you knew any better.

I don't blame anyone for being in defense about something that may contradict what my parents told me all my life growing up. So how often do you put yourself in other people's shoes? Ask yourself where or how they may have grown up? It can be tough, but it makes the difference in people who are capable of understanding and communicating effectively, compared to people who never give a thought or truly listen.

Whether you're in a relationship, debate, selling, or an interview, your ability to genuinely listen and understand makes your presence desired. The fact that this takes mental effort lowers the likelihood of people coming together or ever sincerely understanding one another. That's the ultimate goal, not to get people to agree on everything, but to respect each other enough to reason, appreciate, and embrace one another's perspectives. After all, we're not as different from one another as we consistently exaggerate. Sure, we may get frustrated with each other over different beliefs about how the world should work. Still, we're all merely a reflection of the same thing in a variety of expressions and programming.

None of us chose what skin complexion we'd be, or our appearance upon being born. Still, before judging based on the content of one's character, people stereotype and allow physical appearances to create an illusion of being different. In reality, we haven't gained the proper approach or understanding of how to deal with other people's diverse preferences. We can't expect everyone to think the way we think, or align their actions and morality according to how you may prioritize them. People have enough trouble figuring themselves out, stop thinking people know what makes you happy, mad, annoyed, etc. at least without the proper amount of effortful communication.

Robert Greene wrote a book called "The Laws of Human Nature." It has some valuable insight into emotions and how we should go about handling other people's characteristics. "Interactions with people are the major source of emotional turmoil, but it doesn't have to be that way. The problem is that we are continually judging people, wishing they were something that they are not. We want to change them. We want them to think and act a certain way, most often the way we think and act. And because this is not possible, because everyone is different, we are continually frustrated and upset. Instead, see other people as phenomena, as neutral as comets and planets. They exist. They come in all varieties, making life rich and interesting. Work with what they give you, instead of resisting and trying to change them. Make understanding people a fun game, the solving of puzzles. It is all part of the human comedy. Yes, people are irrational, but so are you. Make your acceptance of human nature a radical as possible. This will calm you down and help you observe people more dispassionately, understanding them on a deeper level. You will stop projecting your own emotions on to them. All of this will give you more balance and calmness, more mental space for thinking."

The point is to take a different approach. Now we have turned our perception of one another into a positive assessment. When you have this in mind during human interactions, you'll be embracing the nature of life instead of hating or quickly condemning, and all it takes is awareness and a desire to understand.

Many psychologists say you can't study someone's brain and mind without studying their culture in the process. That shows how much of an indirect effect our culture has on our thinking. It can completely dislodge our reasoning with one another simply because of our inability, or lack of mental effort to reflect beyond our desires and environment. Despite the lack of energy most times consciously, we do this automatically without thinking subconsciously.

It could be your heart racing as you see someone about to cross the finish line in a big race. My mouth usually waters when someone I wish was me, is eating a delicious meal on the food network. My tastebuds would react, and my mouth would water directly from the thought of eating it. I could taste it, but then I open my eyes. Watching a show about animals in the wild will have you cheerful, the lion finally caught his dinner. And then a bit of mourning for the impala, the lion is suffocating by the throat. Oh, and don't act as if you've never got tear eyed at the end of a romantic or sad movie.

Your brain has mirror neurons that change brain activity, causing you to feel as if it were you. In all of these cases, it was pretty easy to put yourself in their shoes. Empathy or any form of moral concern is usually stored for our inner circle. Outer circles tend to get the opposite effect, defensive aggression. These circles are natural, but looking from a more expansive circle, we all have universal interests and things in common that should display a better overall constructive connection.

One of the top ten books that are recommended to read is Dale Carnegie, "How To Win Friends & Influence People." Nothing in this book, to my surprise, is complicated material, respectively, mostly common courtesy. Carnegie gives countless examples of how to win people over. Simple ways, but extremely useful. For example, remembering someone's name, providing random compliments, genuinely listening to someone when they're speaking, giving a simple smile, or talking in terms of the other person's interest is wisdom. This all seems simple, but we are usually on the defensive end when it comes to others. It feels draining to even think about realistically implementing these reactions during times when we may lack the patience. It isn't about putting energy into doing a "fake smile" or "fake laugh." That's draining.

If we truly have the desire or genuine intention in us to help, with the right balance of rest and self-care, the energy will always be there. While many may say they "don't care" about others' feelings, it can be a counterproductive approach simply because you can't escape other humans. At some point, you are bound to interact. If you don't think in terms of how you can provide service to others, you may never gain real wealth or fulfillment. When you do, you'll always look to capitalize on these opportunities. It is noble and wise for one to aspire for healthy relations, or at least the invested time to become skillful and aware of how to see the bigger picture regarding emotions. These simple skills can take you farther than you may have never thought. This can lead to you becoming more emotionally influential to others that I'll talk more about later in the book.

You only have the energy for the things you have the right attitude about. To think our views can always be consciously constructed should be enticing to you. It is then when we begin understanding the mental steps it takes to be more powerful. Knowing how to deal with other people's emotions is essential in youth and even more important as adults. Always having your guard up can create subtle anxiety that may not be needed in most cases. It's ok to be protective over yourself; it's not ok to be overprotective. Don't hold back on that creative caring, and adventurous nature in you despite the unknown, that is the beauty of life. There is someone else out there who needs that energy, which may inspire them to recreate.

In his book, he says, "Any fool can criticize, condemn, and complain – and most fools do. But it takes character and self-control to be understanding and forgiving." You come off more of a respectable person by your ability to show compassion and forgive before judging and hating. Someone who understands that helping people fulfill their desires will always help them achieve their own has endless potential.

Much of the book is about people that did a great job identifying specific problems, values, and desires. The skill helped them get jobs, materials, interviews, business opportunities, and many other things. Taking a different approach to people's emotions is wisdom. Yet, these methodologies teach something beyond the art of taking advantage of people or gaining personal success. It shows the art of compassion and the power in perception.

Again, empathizing isn't complicated humans use these powers without consciously realizing it all the time. When you begin to combine those natural abilities as you learn life lessons, you become even more powerful. It'll then become a skill in a sense. It takes mental energy, experiences, and wisdom to know how to empathize genuinely. The time spent analyzing someone's emotions or beliefs and gaining a genuine sense of understanding is rarely done. We are instinctive, and most times, too busy thinking of ourselves. We're, in most cases, only seeing things from one point of view and reacting to that initial reflection. It's hard to blame you for this. You will be sure to look out for yourself before thinking about someone else. Society has portrayed a cold world that brings about thoughts to isolate yourself. That's ok. Humans have evolved and become what we are today only because of one thing, which is our ability to help one another.

We need each other to survive. Naturally, we are born to interact. So despite your pride continually saying, "You don't need anyone," in reality, you do. Much of our behavior derives from what we've learned from others. This is only because it is much easier to learn from peers and influential people than spending more time figuring it out on our own. You may not find any successful person who doesn't have a great supportive group or mentor.

Think about how much you appreciate someone who supports your dreams. The more we accept the fact that to a significant extent, our happiness comes from one another; the more we seek this love, the more of it we will create in our life. We have to be willing to understand ourselves to understand others truly. You'll realize how that is true self-love that you can feel. Naturally, we love talking about ourselves. It isn't surprising to know that in recorded phone conversations, the one word that is said to be the most used was "I." Even a therapist may potentially have a therapist. Nobody is exempt from the natural senses that make us who we are. Nobody has it all figured out. Nobody is perfect. Nevertheless, if we have a desire to be better humans, we will become better humans.

The first step is becoming mindful. The more you

practice it, the more you will naturally begin to think in peaceful ways instinctively. It's not that you necessarily have to practice just thinking positively; it's about creatively thinking in ways that keep you empowered. The biggest challenge of gaining knowledge is applying it in your life. This transition is most important. No book can make you change your life or make you treat people any differently despite being informed of a more useful method. It takes effort.

Pay attention to your thoughts after reading this book; you'll notice things about yourself and the way you think that you didn't see before. That is because you've created new neuroplasticity in your brain. You've given it additional information to create a better overall understanding of yourself instead of staying stuck with a flawed perception, due to the lack of knowledge. All you know is what you know. If you never learn anything beyond what you do now, your brain can only operate based on the level of awareness you have. A lot of people don't do better because they don't know any better.

Throughout this book, I will acknowledge many things I may have reacted to differently in the past if I had been more mindful myself. I will put what I've learned to practice. In the past, this may have hurt, left me ashamed, and even embarrassed. This sacrifice is necessary only to display my self-consciousness and the purpose of what I write about. My honesty hopefully makes you more comfortable living free from restrictions. I must lead by example before I can encourage anyone to endeavor in any virtuous transition. I'll use myself as a lesson.

My goal of making this book will not be to convince you that everything I write is accurate or makes sense to you. If this book changes the way you may look at life in some ways, I've accomplished my goal. I leave you with my perception, which is all any of us ever have to give. The amount of supporting facts I have is irrelevant. You can come up with just as many reasons to justify your doubts about my claims.

Studies have been shown that people with higher IQs are great at finding ways to support their conclusions. Hey, it makes for a great lawyer. All you need is one objection to any challenging premise; it doesn't matter how much truth is brought to your attention. A term often associated with this behavior is cognitive dissonance, meaning in uncomfortable situations, you may tend to avoid any challenging core beliefs.

Scientists often find strong arguments that oppose other scientists all the time. Some people question the very ideologies of science and the principles it's based upon. Any book I considered a must-read made me look at life differently. Not because of the information and how factual it was, but the way it was uniquely presented from someone else's perspective. You don't have to believe everything that is in a book, but you will still gain the knowledge of someone else's outlook. Something that can stick with you and even impact your life forever. Some things may resonate with you, and some things may not. Use what you need to help you.

We're all on a spiritual journey, learning lessons at different times in our lives. Never underestimate the influence interactions with the objective world will have on the subconscious mind. Never underestimate the role you may play in someone else's journey towards finding themselves. Everyone has had a moment when they paused and said, "I never looked at it that way". It seems the more perspectives you hold, the more lives you live, the more you broaden your understanding and judgments of everything around you. Besides, who am I to act as if I know it all? If I were someone oblivious enough to believe this, I'd still be speaking only from experience. As many right and wrong ways as there are to write a book, or present any form of expression, the only right way is your way.

Everyone can teach you something you didn't know previously simply because of our unique involvements throughout life. Other people's perspectives can hold a lot of value. Sometimes our beliefs are so strong we never give any other options to see it beyond the way our intuition directs us. Whether that be from tradition or a way of thinking that has become immoral, but sacred. When we are open to suggestions, it can alter the way you thought you saw something. It's one thing to make a sound judgment based on questions and understanding one's point of view, another to dismiss the unfamiliar altogether. A change in your mindset is a change in the way you were looking at the circumstances. I've learned this myself.

I used to blog. There were times when people I show my writings to didn't think I wrote it. They even went as far as to say I copied it. I was getting offended by this. I mean, how hard could it be to write? Why would I have any reason to lie? Then, I looked at it from another angle. If someone reads my writing and immediately thinks it is too well written to be by me, as if a professional wrote it, that's more of a compliment. After all, if it were poorly written, they wouldn't have had a hard time believing it was me. This made me feel like a great writer. That feeling is a direct reflection of the way I chose to view it. It also speaks to the power in how we see other people. Your perception of others can make you bias towards what you think they can or can't do.

I once heard a story of a guy who was loved and chanted by millions of fans in an arena. After the show as he was walking to his car, someone rode past him and said, "You Suck." Despite the many that loved him, he chose to focus on that one person, which made him feel bad. If you're feeling wrong about anything, know that a change in the way you're looking at it can mean everything. Focusing on the wrong things will only keep you from seeing the many who love you.

People will also fulfill a doubt about you simply because they can't or don't have the confidence to do things themselves. More than likely, if someone doesn't believe in themself, they won't believe in you either. Don't allow people's ideas of what is possible and what isn't project the way you feel. When you find yourself reacting to something in a provoked way, take the time to think about how you are viewing it. None of us take disrespect well, but in certain instances, looking at it differently can change your attitude towards the whole thing. It may not even be worth reacting to because of the more expanded perceptual conclusions you've come to. At any time in your life, you can do this.

For every negative possibility you can quickly voice or think of, it is only fair to bring to your attention a potentially positive outcome as well. We often focus so heavily on the bad that it only stirs up these emotions as if they were right, then we react. Thinking justly creates a balance of emotion and probability in your head. Seriously try this, it works. Notice the difference in how you feel based on how you perceive each situation. It will make you more protective over the things you think about.

You'll come to realize it's always your choice and you that defines your happiness. "What if her parents hate me?" "What if her parents love me?" "They keep staring at me; I just know it's this ugly outfit." "They keep staring at me, am I looking THAT good today?" "She loves me." "She loves me not." "He thinks I copied my writings." "Or he sees how good it is written; he's having a hard time believing it's my work." "Nobody may read this book." This book may change someone's life one day."

Whether you like it or not, people will forever formulate illogical assumptions of who they believe you are, or even what they think you're capable of. Good or bad, it could be anything. This is not something you can control. You can only control the way you choose to see. Much of how we feel about something starts with how we see it. You should give props to that friend who always looks on the bright side. Perception is truly an art, a gift.

The power to direct thoughts into a compelling positive vision is in the beauty of each one of us.

It's funny, you know. I once saw a show that was filming a child's finger painting. They decided to take that painting and hang it up in a highly respected art museum. It wasn't long before adults were walking up to the picture at awe, admiring the artwork of this incredibly talented 3-year-old that they assumed was a famous adult painter. The perception of what they saw defined their approval of it.

This is comical because that's how it is in other areas of life. We're more likely to approve of a product that has good reviews over a product that has terrible reviews, even if the product with bad reviews is a lot better. We're more likely to listen to people who have something symbolic about themselves that is linked to intelligence. Someone with a degree in a specific subject would leave you open to anything they may suggest because of your perception of them being more knowledgeable. I've seen videos of people who would do immoral things simply because someone who appears to be smart is telling them to do it.

Much of our preferences and approval for things are linked with the way they were experienced or taught. It could be someone who we were taught to have authority over us or a pleasurable experience that creates an underlying attraction to the unique things we prefer. Most of these urges are so subliminal we don't even consciously know why we approve of certain words and disapprove of others. There are things like food, music, products, games, and movies that I don't have a liking for. It doesn't mean those things have any loss of value because of my distaste for it. I could care less about mushrooms, pop genre, coconuts, and coffee, for example. The beauty in perception is that not everybody would agree with that, so they're still great things.

The world doesn't revolve around me! Just because I didn't approve of it doesn't mean anything. Imagine If people stopped doing something because I didn't like it. The scary part is, some people hold back on doing things because they are afraid of criticism. I've done this. You have to realize that none of it matters. Not everyone has to like whatever it is that you do, but someone will. You could have the highest morals and character, and not everyone will like you. That's just the way it is. So, where does the real approval lie when we speak of something worthy of being admired? It lies within ourselves.

Throughout your life, you will have people who will call you young and old. Someone who's in their mid-fifties would look at someone in their mid-30s as still young with plenty of opportunity and life to live. You may have thought you were an old wreck amid a midlife crisis. People who are younger than you will always tell you that you're old. Our positions in life make us perceive things in specific ways. Depending on the person you're talking to will determine if you are old or not, not your actual age. Notice how you feel better when older people tell you you're still young as opposed to younger people who make you feel like you're growing wrinkles.

If someone is 45 years old and lives until he's 85, that's 40 more years of life and experiences at an age where most would feel like their life is coming to an end. Think about the number of people who may get uncomfortable as their 30s approach as if they don't have more amazing experiences ahead. Age doesn't define our maturity level or mindset, either. It's interesting how age is just a statistic tracked based on time, which is a human-made concept. While there is a difference in adolescence compared to adulthood, how we feel and construct our reasoning based on age is flawed, and all a matter of perspective.

Even in other aspects of subjective opinions, you see a wide range of distinctive views entailed with personal preferences. It all comes down to a matter of how we choose to see it. It gets even more profound when we go in detail of why we feel the way we feel. Just look at music, sports, books, tv shows, cars, and anything else with a wide range of subjective biasses attached to it.

Think about the number of people who will instinctively rebuttal claims that don't match their perception. LeBron is better than Michael Jordan. Kobe is better than both. Rihanna is better than Beyoncè. Chevy makes the best vehicles. Fresh Prince of Bel-Air is the best sitcom ever. Jay Z isn't better than Nas. Stephen King is a better author than J.K Rowling. Ps4 is better than Xbox. Cheesecake is nasty. Android is better than Apple. Pineapples on pizza taste amazing (Not Really). Libras are the best zodiac sign. I think you can imagine people's reactions based on these statements.

The amount of time invested in quarreling to get people to see why they're wrong and why we're right is endless. We all know it comes down to our fondness with these things that have fascinated us or inspired us. Nothing more, nothing less. It doesn't make anyone right or wrong when it's all a matter of perception. What fun would it be if everyone liked what you liked or agreed with everything you sought to be true? Life is beyond just your opinion. The moment you embrace that, you discover far more than you thought you could ever see.

Perception can define the outcome of a game despite any particular rules that are supposed to bring clarification. Did Dez Bryant really catch that ball? It depends on what your perception of a catch is. Fans watch close playoff games in the NBA only to begin arguing about what was a foul and what wasn't. We laugh at memes of the losing teams, and our perceptions swing back and forth about who may potentially win the series. It makes us realize how subjective the game really can be. As much as refs try to make calls as rational as possible, sometimes they can't hide their subjective selves. Nobody's claiming they have to be perfect. It is just a testament to the power in how we see things, especially when it can be debated soundly on both ends.

How often do you take into consideration the things you've enjoyed or may have not appreciated, and how much your present mood played a significant role in how it was experienced? A lot of times the way we experience our days is a reflection of how we feel when we first wake up. Some things may have created a different reaction from you had the timing been different.

If you may be relaxed, fresh out the shower with a glass of wine, a book may be just what you need to cap your night off. The content in the book may hit you differently depending on your mood. Sometimes you feel like reading and before you know it, you're halfway done, but it felt like you just started. Other times it may be hard to read if you're tired, hungry, mad, sad, etc. And consequently, the content won't hit you the same way.

I've read books that weren't initially interesting, then I may reread it at a random time months later, and the words are just what I need. We're continually looking to satisfy natural sensations in some way, and depending on our state of mind will determine what we may need. It makes me genuinely wonder what it is that makes us randomly choose certain activities, foods, people, drinks, etc. Someone's preference at the moment speaks to that moment, not their future attitude that could easily result in them feeling differently.

Depending on what you may be going through will determine the type of stimulation you need at that moment. I've noticed how differently my mind reacts to things depending on when I do it. Reading or even writing in the morning versus later that night can have completely different reactions from you mentally. It is quite intriguing to me, consciousness, and how our moods become everything at that moment.

Another good example is music. You may not always want to listen to R&B unless your feelings or vibrations align in a way that makes you enjoy it and relate to it at that moment. Other times you may need some rap, pop, country music, or whatever you may prefer because we're just in that type of mood. Many people love music because it's a convenient way to release dopamine. When dealing with our feelings, we must understand how it can dictate how we see situations or things. This is why we can sometimes change our minds because, in a sense, our perception has changed.

There is a book called "The Art of Possibility" that gives an interesting concept of our perceptions. It provides an example of two people who go to an area to seek business opportunities. What the two people see and interpret is different. The city was covered with people who don't wear shoes. The first guy sees an opportunity to sell since nobody wore any. The other guy saw no chance thinking they weren't even caught up on what shoes were, so it'd be a waste of time. We interpret circumstances in our own life the same way. Whatever conclusions we come to decide the actions that follow. The possibilities of any situation come down to how willing we are to extend our perception of what can work and what can't. Truth is it's always our minds that construct what is or isn't possible.

In no way does this information mean I've overcome the power in perception. It only reminds me of how amazing it is. The times I may be swayed at any moment despite consciously acknowledging the tricks perception may play on me only speaks to something beyond our consciousness. It's as if the more I understand the flaws and nature of myself and subjective ways, the more I understand others.

If there's anything I ask of you while continuing to read this book, it is that you hear me out. Know that these words were only were formed out of a passion for creating a message that could potentially help change the world. Some of this information will be articulated in more than one way to increase the number of people who may relate under different circumstances. Some things will be expressed in repetition for a specific purpose, while other things may be stated once. I even have random short shorties throughout the book. These stories just came to me randomly while trying to fulfill the desire I have to express in multiple ways.

There was an interesting statement a writer made about the difficulties with trying to provide a message while still growing. "One thing no one tells you about being a writer is how to cope with the fact that your thinking keeps evolving, while the things you have already written stay the same." While the impacts you have as a writer can help for generations, I realize how this book would never be finished because of growth. I'll always have an upgraded opinion or something new to talk about. With that being said, some of these thoughts could have been articulated differently, but have gained an appreciation by me simply because of how I can observe my emotions in different chapters of my life. I've learned more about myself, and it forced me to realize that the critical elements of this book overpower my own emotions, even when I had my doubts.

Just like you, I try to make sense of everything around me. Well, here's the way I see it. I will attempt to explain my outlook on the world in an honest, comprehensive, and straightforward way. Things like my inner thoughts, feelings, expectations, and self-consciousness all in one. Things that may seem impossible to explain, like love and religion.

Remember, the more complicated something is, the more likely it is because of our fixed views about it. Be open to possibility, be open to perspectives, be open to my experiences, and allow it to broaden your understanding. Oh, and of course, my real intention of writing this book. Where did it come from? I'm not sure, likewise to you as a reader, this will be a journey for both of us. And though it appears that I may have already gotten ahead of myself by this long nontraditional introduction, maybe I'll know at the end, as I unify these thousands of thoughts we call perception. It reminds of the artist Drake and his album called, "Nothing Was the Same." In the intro, he would rap longer than the typical intro of an album. He was self-conscious about it as well by stating, "How much time am I spending on the intro?" It's as if you can quickly become too excited to where you want to say so much, but have to save some for later. It also speaks to how so much greatness can come from unique expression, instead of the typical formats.

I often catch myself trying to see and feel the essence of consciousness. What are feelings? What is existence? What is our purpose as humans? I know I'm not the only one who has these thoughts. A lot of times, these questions arise as I stare and admire the sky just looking at the stars, or the sunrise, taking the time out of a busy day to notice a fantastic creation we bypass most days. Life is a beautiful mystery. A mystery overshadowed by a false sense of self. One that still leaves me at awe, feeling like something is missing in life. Then, I may get a sandwich because of my bodily desires bringing me back to earth.

CHAPTER 1

The truth hurts

The Look in the Mirror

This journey we call life is filled with many challenges. Challenges that test our patience, faith, love, loyalty, morals, temptations, anger, fear, and mental strength every day. As a spiritual being with limitless potential, we must overcome these obstacles to grow into the person we desire to be within. The toughest part is getting out of our way and facing the things that we may try to make excuses for.

The truth isn't always something we want to face, but it will always be the only way to prosper indeed. We must critically evaluate the things we believe are right because it could be hindering us. Then we must update any misleading information and begin to consistently restructure our ways of thinking by keeping specific perspectives in mind. Whether it be an unfortunate circumstance, failure, success, relationship, or tragic event, the way you react to it will determine everything.

If we want to see a mental change in our life, learning how to rewire our thought patterns to uplifting beliefs is essential. This is possible once we realize how to reprogram our minds. A great way to practice is by expanding your mind to different positive outcomes on any strong negative beliefs you may have. Notice the way you feel as you ponder on various scenarios in your head. Pay attention to how each situation seems real, whether good or bad. The feeling is as if it happened because we can indeed feel it.

This is a great mind power that guides our actions based upon whichever way we have creatively decided to see. If we took the truth of that information seriously, then we'd prioritize our purest thoughts for a better-quality experience of life. Since we are oblivious and passive towards it, it hurts. The truth isn't supposed to hurt. It is meant to help us grow. When we don't want to face the truth, it shuts the door to self-actualization. We must learn to face the truth with open arms and acceptance with no shame instead of habitually allowing it to hurt us. Denial brings feelings of insecurity, anxiety, anger, and stress, which is rooted in the complexities of emotional and egotistical phenomena.

Even at times when we can consciously acknowledge the things we aren't doing right, why do we continue to do it? A big reason is because of how our daily habits can unintentionally cause us to do the same things from the sense of familiarity or cues. We also have to take into consideration that a lot of bad habits people have excite the pleasure centers of the brain, causing a dilemma or conflict between the conscious mind and subconscious mind. If our desire to do better and study, workout, clean up, start a business, save money, or reach our goals isn't stronger than our urge to gamble, drink, procrastinate, or spend money carelessly, we'll stay stagnant, or better yet, we'll form bad habits.

Life or people don't owe you anything. When we don't make the right decisions, we only make it worse on ourselves. We can overcome bad habits and short-term desires by shifting our focus. Sure, gambling, this money will be a short thrill, but in the long run, I'll lose a lot of money I could've invested elsewhere. The thought of both actions (spending money and saving money) give me great pleasure, but whichever one claims superiority in regards to desire, will be the one that wins.

It's like cartoon visuals with the angel on one shoulder and the devil on the other. They each give you a different perspective of why it's the better choice. It is up to you to make that conscious decision, one that you can live with. There were times where I would be completely content and happy even after gambling at poker, but other times I would be embarrassed by my lack of self-control and not knowing when to stop.

Spending money on experiences isn't something I would never deem as complete carelessness in any setting. If it is the experience you wish to gain, then spending money on those experiences would never be a complete waste of money. I needed a lot of those experiences (good and bad) to form this expression. I wouldn't be who I am today without it. Do you see how I took that situation and discovered more than one way to look at it? Practice doing this yourself to help keep you on the right track mentally.

I've, in the past, allowed short term pleasures to hold me back only to have regrets in the long term. I'm sure you've been there once or twice. Life goes by fast without any real progression, before you know it, you're older, but don't have anything to show for it. A part of me always was somewhat content with those short-term pleasures. I mean, what was I chasing? Money? Fame? Attention? And then what? What did it mean, and at what point does it end? At what point do I appreciate the things I have and realize I'm chasing things that are meaningless and endless. Is it wrong to recognize that people die unexpectedly every day, so appreciate this day?

There will always be someone wealthier than you, but also someone significantly less fortunate. If you ever lose your eyesight or leg, you'd have a robust appreciation for something you used to overlook most days. Stop perceiving yourself as having nothing and start seeing yourself as having it all. Stop stressing yourself out about things you don't have because meanwhile, your life is passing you by, and you've always had everything you've needed within you. This isn't to say there's anything wrong with wanting more, it's a mental understanding of something that'll always be more powerful, which is this very moment.

The memories and the relationships you create from making the best out of today are a success. I'd have a war of thoughts in my head. On one side, I'd feel a motivated urge to accomplish, conquer, and reach my potential. On the other hand, I was significantly humbled and less motivated from the perspective of already having it all within me. The value of my life and the success of it isn't measured by the perceptions of what others see as success. It makes me question what is specifically creating that energy. Is it our desire to prove to others how worthy or great we are? Or is it our desire to prove it to ourselves?

A lot of our energy goes into smiling in pictures or at places and posting it to appear happier as if it's some competition. Why? Because we want people to see us having fun and living lavishly. This isn't always the case. I take pics and use my phone to record memorable moments, which is something that wasn't available in the past. So there's value in the technology, but having balance is important, so sometimes just putting the phone down and being in the moment is better than feeling the need to post everything. This narrative of feeling unachieved if we haven't reached star status or become a millionaire is illogical. Give yourself credit for even your smallest accomplishments.

Life isn't easy, and neither is mastering your mind. The amount of pressure we put on ourselves is a big reason we can easily get stressed in life. When we make peace with our circumstances, you'll realize that it is our idea of what success is that makes us stressed. You may have accomplished many things in your life and overcome many obstacles that you've never given yourself credit for because your life didn't turn out quite as you visioned.

It may seem this way because you always compare your accomplishments to others who may have more. Or you may have a habit of only acknowledging the times you've messed up. It can easily make you overlook how powerful you are.

If you feel unachieved or have a feeling of needing something more, you will inevitably blossom into the person you were meant to be. That energy will continue to build up until you do something about it. None of this is intended to discourage you from desiring wealth or fame; it is to create balance amid your journey so that you don't lose yourself along the way. It is a reminder of how worthy and amazing you are, even if you don't reach that point. By creating an attitude full of consistent gratification will increase the likelihood, you make more money. The way you move will be different. It can be frustrating making this transition depending on how well you deal with these challenges.

The biggest challenge we face is when we look in the mirror. We all can look and see flaws in other people, the mistakes they make, the poor decisions, or even the toxic behavior. Yet, how often do we hold ourselves accountable for things that may have caused us debt, bad credit, bad relationships, loss of friends or family, or even sickness? Instead of being more attentive and responsible for our mental attitude, health, and energy we give, we make excuses that lead us to perceptions that never quite pin the fault as our own.

That is why one of the toughest challenges to face in life is the truth. We may be so comfortable living a lie that we lose sight of what we truly value. We lose ourselves. A lot of the problems we have in life can be fixed, but they never are acknowledged by us because of denial. Sometimes it is your fault, your bad habits, your carelessness, and lack of self-discipline that holds you back. The moment you can identify things you aren't doing right and make a conscious effort to change is the beginning of something great happening in your life. This isn't something that has to be in your physical reality.

The peaceful nature of being alive or those moments when we're extremely happy for whatever reason is something we should strive for consistently. As you continue to read, you will see how even the things you may perceive as adverse circumstances can be the beginning of something great happening.

When I look back at previous jobs I've had; I realize how at everyone, there were opportunities for me to be promoted. Some people would ask me if I was interested because they saw my potential. It was always my attitude that made me hate my job. It was my attitude that always made me feel tired or ready to go while I was there. I always thought that I was worthy of more. The result of this caused a lot of built-up frustration with myself. I didn't want to become consumed in a career that wasn't fulfilling. Deep down, those jobs never gained my full commitment because it didn't give me any passion.

I've realized how the right balance of everything is essential. You could be in a position where you're making a lot of money and be miserable, depending on the people you're consistently around or from the job itself. Someone may take less money to be in a loving environment instead of one that is harming them mentally. Then you have to take into consideration other things in life that we may need to fulfill our happiness. Sometimes we think it's as simple as making a lot of money when there's more to it than that.

While those jobs weren't necessarily what I may have had in mind for a career, my attitude, in general, was detrimental to me. You can't prosper with the wrong attitude because the feelings that are created will always make you act unwillingly. Even if you're not where you want to be, I overtime had to realize that doing your best at everything will eventually get you there. Plus, that job can help support your real dreams. It's essential to understand the difference in the reaction by looking at things this way. You could go to work miserable or excited about the fact it's funding something you really want to do. Sometimes the hardest thing to do is set a goal. At some point in life, we're forced to stop looking for external validation, direction, and understanding. With nowhere else to look, we look inside and discover our true self and purpose. A lot of people will choose to say, "That's just the way I am" and deal with the issues or bad habits that have created the life they have. We think we are happy with this decision, not knowing life has so much more to offer to our happiness and potential.

A lot of times, we go through painful experiences consistently until we may change because of them. The universe will continue to put us through the same lessons in different ways until we realize it is our ways that we must overcome, not the objective worlds. Many people may not be wealthy or be in the situation they want to be in right now, but if we are making an effort to become enlightened and follow our passions, that is a success. Many people share stories of how they were in a completely different situation a year ago, or even months ago. The point is you have to start somewhere. Just because you're not where you want to be today doesn't mean you can't be in a completely different situation in the near future. You must align your thoughts in the right ways.

Many of the things you have and don't have are simply a result of what you desire the most. It will make you question the things that you've prioritized over others simply because of desire. A typical response to this statement is a rhetorical question. Well, why am I not a millionaire? Well, the number of risks, sacrifices, work, or dedication needed to become a millionaire may not be high on your priority list. So while you can consciously say you desire to be a millionaire, the true essence of your beliefs and passions will show in the actions you take to become one. Many people think so much and have great ideas, but never actually take action on them. I've been guilty of this. These days it's so easy to become distracted. When we can focus on a particular task, the number of things you will get done is endless.

Think about a time when you've done some work you've procrastinated on at the last minute in a short amount of time. It was your ability to focus or zone out that made you capable of doing something that generally may have taken longer. The quality of the work, a lot of times, is determined by the time you've put into it, so it's not all about how fast you work. It's about your focus and time management, which takes self-discipline. You may put tasks off because your attitude about it doesn't excite you, which would result in you not having the energy. The energy you have to do it at the last minute is because of the pressure that is now on you if you don't get it done, now that energy is revived.

The goal is to create that energy and love for what we do to where we don't feel the need to put things off day after day. Ultimately when you finish things you need to get done, the feeling is more significant because we no longer have that subtle anxiety of knowing we have something to do. It clears our minds and makes us feel accomplished. Think of those days where you were extremely productive, whether it was cleaning, running errands, exercising, completing work, etc. You felt amazing and on top of the world. Prioritize and practice good habits like rest, mental exercise, hydration, working out, and self-discipline. Balance is essential because you're ability to focus is hindered whenever there's something you're neglecting. Often we can get caught up prioritizing other things before our body. Taking care of your body and mind is what helps you operate efficiently. If you feel as if you don't have time for these things or they're hard to do, then you must learn the skill of focus and directing energy perceptually.

There was a study done on goldfish, and it was discovered that they have a higher attention span than humans. With all the technology and different ways to be entertained today, our ability to sit still and concentrate can become poor. A lot of times, we miss out on important information that could've resulted in better productivity or decisions. Naturally, our minds seem to become distracted quickly. This means we must work at training our brains to function more efficiently. If we can never focus long enough to tune out negative people, temptations, and our monkey mind, then we'll never achieve goals.

This is why eating healthy, exercising, staying hydrated, and meditating can help you gain strength mentally. All of these things challenge our mental and physical habits as well as our self-discipline. You see, the mind is tricky. Your mind and its reward centers in the brain can stimulate you for being lazy and stimulate you for accomplishing things. Don't get caught on the wrong end of this concept. You always feel better when you do something that promotes your well being. When you consider all this, we all should always strive to grow and channel our energy to higher frequencies.

We should always seek to learn more about ourselves. Maybe we all can put ourselves in better situations when we are dedicated and passionate. Without it, it's simply not possible. When I realize what real passion is, I see how it can make someone write a book. I see how it can take someone farther than they thought they could ever go. I see how, without it, we never actually accomplish anything. Passion will overpower any fear or anxiety you may have about failure and doubt.

The look in the mirror can be revealing to many things about yourself you never thought to acknowledge. The purpose isn't to look down on yourself. It is to practice being real with yourself. Nobody is perfect, and it feels great not to try and be. Acknowledging your mistakes and learning from them is the most sensible thing you can do. I've noticed how free I feel after. Creating new neuroplasticity by expanding my perception beyond me always being right instantaneously made me more aware of when I may be at fault. Instead of becoming defensive or hurt by being wrong, I feel a blissful acceptance as if I've done something more powerful.

Often, we get so caught up in defense mode that we find ways to make it seem as if we're always the victim, which is a terrible habit to possess. You'll find yourself being the toxic person among your peers and won't see it. You'll convince yourself that all the bad things that have happened to you aren't your fault. It will give you the false perception of not being able to do anything about your situation, and you never will. You've simply gained acceptance in the wrong way. Throughout this chapter, I will point out many things that we as people have become passive towards. This is the reason why we never see any real change. Hopefully, by the end of this chapter, you won't be afraid of the truth, even in moments when you are faced with having to take accountability.

Intention

> ***"A truth that's told with bad intent***
> ***Beats all the lies you can invent."***
>
> **-William Blake**

One thing I've learned in life is that your intentions are the real purpose behind anything you do. Everything we do has some sort of purpose behind it. It's something only you know. Someone could ask you what the purpose of your actions are, and you could lie to them. People have prioritized using religion for money and control instead of the prioritized intent to bring prosperity and peace to the world. What good is the truth if it's used as an opportunity to manipulate intentionally?

We know water can be used to quench our thirst or drown someone, the intent is the difference. You may approve the actions of someone then feel entirely different when finding out their intentions. While actions always reveal a lot of information, it is the intention that reveals something far more profound. The same concept applies to the real purpose of why we treat certain people in specific ways.

Think about those times when you may have felt love, jealous, or hateful towards someone. What's the deeper reasoning for your treatment of other people? Is it their smile? Is it intimidation? Do you sense weakness or strength? Do they have something you don't have or didn't have growing up? Does their beauty make you dislike them, but really insecurity about yourself? Even if you just don't generally like people, or treat people equally, it is still all a reflection of intent.

Why do you laugh more at certain people's jokes? It could be an attraction or because of their humor and experiences resonate with you. You may find it comical how they naturally speak their mind. Why do you dismiss everything certain people say even at times when it makes sense? They may have said something you despise, so now everything they say is annoying to you. Or they could remind you of someone you had a bad experience with in the past. The better we are at identifying flawed outlooks on a personal level, the better we'll treat other people and see what influenced us to act that way.

Sometimes our actions are a result of how we have decided to see the situation. So self-honesty and the critical information behind the simple question, "What was my/his/her intent?" is everything. An even more profound, more clarifying question to ask is, "What is it that caused or influenced my intentions in this way?". The more we communicate in this way, the more we discover things about each other and ourselves that we may have never acknowledged. This is an opportunity to cure ourselves and perception. When people take an approach to healing, it is a lot of times done in ways that produce temporary relief. Many don't understand the conflict is usually happening in their head. So healing holistically may never be taken as seriously as it should. When we learn how to be in touch with our emotions, we've used consciousness as the gift it was meant for.

The worst type of misguided intention is when we lie to ourselves. A lot of times, we don't even ask ourselves why we do the things we do. When we feel envy, hate, depressed, happy, or even pleasure, how often do we identify the source behind that feeling? Identify the subliminal causes to the things that make you feel bad and eliminate them, identify the subliminal causes to the things that always make you blissful and gravitate to them. Always take reasonable approaches to gain more understanding in any given circumstance.

Our moods can be effected quickly, so becoming aware of these symbolic things can help direct your feelings the way you want. Some people are significantly more content and happier with their life on sunny days as opposed to rainy days. Yet, you have those people who love when it rains and may receive some stimulation from the natural event. Some people will feel as if their day is ruined because of rain while others may see it as an opportunity to do many other things. This is subliminal and symbolic, something that we may have never thought influenced our mood to such a high degree. It may even go beyond the weather. The weather may be only one factor in how it combines with other things making us happy or sad.

Suppose I had a girlfriend who I asked to meet me at a coffee shop for lunch. Only for her not to show. She had been acting weird lately, and I wanted to talk. I ask her why she stood me up. She replies, "I'm sorry I overslept," or "I was feeling sick." Yea, these are reasonable answers, but what are her true intentions behind these words? I continue to ask questions until I finally hear, "I just don't think this is working out." Yes, it may hurt to hear the truth of this situation, but it is essential.

Feelings first come from the way we perceive circumstances. So when our state of mind is altered, it is our perceptions that have changed first, then we start to feel differently. The cause of this change in attitude can be from a vast number of things like lack of effort, bad habits, beliefs, character, miscommunication, etc. The way we perceive people is continually being updated based on our most recent experiences or impressions they've made on us. Depending on what they may have recently done or said can dictate whether you like them more or all of a sudden hate them.

Our perceptions of people can also change over time when we begin to see the things they believe and may prioritize over others. The flaws we have can either cause people to stray away or gravitate even closer to us as if they've found some perfections in our imperfections. It's important to note that the effort you put in to grow as a person is something that can only be personally achieved. We can uplift other people, but there has to be some inner desire or passion for doing this themselves.

The timing, speed, and events that will happen throughout your life may not be in the same sequence as the person you're with. In this case, it's only logical to assume her perception of me has changed. Which explains the lack of passion and love that was once there. Sometimes we think we know what we want, but then it turns out it's not what we initially thought it'd be. How often do we have a perception of something being fun, scary, or boring, then we experience it, and it's the opposite? It happens all the time. The key thing about those experiences is what you take from them. You can use them to help other people in the world. You can use them to drive you to become a more excellent person. It's all within the competent nature of your mind.

Perceptions are never stagnant. At any moment, the

right experience or words can change everything. There are thousands of things that can modify our judgments resulting in a different attitude. I use this as an example because of her initial vagueness. It could quickly leave you deceived to what the real problem or agenda is. Two people can ask the same question, or partake in the same activity, with two different motives behind it. The things people do and say don't always accurately convey their true intentions. Sometimes people's plans can even change depending on what they may end up experiencing. We must ask ourselves what the real motives are behind what we do or say. It is then where we start to see the real art in communication and character.

Always be clear about what you want in life. It's easy to say we want things like money or a great career. How much money? What type of job? What precisely is it that you want that will make you happy? There's an analogy of the mind that I've never seemed to forget. It's compared to a boat at sea. Your consciousness is the captain of the ship. You can direct it where you want to go. If you don't, it'll cast away to wherever the wind and ocean currents take it. That's equivalent to allowing things in the world to control your circumstances.

You can be frustrated about things in life, but if you never intend to do anything about it, nothing will change. I've never given my mind exact direction toward precisely what I wanted to do besides when I've created this book. I may have said things that were either vaguely unclear to my subconscious or never confirmed. When we aren't clear, we leave ourselves confused as to what it is we want.

It's no wonder I wasn't truly ever happy in life. I felt as if maybe graduating college, or getting a corporate job, and material things would bring me the ultimate level of bliss. While those may be great things to have and do, the truth is, the fulfillment I get from doing something I'm truly passionate about is in a tier of its own. There were times in my life where I didn't know my purpose or what I was good at. The experiences I gained in search of myself gave me the ability to form this expression as a writer that always seemed to come naturally to me.

Having a real purpose for what you do goes beyond money and is a far more gratifying experience. Knowing this is something I want to do makes me happy. Set true intentions for yourself and the things you want and be as specific as possible. Don't be vague when it comes to something you desire. Your behavior will only align with whatever it is you think to do. Don't think in terms of what will make the most money, think in terms of passion and intent.

Character Assassination

> ***"Too often character assassination has replaced debate in principle here in Washington. Destroy someone's reputation, and you don't have to talk about what he stands for."*** **Ronald Reagan**

The things that get you condemned, demonized, or character assassinated can be determined by the mistakes you make, people who disagree with you, morality, and even your lifestyle. Sure enough, simply being human qualifies you to be criticized in some way. People, without realizing form quick opinions on others all the time, potentially from a rumor, casual conversation, the things you wear, your accent, skin color, net worth, and the list goes on. Sometimes your observations can be accurate, but it's about those times when we're overly biased that we must take a step back to reevaluate.

Truth is you can never be too sure of anybody and who they are, perception and emotions are just that overpowering. There's a bunch of different types of reasoning that supports our decisions at any given moment. A lot of those decisions we make whether good or bad, are determined by how we feel at that moment. With this realization, you may be able to acknowledge and even stop yourself at times when you need to calm down, eat, drink, sleep, etc. When it comes to others, you'll start seeing their attitudes from another angle as well.

Instead of reacting impulsively to the things people do, you should become more curious about what causes them to act the way they do. Or you could not become too consumed in it altogether. The better you are at taking great approaches and gaining comfort in your skin, the better you'll be at maintaining peace, forming opinions of others, understanding others, and living freely. We're always learning and rediscovering ourselves. The more we understand and mentally work at creating this dominant attitude will be the day humans reach another level of intelligence.

Your reactions to your experiences say a lot about your analytical skills. Whether it be of yourself, other people, things, places, etc. We give our opinions on things which can a lot of times be accurate. Then there are those times when we're flat out biased and reveal information about insecurities, fears, and pleasures which reflect why our reality is the way it is. If we could look beyond our emotional tendencies enough to create better evaluations, things like character assassination may not happen as often or be as powerful.

At times when people may attack your character, it can be because it threatens the control they have. If I have people's beliefs under my wing, then I can control what they see, how they live, who they support, what they think is possible, and who is considered evil.

Character assassination comes in many forms. You'd be surprised how often your name may get brought up in casual conversation or gossip. The narratives people create from their idea of you can be influencing. It's interesting how receiving information from a source we "trust" lowers our effort to analyze situations for ourselves. If someone you trust tells you bad things about someone else, you'll probably feel discomfort or threatened by this person. This happens without you ever genuinely knowing them. It certainly appears logical to take this approach, but we must not confine our judgments to specific narratives in any situation. It's better to be safe than sorry when potential danger is around, it's understandable. Yet, it's the balance we can show that keeps us from becoming too judgmental or creating unnecessary anxiety. People will always try to project the way they see things on to you. Sometimes the information or perceptions people provide can be accurate, but it is up to you to decipher this information by thinking critically.

A simple definition of character assassination is, **"The slandering or vicious personal verbal attack on a person with the intention of destroying or damaging that person's reputation or confidence."**

Notice the examples I'll make in the next few paragraphs about the portrayal of people's character and how powerful it can be. There are many people I could use as an example, including myself. Surely you can think of a moment when people took something to try and ruin your reputation or belittle you. The people I will use as an example stood out to me because of the misunderstood passion. It's the reason why rumors and gossip can spread so quickly. It's why people can become so easily hated.

Ridiculous headlines may get attention due to the emotional disapproval of the allegations. News stations use their platform to spread whatever agendas they choose. Some significant issues and problems never get the amount of attention it needs globally, yet there are irrelevant things that trend all the time on the news, which is merely a distraction from something most people have become accustomed to overlooking. This is all psychological warfare, and some people have mastered this game to destroy other people if needed.

The power of emotions is why it can be easy to change your perspective of someone or something entirely. It can also be the reason you're utterly passive towards the wrong things someone you admire does as well. Both, however, have one thing in common, which is a strong emotion, causing a lack of a more rational analysis of the situation.

For example, we've seen popular speakers like Malcolm X, Martin Luther King Jr, Dr. Sebi, and The Honorable Louis Farrakhan all face character assassination at some point. Some people didn't like the things Malcolm X was teaching, and some of the insensitive statements he made caused controversy. Malcolm X was brutally honest, and it rubbed people the wrong way to hear him speak his truth. It made people question his character and try to pend it as hate. Still today, many people love and respect him, but it was the conflicts dealing with others' character and pride, including his own that caused a tragic death.

There were people who were once close to him that no longer viewed him as an ally. Even when people may have similar aspirations, their approach or methods can still create some animosity. You also can't overlook the role the government may have played or other powerful and influential people in his death.

Malcolm X was viscously passionate about people's rights. Even when our intentions may be aligned in the right way, people whose plans may be the opposite will look to find ways to take you down. Malcolm X appeared to know his days were numbered. Still, he went out fighting for something the best way he knew how to from his understanding. Often it appeared he didn't care who was against him, and he proved that by starting his own group. His ideas and perspectives would continue to grow when he visited different areas around the world. He wanted to establish power in the black community instead of looking for any empathy from enemies. Listening to his old speeches, you felt his desire to create a beneficial approach to establish a prosperous life for his people.

His approach to creating change was by force (if needed), and it caused him to despise anybody and anything that appeared to be counterproductive. Malcolm X would even despise Martin Luther King Jr and criticize him in ways because of how their approach to fighting injustices wasn't the same. Ultimately the fact they both were still fighting for something gained mutual respect.

There's more to Malcolm X than a paragraph could ever articulate, and there's probably more to the story that many don't know. The point is how our approach to leadership, the way we make others feel means a lot. This isn't to say you should sugarcoat the truth or look to be kind in your approach. It's saying your wordplay, how you speak your truth should captivate if anything.

Malcolm X was an inspiration from many people's perspectives, but many others would feel uncomfortable. After all, there were white Muslims who were just as committed to justice as him. Often he would promote the idea of allowing black people to separate from the white man. He didn't think it was possible or necessary to live amongst them. He knew white people were in fear of the black man waking up and potentially treating them similarly to the way they treated blacks. He described it as a guilt complex.

To set good intentions and have emotional understanding is wisdom that can create a more enlightening approach than a threatening one. Still, it's inevitable that our beliefs won't quite align with others which can cause you to become a victim of character assassination. The truth hurts, but it must be acknowledged, or there will never be any real progress towards a greater awakening. We must, at some point, realize the ignorance tied to these emotions. Is mass murders and wars the only way to overcome most forms of tyranny or conflict? Maybe to an extent, but it still means humans, in general, haven't overcome anything truly grand.

The communication and inspiration are where all the real power lies, and it can create whatever we'd like when initiated affectively. When you look back at the events that lead up to Malcolm X becoming who he was, it was backed behind some pain, lessons, and passion. All he wanted was his people to be treated with respect. The more he learned about the world, himself, and others created a vision that fueled his goals.

Martin Luther King Jr, even today, has narratives dealing with his character being brought up. Some people argue MLK was used by the government in ways that kept the people always willing to turn the other cheek. People today may bring up his affairs and how he wasn't as righteous as everybody seemed to think he was. He's most famous for his "I have a dream" speech despite the other powerful statements he gave that may have sparked a different world for the black community. That dream was about to become a reality. After initially standing for togetherness, he realized integration wasn't the best way to uplift black people.

Today many people argue that integration held blacks back. It shows how much during that time self-love was damaged. Our emotions can guide us in ways that leave us taking the wrong approach. As much as blacks wanted to be seen as equal in the eyes of others, it only put them at a disadvantage economically. Instead of spending money with each other within their communities, they spent money with other races.

Some argue that beyond self-love, blacks wanted the resources and opportunities integration provided. That's when black athletes begin going to PWI's making HBCU's less valuable. Black coaches suffered from integration lacking jobs that may have been caused by discrimination. It was a period that had its pros and cons. Even today, when discussing NFL coaches, general managers, and owners, we see a disproportionate number. Some blacks benefited from integration, while others realized it meant blacks might never establish a real community or control.

This explains why, even today, many blacks may purchase items that never circulate in their community long at all. Yet, when we look back at the history of The Black Wall Street, and other vile agendas throughout history, we'll see how a lot of times there have been actions taken to prevent blacks from ever prospering. Nevertheless, even amid a perceived crisis, the mind knows the solution to creating prosperity. We have to allow ourselves to look beyond to truly see the opportunities like MLK.

Martin Luther King had consciously understood the power in unity and where people spend their money. He wanted to bring that value back to black people. He started to become a threat. "Destroy a man's reputation, and you don't have to talk about what he stands for" is pretty clear hear. I think the fact that MLK isn't genuinely represented by what he stood for is very telling. It appears we got the warm-hearted version of him when his ideas went beyond that.

To soften or not fully acknowledge his character in a sense is character assassination. Ironically, he was assassinated physically, as well. People will argue MLK survived the gunshot wound and even argue about who the actual killer was. Even today, there is information that hasn't been released, which could alter your whole idea of the situation. The positive or destructive influence someone may have on people is powerful.

The way in which you aspire to direct humanity to its true potential is the highest form of power and dignity one could reach. One of the most critical messages MLK provided was the consensus of how judgments should be made. He stated that people should be judged based on the content of their character, not by any prejudice misconceptions. He knew the power in character assassination and provided a logical way to analyze each other more intelligently.

Dr. Sebi was a man who taught natural ways to be healthy and proclaimed to be able to heal people from many sicknesses. Despite going to court and winning his trial, many people still discredited him. He said things like HIV, cancer, blindness, and many other diseases could be cured by bringing the body to its natural state. Detoxing the body and ridding it of any excess mucus that can make us more prone to diseases or infections is what you're mostly avoiding. Mucus is our frontline defense against infection, but too much can make us uncomfortable.

Diseases can only survive or even exist in an area of an acid-base. Many of the western treatments deal with acidic liquids, which, according to Sebi's logic, is counterproductive. Some people despise pharmaceutical companies while others believe the medicines generally aren't bad; it just appears to be more prioritized for profit as opposed to actual cures. It reminds me of the principles of power and what it takes to keep it. Completely curing or providing the things that help people become more powerful isn't a goal by people who already have it. This is simply wisdom people use to keep their advantage over you. The point is that even if there may be some flaws or misconceptions regarding which diseases he cured and didn't, it is the assassination of his character that is the problem. Even when you're genuine and want good for humanity, this can make people angry. He even knew this himself which he stated in an interview. The fact that his compassion became so overpowering to where it was superior to any negative emotions is remarkable.

People will somehow become more consumed in trying to discredit you instead of appreciating the nature of who you are. It makes me realize that even when you may have good intentions, it doesn't mean you won't still be attacked in ways to make you appear inauthentic. I sit back and realize throughout history whether you're black or white, rich or poor, perception can make you despise good people and support bad people. Often, there is someone who is black that may despise or discredit other black speakers. They may help justify the treatment they receive from other races or their lifestyle.

Some blacks fought in the American civil war for continued slavery. Many people acknowledge Africans selling their people for money during times when slaves were being sold. It's as if the battle goes beyond skin complexions. Some people will fight for you and some will sell you out. They may even sell themselves to prosper. Many people would wonder what made the moors provide the valuable information they did to help conquer people that looked like them.

Even the white man has gone to war with himself over the lack of ability to overcome bigotry. The Chinese and Japanese wars are no different on a large scale. Millions of people dying and suffering are atrocious. Fear, beliefs, money, greed, and ego can create emotions that cause mayhem when it may prevent people from getting what they want. Yet, it must be noted how everyone gets what they want when they're able to extend their experiences and desires in modest ways instead of prideful ways. We instinctively protect our kind when humans, in general, are one of a kind. In fact, "race" is a very recent concept that I'll talk more about later in this book. I do want to emphasize some general information about it now. Essentially the first human being and all of our origins began in Africa. This is a fact, yet look at how our perceptions of one another make us appear differently.

It's almost commonly known now that the concept of racism is very recent, and history tells us many of our ancestors never perceived each other or even themselves based on these distinctions. It's something we've all lost sight of. If we could track our generation back far enough we will all eventually find someone that relates to us all. That is truly incredible. Try to continuously make yourself aware of this until you've built a strong enough perception to see the bigger picture of "race." The point is we're all more committed to misunderstanding each other even when it's clear how ignorant we are behaving. Be committed to something more worthy and honorable, like growth. Don't become confused about what you're fighting for. You'll fool yourself into thinking you're doing the right thing when in fact it's the opposite.

When we speak of high character, it is used to describe those people with admirable self-control or modesty. When you've been able to tame or master that "bad side," you're in a sense escaping the darkness. Coincidentally many people describe this particular alter ego as the "shadow." Having a reputation of high character is worthy of honor to many because most people know everyone's not as noble as they may present themselves. Yet, the lies, immoral behavior, or bad character we've displayed in the past doesn't have to define us. The high character can come as a result of those experiences. So while we all can find things to criticize and character assassinate each other over, there's a difference in evaluating situations to help them as opposed to destroy them.

The Honorable Louis Farrakhan has been accused of having something to do with Malcolm X's death and is demonized by many influential people because of the authentic messages he puts out. Some people despise the million man march because it never actually accomplished anything from their perspective. Yet, many love, respect, and honor this man for teaching strength and purity in one's soul.

Nobody is perfect, which is why even when there are people who may have changed or are fighting for something important, things can be brought up to make them look flawed. But that's what makes them so powerful. The mistakes they've made, the lessons, and the experience created that wisdom to help others. It's one thing to continually make the same mistakes, but when we use them to come out a better human being, it should be apprcciated and inspirational. Think for a second about how the information about these people rather good or bad could make you support them or discredit them.

It's rare that people are able to create a clean image throughout their life, simply because of how easy it is to construct a narrative negatively. People who do have this perception of being pure, honest, or completely moral can sometimes have their flaws overlooked. Just look at the difference in how people view Barack Obama as opposed to Donald Trump. Obama naturally has more of an understanding, emotionally intelligent and charismatic persona which makes him beloved by many. He always seems to know the right things to say.

Trump would be the opposite. He says things even if it may come off as insensitive, childish, or unprofessional. I think what I'm ultimately trying to convey is how to a high extent, our outlooks of others are extremely bias and more rooted in how these people make us feel. Someone could love Barack Obama for his demeanor and skillful way of speaking and keep that consistent attitude even when bad decisions were made. Someone could hate Obama, not because he's unqualified, but because of his skin color, deep down, they may feel threatened.

Another example is in sports, athletes deal with the constant narratives that get pushed on their character all the time by journalists. It almost creates a love/hate relationship because of how we marvel at the great articles and stories attached to individual players like Michael Jordan. The downside is when pro athletes are being talked about negatively. Think about how LeBron James early in his career got so much hate.

Despite the pressure and higher standards he's been held to his whole career he had many doubters. This may be caused by how much of a pedestal people put him on. When you have someone who is loved and acknowledged as the greatest at something, it can become annoying for some people when that's all you hear. So they become stimulated by being different, or resentful towards that person. To see the person that others have so much hope and faith in fail was satisfying to those people. This can be compared to the success of anybody. People may initially build you up because you're fighting for recognition, and then when you reach the top, they want to see you fall.

There was a popular interview done by James after his first year in Miami. James was desperate for a ring by this time in his career, and for whatever reason, many people didn't want to see him get it. They ended up losing in the finals to a great Mavericks team that year. It's important to note that there were plenty of people who loved LeBron James at that time, and had he been more focused on that, it may not have got to him mentally. He'd eventually make comments about how all those hateful people had to go back to their regular lives. Later on in his career James no longer allowed these types of things to bother him. His initial decision to leave Cleveland, the burning of his jersey, and the many other narratives used to attack his character were endless.

This isn't to say constructive criticism isn't necessary or bound to happen; it's showing how the perception of people's actions create storylines representing that of good or bad deeds. Some people have no problem with how Kevin Durant left his former team OKC to join the Warriors despite recently being up 3-1 to them in the playoffs and losing. Despite winning finals MVP, other people don't even acknowledge the two championships he won while he was there. It's as if he lost people's respect, but he got the championships, which from his perception meant everything when talking about the greatest. Now, the way you got the rings can still limit you in regards to your legacy.

What point is winning a ring if you lose some of your

respect or dignity? It also is important to point out that despite KD being disliked by many over his choice, he had good intentions for himself. He had the right to do what was best for him, but to some other people, it was disgraceful. Recently he hurt his Achilles in game 5 of the NBA finals coming back too soon from an earlier injury in the playoffs. The Warriors were after a 3 peat.

Despite many people who may have resented KD for joining them in the first place, he may have gained some respect for doing something that is truly a test of a real warrior, and that was risking his career for his teammates and making history. It's just interesting to me how the information itself can be painted in a way that can cause hate or admiration. You never know, one day you could be the perceived villain, the next day you may be the hero.

Look at how "student-athletes" have just recently been allowed to make money off of their name, but the school profits millions. It's the perception of them being students and not professionals that hold enough power to actually make them look bad for even getting caught profiting off of their own name. The significant storylines would paint a picture as if they're bad people for doing this. Despite the greed of those in powerful positions, the narrative is as if they're doing the right thing by punishing them. It's as if it displays bad character to profit off your name, but we live in a society that promotes capitalism. It's hypocritical to not let people benefit in any way they can because that's what America is all about right? Now recently, players have been granted the opportunity to make money off of their name after consistent talk and outrage. What changed? Their perception.

Many people argue that today's society is still centered around the concepts of slavery. Instead of the past physical methods of control, it's mental now. As long as the top dog doesn't feel threatened about his control, he doesn't mind allowing the people under him to be productive. A common analogy used is athletes and the millions of dollars they make. Yet, they're still being used in a way that'll never allow them to truly prosper. They'll always have this "master" who can overrule them, throw them to the dirt if they act out, or ruin their reputation if needed. The "master" mindset is what distinguishes people who will always be slaves and the people who see beyond the illusion.

I still remember the first time I read a book called "40 million dollar slave" by William C Rhoden. He emphasized how Jackie Robinson thought to be heroic for being the first African American player in the MLB. He later would have regrets about ever doing this. People criticized him saying he helped destroy the Negro Baseball League by being in favor of white interests. In this case, it was simply a lack of understanding or guidance about what would be best for his community. The list goes on and on.

Why, at some point, do certain people who may have good intentions become despised? It's because all it takes is the wrong comment or action that can create a narrative designed to discredit them altogether. Just because someone has good intentions doesn't mean they will gain others' support, it could be keeping them from accomplishing their agendas. It's not hard to find things we may disagree with about the world. Something small and insignificant to one person can be a big deal to someone else, creating a feeling that makes them resentful.

We've seen people who follow Islam or are Jewish face horrific punishment and demonization because of their beliefs. We've seen famous people's careers ruined off of a wrong decision or because of someone's planned agenda to ruin their reputation. Everyone's immediate reaction to Kanye West talking about slavery hit people at an emotional level. If something isn't articulated the right way, or it is presented in a way that comes off insensitive, it can cause a lot of problems, even if there was some truth to it.

Nobody has any true control over the way we are perceived. Even when people make attempts to show how much they give or donate, many despise it sensing it was more ego-driven than genuine. They may question why you had to record it or announce it. Some people who give are proud of it which is why they may do that, others simply understand perception and want something good attached to their name and image. On one end, it's not essential to have to show everything you do, but on the other end seeing is believing.

Some people made Dave Chappelle out to be crazy or on drugs after he vanished to another country and turned down a massive contract with Comedy Central. He was in interviews explaining how he didn't want to wear a dress and how they were committed to convincing him to do so. They claimed how funny of a scene it'd be, but not to Dave. Could it have just been funny? Possibly. Could it also have been a set agenda with intentions beyond to make people laugh? Possibly. It's not rare to see a lot of famous males at some point in their career wear a dress, so who knows. Even after all that, he still gets criticized in many ways because of his straightforward jokes. Even at times when he makes true statements, it doesn't necessarily mean that people will always acknowledge it. If it brings feelings of discomfort or anger, then many will become more hateful.

Michael Jackson was always criticized for the skin disease he had, causing his skin complexion to become lighter as if it were indeed bleached. Many were skeptical of this being something he did purposely because of the perception that dark-skinned isn't as appealing as being light-skinned. He had been called a kid molester half his life as well for allegedly touching minors.

It's still being brought up today, despite no evidence ever being found of the allegations. Many people may never get enough insight to know what happened honestly, but that doesn't change the power in how their perception of him can still be shifted. Speculation and doubt are enough to create a lasting image of hate. The accusations alone are a lot of times enough to make people look at you in disgust, even if you are innocent. The fact your name is even associated with something disgraceful can ruin a reputation.

Sometimes I read the Bible and think to myself, wow, they took something great Jesus was doing and twisted it into something terrible. Something that stood out to me from the Bible was how easily the narrative can shift. The people's approach to life was always mutually exclusive to their ideas of what it meant.

For example, when you take heed to the things that made Jesus disliked, it was rooted in much of what this chapter emphasizes. Pride, jealousy, fear of losing power, and their way of life caused people in power to demonize him. In Jesus's case, despite being disliked for being so loving, it was his lack of intimidation of their power that made him a real threat. It was the fact he expressed how he was the Messiah. That claim alone made it mandatory that something had to happen, or it would be the beginning of the end for them. The jealousy came when other people started believing in him. Rulers know how powerful this is which is why it angered them. The miracle workings he did on the blind, sick, and possessed individuals didn't sway the rulers in any way. In fact, instead of acknowledging his deeds as miracles, it was associated with Satan. That is the narrative that allowed them to put him to death.

It should be noted how much of their religious views helped support their reasoning behind their disliking of him. For example, the rulers connected helping sinners to blasphemy. The rulers also associated working on the Sabbath day as a bad thing. Jesus would go against these concepts knowing they were man-made. When he was confronted about these deeds, Jesus would respond, "Is it lawful on the Sabbath to do good or to do evil, to save life or to kill? But they kept silent. So when he had looked around them with anger, being grieved by the hardness of their hearts (Mark 3:4,5)."

It makes me wonder why man's ego is so overpowering and why their sense of true identity and power is limited in theory to their own concepts. We can make claims to the material things this world provides, but who made this possible? Who created this? Surely not man, so it is inevitable that our egotistical rationalizations of how this world works eventually creates conflict with something that goes beyond them. To be able to have money, power, rulership, religion, and influence the way of life is something many aspire to do. I question why it ends there. To ascend beyond these desires, we must realize how to expand beyond our ways of thinking. Man has been content basking in his ignorance, murdering, deceiving others, and even himself for the false sense of power it gives him. Despite it all, as a writer, I can still sit back and admire the challenge and beauty in how our perceptions always play the role of the director.

We have our initial reactions and whenever we are presented with new pieces of information it creates a plot twist. That new information can change the whole reaction by you. The tests life will throw at you is only a representation of the unknown, which causes worry a lot of times.

The beauty in consciousness and the possibilities within any given moment are always creating miracles. Know this and realize many things are going right for you, so don't let one bad circumstance make you overlook that. There is a power within you that can guide you places. You may not even consciously be able to explain how it manifested. You were just so in tune with yourself, you realized nobody was ever in your way besides yourself.

Why does the Bible, a book written so long ago, still convey accuracy in much of its principles? Because it's nothing new under the sun. It is the very nature of ourselves that we are always at war with. It's a reasonably logical explanation as to why history repeats itself. Until we realize this we'll continue to be misguided and take the wrong approach. In many instances in the Bible, there was a challenging circumstance. The people would have a hopeless reaction to it and Jesus would shift the entire possibility of what can and can't happen by simply changing their belief. You had people who admired Jesus for the things he did and people who hated him because of how they decided to perceive or make sense of his actions.

Rarely do we have the full details to a lot of stories, but it doesn't stop us from throwing our opinions around and criticizing others. We're quick to throw people under the bus as if our moral light is always on. Our initial reactions should be to try and gain as much understanding as possible before condemning or even praising anyone in any situation.

Kevin Hart went on the Ellen show to express how someone looking up an old tweet of his was an attack on his character and career. People will search and try to find times in our life where we have done wrong or were down. Often, it's not hard because we all make mistakes or have been there. The power in perception can make you hate or dismiss anything someone may say because you have this perception of them as immoral. Yet, who are we to really judge? Even in certain cases when people have done their time in prison, people's perception of them still will never change.

Some people will never see Chris Brown beyond a woman beater despite the relationship being abusive on both ends. Even today, some people are still angered by Mike Vick and his dogfighting ring despite doing time. It's not to say just because someone does the time they've somehow changed or are any better of a person. It simply speaks to the power in how one particular event can become the highlight of who someone is. It's something many people don't ever escape. The irony of it all is how many things are spoken about people that many of us don't even know personally.

There's a reason people often say there are two sides to every story. Or maybe three? Your side, their side, and the truth. It's interesting how we tend to react aggressively initially at times and then calm down after we take in more information. You may be resentful toward someone upon meeting them, but after conversing, you understand them in a way, you couldn't before because you lacked information, which would give you better proper understanding. People's perceptions only extend to the level of information available to them or to the unique experiences you've given them. It creates flawed outlooks of one another all the time. This is why you shouldn't spend a lot of energy trying to prove things to people. While being misunderstood is frustrating and can hurt, understand that perception will always inevitably overrule your desire to be loved and respected by everyone.

The things that create the most reactions are the things that hit people on an emotional level. It doesn't matter how ignorant the topic is; people will entertain it. Businesses will go to high lengths to protect their reputation, or at least create marketing ideas that give people the impression of their products being of high quality. Most times, people only like certain places of business because of the way they feel when they go there. It's almost as if the image has more value than the authenticity and natural energy in a lot of cases.

We all want the world to reflect how we think it ought to be, or at least what we've always been told. The primary methods of control strive on the divide and conquer agenda. It causes confusion, hatred, and conflict. If the truth does hurt because of this, how much of our lives are portrayed on the basis of lies and deception? A difference in beliefs shouldn't result in millions of people being killed, or someone being character assassinated. In some instances, vile humans do downright bad things that deserve the outrage it gets. We should expose the traits of people's inhuman character and look to improve collectively. We should also become more responsible about how we go about placing judgments on others.

Embracing life and the beauty of it means not everything will be aligned with your perception. It doesn't make it bad or should have to cause hate. It's interesting how we can hold on to grudges or hold things against others for long periods, but want to forget the things we've done wrong quickly. Ultimately this signifies a huge mental growth when we can combat our differences and still appreciate one another. When there are times when people have done wrong, how many times have we tried to help cure any emotional issues that may have caused that behavior instead of immediately bashing them?

We must take into account the things people have been through that may have traumatized them or created the attitude they possess. After all, if we truly did know better, we'd do better. This doesn't mean that when people act in wicked ways, they don't deserve what happens to them. Going about gaining understanding and trying to target the source to these actions is what can solve issues that are often repetitive in society.

We hear about school shootings and terrorist attacks that often no longer even come as a surprise. This isn't normal and never will be. The conditioning of the mind that causes this behavior shows the power in perception and how it can make someone do something so psychotic.

Use these examples to help create a better understanding of life and the way you go about making sense of others' behavior. Always seek to understand and assure you are using a lot of information before concluding.

Cognitive Dissonance

> ***"Sometimes people hold a core belief that is very strong. When they are presented with evidence that works against that belief, the new evidence cannot be accepted. It would create a feeling that***

is extremely uncomfortable, called cognitive dissonance. And because it is so important to protect the core belief, they will rationalize, ignore and even deny anything that doesn't fit in with the core belief." - Frantz Fanon

The moment you hear something that objects to your core beliefs is the moment you begin to defend them. The arrogance attached to perception causes us to feel as if we're always right. This always reminds me of the famous quote, *"I am the wisest man alive, for I know one thing, and that is that I know nothing."* Socrates was a man who was open to the possibilities of everything. He knew that the moment he thought he knew it all would be the day he knew nothing. Usually, the man who becomes egotistical as if he knows it all is quick to bump his head. When we model our intelligence based on projections and theories that have no true answer to life, we are only feeding the ego, fooling ourselves with awards that never gave any true depths of illumination.

The moment we begin to accept detrimental philosophies is when we start to cut off possibility. It's the moment we no longer question, which is a sign of a society lacking inquisitiveness. Albert Einstein repeatedly informed people how he was no different than you, only passionately curious. Instead of just accepting many of the things Einstein was taught, it only increased his questions about them. He never allowed a belief to become so strong that he no longer took heed to other possibilities. He realized just how infinite and magical our thoughts are just by being curious. He didn't get offended when things he thought were true ended up being false. It fascinated him to discover beyond. The knowledge we gain is essential, but not as necessary and as powerful as our imagination.

I would agree that the truth hurts those core beliefs, but is it the truth that creates this pain or makes you uncomfortable? I don't think so. It is the discomfort you get from being perceived as wrong. It insinuates a dumb person. Though it doesn't mean you are dumb at all, it's how it makes people feel. This feeling is directly associated with other emotions like self-esteem and pride. People like to feel right not wrong, so we defend ourselves before ever trying to understand one another truly. It is said that ignorance is bliss. People are content with living under their fabricated illusions if it doesn't tamper with their beliefs, even if the expansion of thought results in a more harmonious life experience.

It is critical to be able to unlearn and relearn information. Cognitive dissonance causes you to defend yourself instead. At this point, it is no longer about what is true or false. It is habitually at this point where humanity fails to accomplish any real success at communication. We consistently fail to see beyond what we've always known. No actions can take place if we can't even come to any reasonable conclusions. We'll spend hours trying to convince each other who is right. We will end up arguing about something completely off-topic.

It's a matter of time before someone indulges in a typical attempt to win a debate. Attacking someone's appearance, making jokes, or tapping into the audience's emotions to get a specific reaction are common tactics. These are attempts to make you look at that person differently. This can go on and on. A homeless man on the street could speak to you elegantly and truthfully. Many would despise the knowledge he would spread because they already have this perception of him being unqualified. Meanwhile, the people you see with money, or positions of power are easily able to influence with lies because of the perception of them knowing more than you.

What subliminal cues are you using to form your conclusions about people and things? Why are words more meaningful depending on who says them? It all lies in our perceptions defining when, where, and who we accept this information from. What does writing a book mean to someone you perceive as unqualified, even if the information was very informative? Realize as much as it appears like you're always right; your brain is just trying to make sense of any daily interactions with the objective world, which is often extremely subjective.

Deception

> **"All deception in the course of life is indeed nothing else but a lie reduced to practice and falsehood practice from words to things."**
>
> **– Robert Southey**

Most of the cars, electronic devices, and even track times were at one point in time seen as impossible to create or break. A compelling vision is one that isn't discouraged by people's lack of belief in the idea. We all, at times, fulfill this doubt towards the things we don't think are possible to do. Nelson Mandela once said, "It always seems impossible until it's done."

Deception comes in many forms, and it starts with ourselves. Deception poses a limit on the things we can do. The fact that we've never seen something done before fools us into thinking that it could never happen. Beyond our self-doubt, this way of thinking could have been motivated by the things we were taught during childhood. As a child, you were open to many possibilities. A lot of times, you were told, "that's not how life works" or "you can't do that." The result of that is deception since it changes your beliefs, preventing you from attempting thinking it is already impossible.

The things we are taught to value and perceive growing up creates the type of cultural experience developed within an area. You have western philosophies and theories that routinely distorts the authenticities of nature and its real purpose. They become so repetitive that we lose the ability to fathom how flawed our ways of thinking have become.

Perspective is one thing; a fact is something completely different. It's easy to get these two confused. It's almost as if they coexist to form our definition of why things are the way they are. As a man who seeks people's true intentions and the truth, I find it a bit weird how quickly you are crazy or a conspiracy theorist for exploring the dimensions of possibility. As if the possibilities of your very existence aren't enough to leave you speechless. Males release millions of sperm cells, but only one fertilized an egg to create, you. The earth is floating in space at the perfect distance from the sun to create, life. Anything swaying you to feel below the powers you possess is deception and should be confidently dismissed immediately.

You know, it sounds cliché, but the truth shall set you free. Think about the level of confusion and deception that can leave a country or even humanity distraught. A simple thought or suggestion can end up being the explanation for something that was never legitimately verified. The bible compares the people to sheep, with a shepherd. I often sit back and reflect on that analogy. Sheep don't think for themselves. Sheep can easily be led in the wrong direction. It is a sad but accurate comparison to life simply because of the process involved with learning.

From the moment we've been born, we've always been led to believe, instead of shown how to see. Honestly, there are many truths about ourselves and the world that we fail to acknowledge. Would you call that ingenious manipulation by the few with power or denial of the masses? I'd say both. We feel as if the world and the changes that we dream of are out of reach. How much of this is because of our perception and belief in a deceptive fate? The truth is, change is inevitable, our dreams are conquerable, and the world is yours.

If you've only seen the false depictions of life, it'll be hard to see beyond it. Much of what you see on television isn't real, just a box that's programming your mind. The average American watches 153 hours of TV a month. I know this makes you feel uncomfortable. Watching TV is relaxing and entertaining, so I expect a quick defensive reaction. To say TV does not influence the things you drink, eat, and react to emotionally like the news, is simply passiveness.

We'd all like to believe we consciously make decisions on our own. Usually, it is from some type of influential engagement. The things that go beyond our awareness is the true depths of psychology and the reason you do things unnoticeably. It is the reason you see the world in whichever way the people who manipulate you choose. It's no wonder they spend billions of dollars on marketing.

When television and news first begin to become popular, it was seen as an engine, according to John Adams. We flip through the channels, and it paints our reality in a way we don't realize. If you're always watching reality TV, and they consistently show men cheating, you may form this certainty of men in general. Or you may flip to the news and hear breaking story after another of murders, bombings, or even terrorists. How does it make you feel? Not safe, I can guarantee you that. Fear makes us crave a psychological dependence of feeling protected. This could easily allow leaders of our world to lead you in a misrepresented way, ambiguity, or I think they call it being politically correct.

Even some of these apps you may get on every day can create a belief that may not be as true in reality. The more someone takes control over your perception of the world, the more your actions follow it. The more they control you. That is the only control, deception. Truth is, we believe what we perceive. Something that often leaves me confused is why we run from the truth. As if it's better living under our deceitful principles rather than the ones that craft our happiness. That happiness that everyone in life is looking for. The truth will always be there patiently waiting for you to acknowledge it.

What is happiness?

> "**Happiness is not something you postpone for the future; it is something you design for the present**." -Jim Rohn

We may all be able to agree that corrupt systems play a big part in how it can destroy the world, or at least cause mayhem. In that same sense, partiality, greed, and ego corrupt the heart. And despite that gluttony, it still doesn't make a millionaire completely happy, or someone under tyranny completely depressed. I've seen millionaires stressed as if they have not a dollar to their name. I've seen people with not a dollar to their name, still appreciating the beauty of life itself. What's the difference? A matter of how you are looking at life, and the things we show appreciation towards at any given moment.

There is so much to appreciate about just being alive, yet we get caught up in the things that don't even truly define who we are. "It isn't what you have or who you are or where you are or what you are doing that makes you happy or unhappy. It is what you think about." That's a wise quote from Dale Carnegie. When you think about it, he's right. Nobody is upsetting you but you and the things you are thinking about in the present moment. These thoughts you have literally change your brain.

When it comes to anything, we hold the key to whether it is possible within our mind and will to do it. "Whether a man thinks he can or can't, he's right" - Henry Ford. If you can grasp the concept of this, you can truly change your life for the better. It's hard for me to be mad these days, I'm more at peace than I've ever been in my life. Embracing the challenges you face and turning unfortunate situations into opportunities to learn changes your whole approach. You will always find the beauty in life through the vastness in perceiving any circumstance. You will unlock the key to possibility.

Imagine not being able to go to a concert with your friends. Your parents didn't allow you to go. You may feel anger built up. Later, you find out your friends had been in a wreck from drunk driving. That may change the way you feel about the whole situation. You had initial anger for not being able to go, but then a feeling of relief knowing that could've been you. Even if you do still wish you had gone because maybe you could've been the responsible one, who's to say how things would've played out? Only the universe, something beyond our perceptions, predictions, and understanding, has precise control. This is why I've learned to trust the universe.

As I've looked back at my life, the events that lead up to this very moment seem purposeful, or fate if you will.

The moments I could've potentially died, gone to jail, or been caught in a situation that could've ended bad shows how there's a higher power guiding us and a little luck to be reasonable. It's as if good or bad there's a bigger picture life is trying to reveal to us all based on our desires and true purpose.

Once again, thoughts are directly linked to how you feel, and I've repeated some of these statements for a reason. The brain picks up on things based on repetition. Therefore, the more you read this book, the more likely you'll eventually gain acceptance of the truth because of the number of impressions it has made on your subconscious mind. The same way repetitive lies will eventually form an acceptance by your subconscious mind because it can't differentiate from what is real and what is fake.

Think about a time where you were extremely tired. At the moment, if someone called you with great news, say money or something of that magnitude. How quick would your mood change? I don't think you'd be tired after this news, you'd have a burst of energy. Everything is energy, and it starts with your thoughts. You may think the money is what created this energy, but it is your attitude about money that created this energy, which is nothing more than thoughts.

It's critical to pay attention to how negative you are because that attitude becomes a reality for you. Not only do you feel bad, but that's what you will notice in the world. There's plenty of beauty among us, but if we focus on the bad, we'll feel like we are living in hell. It may seem as if you have no control over why you see life this way, but we do. Try to actually look at things from another angle and you'll begin to see! You will start to speak to yourself differently and become more detailed in what you want out of life.

Our happiness is usually defined by vague things that give no indication of true paradise. It's easy to say we want money, cars, and clothes yet; you can't put a price on your happiness. The biggest eye-opener is when we see millionaires depressed. Jim Carey once said that he wishes everyone could become rich and famous, so they could see it isn't everything. NBA players like Kevin Love and Demar Derozan have been the center story around depression in the league. People were saying, "How can you be depressed? You can buy anything you want." Demar's response to that was, "I wish everyone in the world were rich so they would realize money isn't everything."

Still, I must admit, I'd rather be sad in a Lamborghini than no car at all. Also, being depressed about lack of food, or ability to pay bills is more severe than millionaires complaining about any first world problems, they could easily seem a bit unappreciative. Yet, I'd also be missing the point. We become misguided about the fact that money does make you happy, but it isn't the source of your happiness. We also tend to overlook the responsibilities, loss of friends, time, pressure, and amount of problems that come with having a lot of money. Many people desire money, get it, then live their life in complete fear of losing it. Think about how it's always some sort of emotional attachment to something with a perceived gateway to freedom or happiness. It is our minds that possess the actual true gateway.

Everyone has this idea of traveling and living happily ever after when life will always have challenges rich or poor. It will always be our attitudes that make us happy or sad. Our perception of people with a lot of money is that they have this perfect life when this is the clearest example of how thoughts overpower any amount of wealth we may get. It works the same way with people who are consistently stressed as opposed to generally being happy most days. What type of thoughts about the world are being entertained the most to make them feel this way consistently? Negatives ones. Most don't even have to be accurate, and most of them aren't, but what difference does is it make if you believe it and continually entertain it?

I've seen multiple stories of people having millions of dollars and losing it all. If we have a terrible mindset upon receiving money, it won't be long before we lose it. In that same sense if we have the right mindset before having wealth, it will eventually come to us and potentially stay. I've read stories of millionaires committing suicide and doing many other things that would make you sit back and say, "They were rich, it couldn't have been that bad!"

A lot of people get money and remember their happiest moments when they were broke. When things were a lot simpler. This isn't to say you should be satisfied being broke. It is to remind you to never forget who you are. Don't get lost chasing something that isn't the true gateway to your freedom and peace of mind. This reminds me of a book called "The Social Animal," written by David Brooks. He was emphasizing happiness and had some interesting points about how we misjudge what makes us happy.

"Relationships between money and happiness can be complex. Richer countries tend to be happier countries, and richer people tend to be happier than poorer people, but the relationship is not that strong; it depends on how you DEFINE happiness, and it is the subject of fierce debate among the experts." Immediately we can see how misconstrued we can become when we attach money to happiness. "Winning the lottery produces a short term jolt of happiness, but the long term effects are invisible. People are pretty bad at judging what will make them happy. People vastly overvalue work, money, and real estate. They vastly undervalue intimate bonds and the importance of arduous challenges. The average Americans say that if they could only make $90,000 more a year, they could "fulfill all thcir dreams", but the evidence suggests they are wrong."

Our happiness always comes from within. You'd think otherwise watching music videos, commercials, and people with money who seem blissful. Materials are nice, but it will never complete you. Sometimes it may take people to have these things to realize something is still missing. It is the connection with our true selves and nature that brings the most fulfilling sensations known to man. Even at times when I may be happy about the money I have when I'm able to use it to help others, it gives me a feeling that goes beyond money. It truly is the simple things that make us happy. I guess the best things in life are free. After all, we do have the free ability to see life any way we choose. It's all rooted in our emotions. It causes us to do things and think in ways that don't even have to make sense.

Emotions can overpower sensibility. I'll discuss this issue later on in the book to hopefully bring more understanding to money and happiness. We've gotten so detailed with life and the way it ought to be lived. Life is defined beyond your culture, beyond just money, somewhere where all possibilities are considered. It's tough for some to even picture a life beyond the one that has been defined for them. It only shows how much we have been taught to shut down our creative minds and conform. Once you start thinking for yourself and looking beyond the propaganda you've always known, you'll never be the same.

Pride

"Pride is the mask of one's own faults."

Perception is individually unique but extends to perceptions seen by a race, group, or even religion. The conflicts with religion, culture, corrupt governments and the color of our skin have created dishonorable hate for one another. I must say a quote from a great revolutionist Thomas Paine. "Eloquence may strike the ear, and the language of sorrow draw forth the tear of compassion, but nothing can reach the heart that is steeled with prejudice." What a powerful message. We often look beyond the facts to defend our ways of thinking.

If in your heart, there is a shield of preconceived opinions that are not based on reason or experience, it is like talking to a wall. Sadly, this is the type of attitude people have towards each other. Anything that has been taught to you based on hate or destruction is non-beneficial. What's in your heart defines your character. Character is the moral guideline of our intentions at any given moment. What is truly in your heart?

He also said, "To argue with a man who has renounced the use and authority of reason, and whose philosophy consists of holding humanity in contempt, is like administering medicine to the dead, or endeavoring to convert an atheist by scripture." Paine understood the power in the way people have constructed their perceptions in that analogy. Most people don't want to see things differently because of the comfort of their fixed views. They are only harming themselves.

The way we see life can cripple humanity itself. Paine had a unique way of writing, he called most of the information common sense. A book written in 1776 with relevance to the times of today shows how common sense isn't that common, I guess. It seems as if at the end of the day it comes down to reason. Nobody likes to feel wrong. Nobody likes to feel forced to do or believe anything. It's a never-ending battle of perception. Think to yourself how you may scorn upon another perspective or reality because your viewpoint is the only reality you see.

I wish we did consider reason over pride. Or better yet, I wished we'd take pride in the right things. Pride can be useful when it's aligned with the right attitude. We should be taking pride in being better humans. We should be taking pride in how we will be remembered on this earth and the people we inspire. We should be taking pride in overcoming ignorance. Have we ever considered understanding before condemning? What type of permanent and flawed rational thought consensus have we created? Not a reliable one, but a surprisingly conservative one. The consistent teachings and repetitive vile philosophies make it clear that it's hard to look beyond the way something has always been done. Tradition is valued, but illogical to suppose it will always be the correct way, despite the unpredictable circumstances that lay forth. The one thing that will forever hold the people back is our pride as opposed to unity.

Unity

> **"He who experiences the unity of life sees his own Self in all beings, and all beings in his own self, and looks on everything with an impartial eye."** – Buddha

The power of unity is beautiful, it's a step towards

another level of consciousness, it's an art, it's life. No matter the scenario one thing is for sure, if something can grow, one is able to become more powerful. This can lead to new discoveries, new possibilities, and new ways of living. As human beings, we want to belong which is why groups and brands represent us in many ways. Not just the groups and brands but the pride, reputation, and uniqueness associated with them. We don't want to feel left out and at the same time, we don't want to be a part of something that doesn't have any respected representation of us.

The true challenge is using the ability to come together and unite in ways that can better our world. Indulging in the subjective ways of winning over arguments or determining what is true or false is a thing of the past. Focusing on what we can objectively agree on, and the root of what makes us feel so differently about why we may be disagreeing is a better step.

I once noticed a picture of a white baby holding the hand and smiling with a black man. Not a clue of what hate is or the difference in them both. One day though that baby will be taught this vile way of thinking and perceiving the world. What are we teaching our generation of kids for them to grow into the same faulty way of prejudiced thinking that makes this world so corrupt today?

We study the past, at least what is given to us through formal education, instead of teaching a new wave of concepts that can change our world for the better. The kids are the future, just like we were at one point. Imagine if we were taught to view the world in a different way, rather than the perception of the world, many are trying to escape from now. When we truly grasp the essence of this human experience, we'd realize how we're all experiencing it together. When you understand the unity that's attached to life you will look to understand others before condemning. This approach to others is critical to implement in your character.

What makes you Intellectual?

> **"The problem is not that people are uneducated, the problem is that they are educated just enough to believe what they've been taught. And not educated enough to question what they've been taught." – Unknown**

What is it that makes us perceive someone intelligent? By definition, intelligence is simply the ability to AQUIRE and APPLY knowledge and skills. Many people don't continue to learn new information, so they're always in a limited outlook. Not only that, taking in information isn't where it ends, applying it in your life is where the true essence of intelligence shows. It takes persistence to apply these principles

Beyond the definition, we sometimes become fascinated with the anecdotes that create this narrative of people being of higher stature mentally. What if it's always the storyline attached to specific people throughout history that makes them appear like some genius? Many people marveled at the story of how Christopher Columbus discovered America. After learning more information, many people's perceptions of him became inauthentic to the point they don't even care to acknowledge the holiday.

Someone could be labeled a genius in a vast number of ways. If they're able to shift a way of thinking or influence millions of people they could be called a genius. If they made a miraculous discovery or invented something that changed the world, they could be labeled a genius. I'm willing to go as far as to say that war hero's, scientists, engineers, and even rappers could be geniuses in a sense. The definition of a genius is someone with exceptional intellectual or creative power or other NATURAL ABILITY. We all have natural abilities that we can tap into.

When we look at the past, we often appreciate the great fortitude people show, whether it be patriotism or rebellious acts. We admire people of the past, which is understandable. The times that they were misunderstood and kept fighting until their passion finally became a reality inspires us. We grow fond and attached to their integrity, morals, or simply put, their desire. That courageous spirit is in each one of us; we just have to figure out what brings out that energy. What will we do in this present moment that gives people of the future something to admire about our inner genius? Many of our ancestors dreamed of having the technology and opportunities we have today. It is a dishonor to them not to live passionately and conquer whatever goals we set out for ourselves. You're more than capable.

We grow up still asking questions about life and still finding ourselves, yet we thought this was the sole purpose of school. School isn't designed to help you find yourself, it's not even designed to help you understand money. Life, as well as your spirituality, will always go beyond the things you are constructed to learn. Many will argue that the only purpose of school is for the interactions. After all, we're social animals. Is that why many people often recall their greatest experiences when they were in college?

Many times college students are under complete distress from work, school, and maintaining a social life. What is it that makes it still worth it even if it may cause us some debt, late nights, and extra time? Obviously, money and potential careers are significant. I'm willing to argue it goes deeper and beyond that though. The experiences and relationships that are established during that time can last a lifetime. Beyond the degree, many people will tell you it is your networking ability that creates job opportunities. Knowing somebody that knows somebody is how opportunities are created.

As you get older, you'll realize how much more information there always is to learn. It never truly ends. Since we still grow up not knowing a lot of things that are critical to know about life, it makes me question what being smart is. What really defines intellect? A 4.0 GPA may be a common answer. Some of the wisest speakers, artists, authors, and philosophers, didn't finish school. Even today you see blogs about how Google doesn't hire potential employees based on whether they have a degree or not. It's more about their skillset and experiences that are valued, not how the skills were necessarily attained.

This also brings a better perspective in realizing degrees don't necessarily mean better quality work. There has been an increase in a variety of self-paced courses as well as opportunities to take free classes from different colleges. It's important to understand that it isn't just about getting a degree, it's about having a plan. Opportunities to build your resume` and relationships are unlimited, you have to expand your thoughts to see them. The energy someone puts in to genuinely learn things that they're passionate about is real intelligence. Many (not all) don't have a real passion for things they study in school. Their love is for that paper that says they graduated. In some cases, you may say a degree is necessary, but in other situations, it is used as a tool. We talk about corruption in politics, religion, and government, but rarely do we acknowledge the corruption in academics. The amount of people who actually "learn" isn't indeed prioritized as high as money or control is.

For example, there's been a new rule made by the NCAA requiring agents to have a bachelor's degree. People are calling it the "Rich Paul Rule" because Rich Paul is one of the best agents in the NBA, and he doesn't have a degree. This created a lot of outrage. People like LeBron James and many other NBA players were questioning the intent of the rule, arguing an agent like Rich Paul has done well without it. He did, however, get a certification which was the only initial requirement. They would eventually change the rule back. The idea that someone isn't capable of succeeding in something without a degree is illogical. It also shows how rules like this can be made to keep a particular type of people down.

Think about how young adults are preyed on to accrue tons of debt by going to college and given loans. Yet, if they were to go to a bank and look to receive these loans to start their own business, they may a lot of times not qualify. Are we trying to build a productive society by allowing millions of people to be in debt? Today many political candidates pose solutions to end college debt which only shows how wicked it was from the start.

Balancing life and going to school, especially for something that you're not passionate about, is difficult. I commend people who've gone through this process. You learn a lot during this chapter in life, and whether college makes you or breaks you, it can still result in you finding your real purpose. The passion to graduate can leave a lot of people willing to do anything. Many kids cheat through college. There's even been a recent college scam where kids who hadn't gone through proper testing had been accepted into schools because well, money talks.

It's as if everything in life and the power it has is always associated with the image rather than the authentic nature of it. The point is someone who is genuinely taking the time to learn something with no reward probably would be more knowledgeable than someone who may have a degree in that subject but isn't as passionate. Many people only feel the need to have a degree because of the power in how potential employers or clients will perceive them.

We all need something symbolic that makes us feel more comfortable about our decisions when identifying who's qualified. The problem is in how this can still be detrimental because of how flawed the approach is. Just because someone has the title or credentials of a teacher, politician, or lawyer doesn't mean they're a good one. You have people who will abuse their power. A lot of times beyond the credentials, we have to find the right person for us. You may have to change therapists, doctors, churches, etc. before you find the right person who resonates with you the right way. Look beyond titles, look deeper into their character, past work, passion, and intent so you can make an excellent overall rational decision in any given situation.

The popular route to attaining success has hurt more people than helped. It's why college debt surpassed credit card debt. You could say going to college has become a trending thing, just like any other trend like fashion, music, and dances. There's more than one way to prosper in life. Many times the things we think about but overlook could be life-changing decisions had we took them more seriously. The ideas we never write down could be million-dollar ideas. The chances we were too timid to take could've put us in an entirely different situation than we're in now. You're always one right decision away from doing something amazing. We just have to decide to do it.

There's a book called Nature God that I happened to come across in the library once. This book was written by Mathew Stewart. One of the most intriguing things to me about this book is how he emphasized a lot of misconceptions about not only God but intelligence. A lot of times, people are overlooked because they lack credentials that determine if we perceive them as intelligent. Dr. Thomas Young is one of the wisest men I've ever read about and isn't talked about in our history books. When we study the history of America, it is presented in such a way that fits the narrative. Those meaningful events or people that get swept under the rug leave a gray area. His beliefs went beyond religion, but it kept him from becoming a popular and honorable figure then and now. When America first begin to form, the biggest and most significant war of that time was the war on perception.

America's fate always seemed to be attached to its forefathers in one way or another. It kept them from ever becoming the truly prosperous, righteous, and free country it always intended to be. The intentions were flawed from the start when you take into consideration how this land was colonized. Yet, there still were people like Dr. Thomas Young that could've potentially created a country that was established with the right principles. He and Thomas Paine were two people you'd consider to be ahead of their time. They were often condemned because of how strong the American people's core beliefs were when it came to religion. Not only that, the people with the power to make decisions during that time weren't completely embracing the ideas both of them were teaching.

Instead of using this opportunity to expand our

way of thinking, America became resentful toward new philosophies. Young's beliefs could have very well changed the whole culture and history of the U.S. In fact; some Presidents had Young's books in their book collection. While acknowledging the truth of his work personally, presidents kept it to themselves to avoid the emotional demonization that may come as a result. During the revolution, the ways of thinking would either lead to prosperity or destruction.

Young was the actual leader of the Boston Tea Party. He and Thomas Paine crafted their pamphlets, describing the true essence of equality, and these concepts help create things like the Declaration of Independence. He even played a critical role in the abolition of slavery. Young never finished school. He was always discredited for his lack of school background despite his authentic wisdom. He fought for the right to be free. He was a freethinker who consistently stated how he was simply a natural man. Young didn't like the idea being pushed of him being a born sinner. He also felt that it gave people the wrong idea about God and the true nature of what it meant. He felt the teachings misguided people emotionally.

It's why many of the founding fathers were deists, but many didn't openly admit it. It appears to me as if deism still closely resembled Christianity but with a more expanded perspective based on reason. They would dismiss the miracles like Jesus parting the Red Sea or doing any other supernatural occurrences but still believed in a God. It reminds me of the book, "The Kybalion". In this book, they distinguished the difference in religion and theology. To be religious is to simply acknowledge something beyond our understanding, an infinite power that has manifested itself the conscious ability to marvel at its own power. Theology is the result of man attempting to theorize as some "middle man" to bring purpose to it all. Whether by characteristics, personalities, or qualities, it is to create fulfillment, but with a subjective approach. This doesn't mean we've gained any real depth in regards to enlightenment; it is our ego that feels content with these concepts because it gives us a basis of understanding.

The Bible uses many metaphors so the initial ideas of many statements in the book are a result of how it is decided to be decoded. You may think at the surface level that much of the Bible is simplistic, but it is more esoteric. When it comes to the translations of these teachings, it can be flawed depending on how it is interpreted. Many words in English derive from other Latin, Hebrew, or Greek words, which a lot of times have entirely different meanings after identifying the source to where these words originated. It gets deeper than the surface level.

You also have to consider the fact that much of the inspiration for these stories could be derived from constellations and observations of different planets. This is why many people have this sense of connection to astrology. People like George Washington, Thomas Jefferson, and Neil Armstrong, were considered deists while there still lies some confusion on who was and wasn't.

John Locke was a popular philosopher during this time. He was extremely passionate about creating a reasonable way to describe life, God, and the nature of humanity. Many would say he is the "Father of Liberalism". Many times he would go back and forth between conclusions after finding flaws in his philosophies.

Sometimes the debates he would have with other philosophers like Thomas Hobbes would be endless. When they would think they had the perfect philosophy to life, there would always be something to question, thus creating a flaw in it. I think this only shows the beauty in perception. It all came down to the type of conclusions they came to. You can see now how we all even today have these particular beliefs that all started somewhere by some influencer. Yet, do any of us truly know?

Albert Einstein said, "Everyone is a genius. But if you judge a fish on its ability to climb a tree, it will live its whole life believing it is stupid." This is because intelligence isn't a single thing. It is a combination of different abilities. Finding and embracing your abilities is important. Your experiences can put you at an advantage at any given moment compared to someone else who may be lacking it. Identify your strengths and embrace them, stop thinking you don't have valuable information to provide to the world.

Intelligence seems to always be observed in such flawed and shallow ways, it's no wonder many people are overlooked. You'd be surprised at how culture plays a big part in determining if someone is intelligent. If someone could respond quickly in conversation, or with quick sarcasm, they may come off as intelligent. In another culture, if someone responds really quickly they may come off as having a lack of understanding or true depth of thought.

Perception is everywhere and defines who we believe is smart or dumb. It defines who is talked about in the history books. It defines who we love and who we hate. It is all usually rooted in misconceptions clouding our ability to logically analyze and override any flawed conclusions. It starts with our learned way of life. Many of us consider ourselves smart but lack emotional intelligence. We all are intelligent in some way because of our different connections and habits.

Interactions with physical reality create changes in our understanding of it. It makes us more mindful and better at whatever we are doing. That's why it isn't enough to hear about different cultures. When you actually visit, it's a completely different level of understanding. Our subconscious mind picks up on so many things that we feel some sense of connection to the people we thought we could never relate to. It's only your mind fooling you into thinking we're different when we're really just different versions and expressions of human.

The process we go through to determine who's smart and who is dumb is driven by ego. It lacks useful purpose and real critical subjects. As I pointed out earlier, school doesn't teach you how to make money. They'll teach you how to count it. They'll teach you how to manage it. They'll teach you how to work for it, but not how to truly make it work for you.

I'm sure we can all also agree that GPA doesn't define someone's intelligence. A lot of jobs may not even look at your GPA as a deciding factor during the hiring process. The things we learn and study are all constructed concepts that don't give you a real advantage in life. It's an educational system that lacks true authentic material relating to life, history, and spirituality. We are taught how to conform to a system, not how to create one of our own. Nelson Mandela once said, "Education is the most powerful weapon which you can use to change the world."

It's true manipulation at its core when not provided with the gift of truth. It almost confines your imagination, imprisons your thoughts, and creates a conditioned perspective. After all, what other information have we been trained to learn or value? I will say a 4.0 does illustrate critical self-discipline and commitment. This deserves admiration because nothing great will come to you without either. Most of our grandparents didn't attend college, yet they're able to provide you the best advice and knowledge.

Life itself is the best teacher you will ever come to know. We live and learn from our experiences. Life and what I have experienced have brought me to this very moment of writing this book. It took experiences with love, hate, religions, school, lies, movies, books, people, etc. to come to many realizations about who I am and each of our true purpose in this beautiful world.

All of the life-changing events that may have come throughout my years have had an impact on my perception. Even as a writer it's tough to write, sometimes you must take a break and experience life to fulfill that expression. The most significant impact of all comes when you open your mind beyond the norm. I've realized how continuous learning is so important, even after school, it doesn't stop there. You can never learn everything no matter how much you try in a lifetime. There will always be something new to discover.

It's all infinite, your mind, potential, the universe, even money is all limitless. Abundance is everywhere. This only shows the endless growth we should continue to do as we age. To stay stuck in one belief, not embracing new information to broaden your perspective of life is like putting your mind in prison. Life is like an illusion. You begin to control this illusion by dismissing bad energy and seeing the unlimited capacities of what you can create within this matrix. These different dimensions of thinking begin with how you see the world. It'll define what you create. It will define who you become.

True Leaders

> **"The task of leadership is not to put greatness into people, but elicit it, for the greatness, is there already." - John Buchan**

The real leaders in this world use their awareness to spread knowledge and help others. Many people get in situations where they have money and power only to take advantage of it. It makes me wonder why civilization after civilization eventually came to an end throughout history. Change is inevitable, but something consistent throughout history is tyranny, greed, and corruption. Even the consistent wars only show the ignorant level of vibrations we choose to embody over and over again.

Why have there been so many civilizations that have, in some sense, manipulated or shorted the people? What type of leader hides the knowledge and spiritual guidance for themselves instead of helping others see? What makes people desire power and posses so much greed as if there isn't enough for everyone? Why do people try to claim territory and rights to this earth as if they'll be here forever? Why is it always the villain, or psychopath at the top with bad intentions and agendas?

Wouldn't a great leader or even villain realize treating people wrong only increases the chance of your plan failing once the people wake up? Imagine a society with leaders who have morals, a society where citizens treated each other with respect, a society where people weren't constantly stressed out about debt, or fear. It's not a perfect society, but it is one based on a healthy level of respect for the people and each other.

The corruption happens when good people become passive towards the evildoings. They allow people who have no intention of uplifting humanity and are careless towards the damage done to earth hold powerful positions. We must expose and take action toward those people we know are poisonous to society. The same way our body attacks potential sicknesses that enter, imagine if your white blood cells were passive half the time. We must act like white blood cells when dealing with manipulative people.

Many times people who do these evil acts continue because they're never faced with any obstacles, outrage, perspectives or energy that makes them uncomfortable. When kids are growing up, they often do a lot of things (good and bad) in a carefree way. It is not until moral guidelines are comprehended after repeated disciplining that kids often learn how to cope with their feelings and environment. The bad or corrupt decisions people in powerful positions often make is due to the lack of accountability associated with the act.

People that feel like "they can get away with it" will do some immoral things you wouldn't believe. In a lot of numerous and scandalous situations, there are also many people who never say or do anything about vile behavior, and you could argue that equally as disgraceful. When they are forced to face their own demons it's comparable to the disciplining of a child who does bad things. You ask the child why they made that bad choice and they may shrug their shoulders as if they really don't know why. There's a side to us that can take over causing us to do things that may be out of character. To me, it only shows how powerful and intense our emotions can be at any given moment.

As an adult, you may despise people's childlike tendencies because they're older, but age has no true control over people's perspective. That's why, even as an adult, we have to continue to grow and work on our mental attitude every day. Many people don't take into consideration that the brain isn't fully matured until around the age of 25. Often people debate the nature of morality and what exactly is right and wrong. Some things are downright morally wrong, but in some cases, depending on the intentions, reasoning, and circumstances, it may have been the right thing to do. A kid doesn't necessarily know what is considered harmful until they've been taught these things from cultural influences. Yet, the nature of higher vibrations and the feelings that come as a result can guide us to the right decisions. Despite people that may become stimulated by bad behavior, it is only because of their mind and how it has been constructed to make sense of what they do. They've perceived something good about their behavior. Often deep down they know when they're not doing something that is "right". It is a matter of them caring enough to acknowledge it.

People often don't notice, acknowledge, or do anything about their flaws until people apply pressure to them. Some people may need that, others don't care enough to create the energy necessary to be better. Some were never truly taught how. Why do people do bad things? It could be out of habit or their perception of what is good or not, not any moral guidelines. In a society where people will make it known that the world doesn't care about you can make you careless towards others. I can only imagine the approach to life upon this realization. It's no wonder why the empathy humans show for one another seems to be significantly low.

While capitalism has its pros and cons its critical to point out how it plays a part in how people prioritize their motives. If the ultimate goal is profit, then some things will always come second to this desire. The result of humans not responsibly taking pride in the health of the earth, food, air, water, and each other is a result of something that appears to be more important to them. The whole approach to life or the concepts we create can cause our suffering as if we aren't the ones who've constructed this way of life, to begin with. How we choose to lead can be costly. It takes the right person who's able to analyze the world and human emotions at an above-average level to be a great leader, not just money or power.

Even if the ruthlessness gets you success, it may be at the expense of feeling empty inside. Real leaders know what is truly fulfilling in life. A costly decision may cause a wealthy man to lose all their riches, at the same time, across the world, someone with nothing who holds faith can gain it all. Any particular idea of power or the fact someone may be rich or poor means nothing to the universe and the events that may follow. The possibility is within us all at any given moment.

Leaders don't take pride in just being someone who has the power to overrule many. They take pride in guiding others to the light and showing them the powers they possess. People's perspective of power is ideally associated with money and land when they're both just illusions of power. We don't keep these things forever. The real power is in how we master our energy and perceptions while elevating human intelligence.

Know your worth

The things and people we put on a high pedestal can be bad for us. We'll end up searching and wishing for materials, or a life like a particular person has, instead of valuing ourselves. You deserve wealth, good health, vacations, a great lover, great sex, great food, and great spiritual energy. We have to know this and really feel this way.

Sometimes we don't attract these things to us because deep down, our subconscious mind feels undeserving or not worthy. There are people who are doing what they love and are no different than you. The only difference is your perception of them being deserving or better at whatever they're doing when you can do the same things. Never underestimate yourself and the value of your soul, beliefs, and energy on this earth.

Put the same energy into your talents as you do celebrities or people you look up to. The admiration and love you show them needs to be that times ten when it comes to yourself. Some of the most inspirational and informative videos barely hit a thousand views, but your favorite music video has millions of them. It shows how much of a role celebrities play as influencers. Idolizing people who are no different than you is senseless. We sit back and say, "I wish I could sing like her." "I wish I could dance like that." It goes on and on.

Embrace the things you are good at. It could change the world someday. We all have something inside of us that can change the world. Unfortunately, this countries definition of success is determined by how much you don't know about yourself. The pineal gland, the natural body frequency we give off, brainwaves, and the power of emotions aren't studied enough. Why? What are we afraid we might discover? The true power of yourself? Truth is, you are worth more than a 9-5 job. You're worth more than just another body used in a war.

You're worth more than tyranny. You're worth more than money, a piece of paper, could ever buy. I'm sure you've heard people say, "If you want to hide something, put it in a book." Sadly, we must go searching for the truth in a book. But who reads? The library is the only place that lets us know people are still thinking. Conditioned thoughts have become almost impossible to overcome. Slowly but surely, I see a generation that is waking up but still stuck in a conditioned mindset.

There are many good people in the world, but we have become isolated in attempts to protect ourselves. Despite me not wanting to, I notice a high level of distrust amongst people of this generation. Many people aren't loyal or genuine. Everybody is for themselves, and we call each other snakes. What type of people are we going to meet if we already have it set in our mind who they are? "Men are trash!" "Women ain't shit!" We are telling our subconscious minds to notice these things more, and we will never see the good in these people because we're focused on those characteristics. We all assume we have haters, why not assume people like you?

I don't bring this to your attention to make you feel wrong, only to show you the many angles we can choose to see and attract this in our reality. We are attracting the very things in our life that we expect or already believe out of people. We have these thoughts, but subconsciously want to feel important, loved, and respected by others, even if coming off as heartless is what gets their veneration. When you get in the depth of perception, you can see how you can hold yourself back. Everything is mental. It is essential to be mentally aware. "I had to get out of my own way; I was my worst enemy." Sound familiar?

The more I write, the more I see the beauty in each one of us. The more I challenge everything that is supposedly the normal thing to do, the more I feel abnormal. I used to want so many things, only to find a passion to change the world. It's not as impossible as it may seem. An idea, a popularly believed perception of the world can last for generations. The truth is, everything is a creation, so create the world you want to see in your physical reality because the potential of your mind is something no man can foresee.

CHAPTER 2

Love

What Is The Meaning Of Love?

Love is defined by our perception of what we think it characterizes. Whatever descriptions are attached to your perception of love is the reality you expect it to exemplify. What visualizations do you have when the thought of love comes to mind? It could be getting off work, going home to a wife who has cooked, wants to hear about your day, motivates you, and then massages you to sleep.

It could be that romantic movie with a happy ending or your man opening the door for you. It could be your dad showing up for your football game. What about those mothers who start their day early getting the kids ready, cooking, running errands, going to work, picking the kids up, making sure they eat, only to do it again tomorrow? It could be the little things that mean everything like support or compliments. It could be patriotism despite the transgressions. It could be a false feeling that comes off as love but is lust. It could be any act of kindness without any expectations of anything in return. It could be any righteous deed. It could be someone dying for another person, or even killing for another person. I give many examples because love has no true definition, it's more what love essentially means to us.

Think about a time when you were younger and couldn't understand why your parents would do certain things. Whether it was to protect you, discipline you, condition you, or simply because that's how they were raised, you may not have understood why at the moment. You just wanted to have fun and explore possibilities. It may have not sat well with you that they may have hindered you in a sense from your explorative ways, or even in your creative ways. The beliefs of our parents hold a lot of weight when we understand the power in perception.

Many may spend their adult years breaking free from many beliefs that had been strongly instilled in them from birth by their parents. They could be doing this to rebuild their own self-esteem or insecurities. As you get older one of the most exasperating things you'll come to realize is that your parents aren't perfect. They're biased and have their own flaws that make them human just like you. Nobody is perfect so we cannot fault others, we must continue to learn and update information. If not we face the challenge of having to overcome generational ways of thinking that continuously create the same attitudes or results.

While some things that were taught to you could have been damaging there are many things you may have been taught by your parents that saved your life. As you got older you appreciated the morals and discipline they instilled in you even if there were some downsides. The ability to see this love indirectly isn't something many people grasp until they become adults.

We express love in ways that aren't always on the same page as the receiver. Even those times when they may seem to be too hard on you, it is still a form of love from their perspective. It's just not being given in the way we'd like it to be. Deep down, they want you to be great, even if that means disciplining you. From their perspective, they turned out just fine, so they may instinctively treat you in similar ways. Just because they turned out fine doesn't mean it's always ok to put someone else through it.

Many people have overcome traumatizing events during their childhood that may still rub off on others in harmful ways. It's hard to put a complete end to the cycle it creates from generation to generation. Once we've become more aware of the things that still hurt us, we can heal. This will create a different approach to how we love ourselves and others.

The essence of love is in the effort we put in to learn how. Admitting when you're wrong and putting effort into understanding others isn't easy to do. It's either you don't show that effort often enough, or we do it too much, leaving ourselves vulnerable, increasing the chances we get taken advantage of.

If we haven't healed properly from things preventing

us from loving ourselves then it'll be even harder going about loving others. It all seems so simple, but there are a variety of expressions and experiences that can cause us to take the wrong approach to love. There's so much to love that involves understanding that no wonder we become misguided about how to go about giving or receiving it.

Parental propositions when it comes to raising successful kids vary from race to race and culture to culture. A lot of times, despite the love many parents try and express, it comes out in damaging ways that they may be blind too. Parents are always right, so in a lot of cases, kids never here, "I'm sorry," or "you were right."

Tough love isn't always the best way to go about showing love indirectly, although it is necessary at times. Most times hugs, kisses, and a simple reminder of how much you are loved is all it takes. I've heard many stories of kids who can only recall hearing their parents saying, "I love you" a few times if that throughout their childhood. It doesn't mean their parents didn't go above and beyond to provide for them. There's simply an imbalance in the way they've chosen to express it. Love is only complicated when our ideas of what it represents get misconstrued.

Think about people who grew up without a parent or even both and what it did to them psychologically. One must, at some point, wonder why you would never want to be in my life. Why did you never come back? Why did you never try and see me? Why don't you love me? It can make them set flawed expectations for people they meet in the future. They'll get in the habit of assuming people who are in their life will always eventually leave them.

They may end up pushing someone away that cares for them, and it came from that bad experience growing up.

Just putting myself in someone's shoes makes me so empathetic. It reminds me of that episode of Fresh Prince of Bel-Air. Will had linked back with his dad, and they begin to hang out. It wasn't long before his dad went back to his old ways, those old ways of not being his dad. The level of hurt in that particular scene spoke to millions of young women and men around the world who are damaged by not feeling loved. This is why love is so powerful. It's what we all desire. Love is expressed in so many ways it should never be overlooked or unappreciated.

When kids are young, they may have parents that continuously work. They could easily assume they don't care because they're always gone. This is an example of how we can overlook the sacrifices people make for us. Simply because that love isn't presented in the way we have love perceived in our head. A man working countless hours to provide for his woman is love, but she still needs attention or will seek it somewhere else if you don't balance your time wisely.

Many men have lost their wives for being so caught up in working, gambling, drinking, that they lose themselves and never have time for the people who care for them the most. We must get on the same page with one another in regards to what matters the most to us. Like much of what I've been stating in this book, taking an understanding approach is growth. When we expand our ability to see love beyond just one way, we recognize it can still be love, just not our perception of what it's supposed to represent.

It's important to note that someone mistreating you isn't a form of love. Identify what may be causing someone to treat you the way they do. They could be damaged or don't know how to love you the way you would like. Never become blinded by your emotions, thinking someone cares for you but mistreats you.

Heart vs Mind

Much of this book is about perception and how we can construct our thoughts to bring us peace. It can be challenging to navigate through our perceptions because of two powerful energetic fields. The heart's frequency is so powerful you can argue it more powerful than the mind. Yet, what is the mind without the heart, what is the heart without the mind? When we speak of passion, intent, character, auras, spirit, etc. These are things broadcasted from the heart. It is then where the mind comes in and creates masterpieces based on these frequencies. This is why it is important to be in sync with the two. Don't allow the fact that you have a good heart make you act too willingly or unreasonably.

This is why just having a good heart isn't truly complete without the use of our mind to make critical decisions. As much as I've emphasized the mind, it is the love and desire I have to spread knowledge to others that created the way for me to write a book. This all started from the heart. Sometimes we can become confused about what decisions to make because our heart is saying one thing, and our mind is saying another.

This is the reason why we must get in touch with ourselves to understand how we should go about creating peace in our life. We can make decisions from the heart that can still result in undesired outcomes because we weren't rational. You can make decisions strictly in a rational way and still feel as if there are things missing in life because you've dismissed your heart's desires. Even when we talk about the chakras, it is a balance that is needed. Never become too consumed in one thing because it'll result in some negligence in other areas of your life and spirit.

Self Love.

The way that we move and act is always according to our state of mind. You will attract things in your life and may not know exactly how you did it. When we're in a state of genuinely believing something, the things we attract happen so naturally. People will see the confidence and belief you have, and a lot of times, it can be influential.

That's why it's essential to sit back and evaluate the way you see yourself. What are some things you think you're capable of and some things you think you're not? It'll in a way show why you may not have those things that you want. It's because you don't honestly believe it's for you. When someone truly has this mindset that they are worthy and are confident about it, people notice. It will cause you to do things that you usually wouldn't do because of the state of mind you're in.

The more we are consistently in a state of mind of feeling worthy of anything the world has to offer, the more the universe will comply. An excellent example of this is how approaching someone you never spoke to before can be intimidating. This will make your whole approach off and that person will probably easily tell. So whether you're trying to sell them something, flirt, or mingle, you'll create an awkward vibe.

Now imagine approaching someone with the state of mind as if you already know them. As hard as you may typically think about what to say or position your body, simply being comfortable and confident would change your whole approach. You'll start a convo so smoothly, and before you know it, you'll be laughing, and the conversation will flow naturally. Do you feel worthy of their attention?

Receiving attention from many people can be great, but self-love should never come from the validation of these other people. Whether people like us or reject us, it doesn't change how worthy you are of having whatever it is you want. Everything isn't meant for you, and being mature enough to understand that people have preferences is never a knock against you, it's how life works. Being able to reframe from pridefulness whenever you are turned down or offering a good deed to someone unappreciative is a fantastic power.

It's like you've created a forcefield around your feelings or perception. This makes it less likely that someone else's attitude will affect yours. Whatever you're doing, do it because you want to and not because of the expectations of how you want it to turn out. It will free you from the anger you get when you do something nice but don't get the reaction you'd like. The consequences of what will happen to someone with the attitude they possess will always hinder them or catch up to them at some point. Understand this and always remain blissful and confident, no matter what.

We must always show appreciation for the people who truly act out of the kindness of their hearts. The people who genuinely love themselves usually extend this love to other people because they understand how connected we all are. To hate others in a sense, is to hate yourself. Too many times, people get taken for granted for being so loving, but that's just one way to perceive it. Are they being taken advantage of? Someone who offers love, in my opinion, can never be taken advantage of. It is only the people who overlook this love or take advantage that will never prosper.

You may think these people who scam, lie, and are cold-hearted always get their way. In reality, they're miserable. You may be that person being taken advantage of because you naturally have a good heart. You make life possible. Genuine people are the most influential people I've come to know. Think about how easy it is to hate. The people who choose love over hate have the most strength that I've seen. Love is the greatest feeling in the world. This includes self-love.

The most important type of love is to the extent

to which you love yourself. A woman can be confident about going to a party and getting numbers. Yet, her self-esteem, the way she feels about herself, has nothing to do with it. Self-love is important because we usually look for someone else to fill that happiness when it comes from within. You are the key to your happiness. The love you have for yourself will be the love you see in other people.

Even in relationships, we often don't have the right ideas about what love truly is. The perceptions we have can create temporary emotions and feelings that cloud our ability to see. The thoughts of being alone can make people fearful. It can cause you to deal with other people who mistreat you so that you won't be alone. A lot of times, solitude is the key to serenity. Many people project their emotions and ways on to you, which can be draining. The comfort in being alone not only shows how much you love yourself, but it can also free you from thinking life can't be fabulous without other people.

Limerence or Love?

I once came across a book called, "Understand Psychology: Teach Yourself". This book was written by Nicky Hayes. It gave me some fascinating insight on love and what we may confuse it with. The book immediately compares the public's image of "love" to how it accurately reflects reality. It argues how long-term love is different from that short term love we often experience.

Many psychologists have concluded that we misuse

the word love to describe a variety of misleading emotions. That short-term infatuation is a separate term called limerence. While long term affection and partnerships reflect a more accurate conveyance of what love truly is supposed to embody. Limerence is a robust and intensive passion with a strong element of fantasy attached to it. This may be why someone appears so perfect to us as if it were us in a romantic movie.

The book states, "When two people experience limerence are together all the time, the emotion tends to die away." This is because of the intense longing for the person, which means they must be unreachable in some way, or it tends to die off. It goes on to explain, "Limerence signifies a preliminary divine period that is replaced by a deeper kind of loving which is considered long term love." This may be considered "real love" after we've experienced their flaws and are still in love because that's what makes them who they are.

During short term obsession, it's hard to tell what you may have in common with your partner. That's why many people go on to make commitments while they are in this state like marriage, only to later get a divorce. What sticks out to me is how the limerence dies off the more time is spent with one another, but it can be maintained if the couple is prevented from being together as much as they would like.

That's something to think about. I mean, everyone needs their space. That space makes time for you to miss each other. Yet, if you do spend all your time around your partner and that phase of infatuation dies, but their presence still brings you happiness, it's a deeper long-lasting kind of love. This observation was done by a man named Tennov. (1979)

Just thinking about the vast number of reasons any given person could find someone else attractive is interesting to me. When we try to understand love and the differences, we must look to the source of our infatuation. It has a lot to do with the way we perceive them. If someone's actions don't align with the characteristics that are synonymous with your perception of love, then it may not work out. And since love isn't something that fades, it's always fair to ask yourself what was it that caused me to be blinded by limerence.

Maybe we overlooked the signs or perhaps the visualizations of what could be led us to the trap. The higher the hopes we have, the more distracted we are when the reality hits. Falling in love is a sacrifice you make to experience something amazing. Whether it's starting a business, writing a book, working out, or even falling in love, there's some sacrifice attached to it. To feel those accomplishments takes many risks that you can't ever be afraid of. You have to be mentally strong enough to handle the outcomes either way. Try to have a great balance of logic and emotion to avoid putting so much energy in a situation that'll leave you drained. While some people can move on, a lot of people can't. Their past haunts them and prevents them from trusting or having the same high hopes for any future relationships.

Contentment

Love, in a way, is a mere level of contentment because, without it, you may feel inclined to seek beyond what you currently have. Contentment isn't settling. That is a big difference. If you feel like you deserve more then find better. To be realistic, there will always be someone who appears to offer more than the person you're with. When we speak of a real connection, it isn't as replaceable as we'd like to believe. At some point, contentment is necessary.

There's always someone that is looking for love. So if you've become comfortable in a relationship, remind yourself that there's someone else that wishes they had a lover like mine. It'll keep you in the right state of mind so that you won't have to lose that person before you realize how careless you've been.

Many times bad things have to happen to us before we understand because we never put ourselves in other people's shoes. Always remember how powerful our state of mind is in any given situation. I know constantly being compared to others can leave you feeling like you're in constant competition. If you're doing the right things, those people will never become a real threat to you.

People's inauthentic idea of love is what causes failing relationships. People's ideas of what they want and offer to someone can gradually change. You can't choose how long someone decides to love you, unfortunately. Suppose you wake up one day and don't have that same spark of attraction to your partner. You may still have a love for them, but you aren't in love with them. The same way we can't help who we love, we can't help who we don't.

While we can all recall the times we've been fucked over, have we ever counted how many hearts we've broken? Or what about the number of people's feelings we may have hurt intentionally or not? If the feelings have become so opposite, it leaves one of you hurt; the communication was never at its potential. We must continuously communicate. It gives a relationship better balance and clarification. After all, without communication, each of you will come to your own conclusions about how you feel. Which is usually inaccurate.

When you throw in the many analogies that can be linked to that "love" feeling, it can become confusing. We all want to be happy, but as life goes by, things change, we start thinking differently. Our perception of life and the things we want can change. Our perception of what makes us happy can change, leaving the person you once had a connection with on another page as you.

It isn't always our fault. We're dealing with the inevitable nature of the mind. And sometimes things don't work out. Even if you may have experienced a relationship where you or the other person cheated, it's deeper than you think. Sometimes we can get too comfortable, yes, but we also can fall victim to desire. Desire to experience something we never have before. Risking everything we've built at the expense of a thrill.

Ted Talk

I once came across a Ted talk video of a lady describing love and why people cheat by a woman named Esther Perel. She asks critical questions and gives more critical feedback when it comes to cheating that you may have never have thought to consider. It will broaden your perception of cheating, love, and the nature of ourselves.

Whether it be through loneliness, boredom, or instincts, she makes it clear how our misconceptions of cheating and love have caused us to overlook the inevitability attached to the concept of marriage or commitment itself. I want to quote most of her speech and elaborate on the things she says only because of how important it is to understand most of the statements she makes.

"Why do we cheat?" "Why do happy people cheat?" "Why do we think men cheat out of boredom and fear of intimacy, but women cheat out of loneliness and hunger for intimacy?" She goes on to explain, "Adultery has existed since marriage was invented and so too the taboo against it. Infidelity has a tenacity that only marriage could envy, so much so, that this is the only commandment that is repeated twice in the Bible. Once for doing it, and once just for thinking it (crowd laughter). Monogamy used to be one person for life, today, monogamy is one person at a time (crowd laughs and claps)."

Interestingly, she makes a critical statement regarding love and marriage. She says, "***Depending on what your***

definition of cheating is will depend on the percentage of people who do it, which is between 26-75%." What is cheating on you? Is dancing with someone else cheating? Is flirting cheating? All of these may be a big deal to someone and not a big deal to others. Even today, we see people who have open relationships. This is why the more you express what you like and don't like, the better chance your relationship will be successful.

She highlights a big contradiction as well, ***"95% of people agree that it is terribly wrong for our partner to lie about having an affair. Interestingly, about the same percentage of people also say that is the same thing they would do if they were having one."*** **When we feel love we don't realize the power of it lies in our perception.** ***"The kiss that you only imagine giving, can be as powerful, and as enchanting as hours of actual lovemaking. As Marcel Proust said, "It is our imagination that is responsible for love, not the other person." "The very concept of love in this era has been shifted from prioritizing economically, to emotionally. This only means instead of infidelity hurting our economic security, infidelity hurts our emotional security. Damaging us to the point where we'll question if we could ever trust again."***

The big contradiction happens depending on if you're the one being emotionally neglected, or the one who has lost their passion behind the connection. After all, the connection to two people have is stimulated by their intertwined perception. As I've stated earlier, this can change quickly as well. The lust at some point must be tamed to allow true love to develop. Or we can realize that people don't stay in our lives forever, so become stimulated by showing appreciation to them consistently, every day. Those people will at least last a lot longer in our life.

While I disagree with her take on people's priorities toward relationships, I do partly agree. People today still may form relationships on the basis of financial reasonings. To have someone help pay bills is still valued. Even people today may stay together for the kids or the thought of being alone. I do agree that the emotional end of love has become prioritized to a greater extent. Many millennials know that they have trust issues and don't see the approach to becoming more understanding and at peace after relationships.

When it comes to marriage we put ourselves on some sort of fantasized pedestal of being "the one", or irreplaceable. We have a romantic ideal, in which we turn to one person to fulfill an endless list of needs. To be my greatest lover, my best friend, the best parent, my trusted confidant, my emotional companion, my intellectual equal. Infidelity tells me, I'm not. It is the ultimate betrayal. It shatters the grand ambition of love. Throughout history, infidelity has always been painful, but today, it's often traumatic because it threatens our sense of self."

We see so many couples who are willing to break it off and not fight for their relationships. We may give up easily. Esther points out this may be because, in this era, we feel more inclined to pursue our desires; we have the mindset that before anything else, "I" deserve to be happy.

So, many times the advice we may receive from others is to leave. Maybe we should all question our expectations out of love because it will always come with sacrifices.

"And if we used to divorce because we are unhappy, today we divorce because we could be happier. And if divorce carried all the shame, today, choosing to stay when you can leave is a new shame."

The interesting thing to me is the difference in decisions that were made and how they interchanged depending on the perceptual value. Often this shifts in different eras. It may have been generally seen as the "right" thing to do for so long before a new concept or "mood" toward a particular idea is changed.

"So if we can divorce why do we still have affairs? Now, the typical assumption is that if someone cheats either there is something wrong in your relationship or something wrong with you, but millions of people can't be pathological. The logic goes like this, if you have everything you need at home then there is no need to go looking elsewhere? Assuming that there is such a thing as a perfect marriage that will inoculate us against wanderlust. But what if passion has a finite shelf life? What if there are things that even a good relationship can't provide?"

As much as we want to be good enough for our lover. Many times it isn't you. It's a personal battle that each person deals with on a subtle level with themselves.

"Affairs are an act of betrayal and also an expression of longing and loss. At the heart of an affair, you will often find a longing, and a yearning for an emotional

connection, for novelty, for freedom, for autonomy, for sexual intensity, a wish to capture lost parts of ourselves. Or an attempt to bring back vitality in the face of the loss of tragedy."

Think about these deep desires that can cause someone to cheat. We all at different unpredictable moments may have these urges to do things to capture or redefine the essence of our happiness, even at the risk of losing someone else.

"When we seek the gaze of another, it isn't always our partner we're turning away from. But the person that we ourselves have become. And it isn't so much that we are looking for another person as much as we are looking for another self."

She goes on to explain how many people who have come to her describe it as "feeling alive." Some tragic event has happened in their life that makes them question if this is it. They, in a sense, use cheating as an antidote to death.

"**Contrary to what you may think, affairs are way less about sex and more about desire. The desire for attention, desire to feel special, desire to feel important. And the very structure of an affair, the fact you can never have your lover keeps you wanting. That in itself is a desire machine, because the incompleteness, the ambiguity keeps you wanting that which you can't have."**

Because she believes there is something good that can come from affairs, she says many people have asked her a weird question, which is, "Would you ever recommend it?" Her answer to this was, "**Now I would no more**

recommend you to have an affair than I would recommend you to have cancer. And yet we know that people who have been ill often talk about how their illness has yielded them a new perspective."

There are gifts of wisdom and peace that can come from bad experiences. In any particular situation, we are in. We must be able to analyze and come to better conclusions about ourselves and other people. None of us are perfect, protect your feelings in a way that doesn't leave you so hurt. It's easier said than done, but many times people have this moment when they're depressed, and they feel terrible. Then after a while, they begin to explore different perspectives and feel better.

Unconditional Love

Love from my point of view is unconditional. It's easy to view love this way, but another to apply this way of thinking into one's character. How many assumptions, expectations, and blemished definitions of love must I free myself of? All of them. Love has nothing to do with attachment. Attachment can cause unhappiness if ever detached from its source. Love isn't stemmed from any pleasures beyond the gratification of seeing someone else smile. Nothing in return is ever expected. Never form expectations because expectations lead to disappointments.

Bob Marley once said, "The truth is, everyone is going to hurt you. You just got to find the ones worth suffering for". What is he trying to say here? I think it is that nobody is perfect. If it is love you wish to spread, do so with no accountabilities. Do so with no marks of who is deserving and who isn't based on biased instincts. It's easy to hate someone and overlook the good in them. That's why there's the famous saying, "There's a thin line between love and hate." If we're willing to be there for people who have hurt us, it's because they at some point have been there for us when we've been irrational or toxic. It's easy to love when everything is going great, but the real test of our love for people will be when their flaws show or during troubling times when they need us the most.

Loving unconditionally means we understand we are all unique people with different personalities. To assume that a skin complexion, culture, or religion defines the intellect, humbleness, or specific persona of an individual is absurd. We are a reflection of our experiences and beliefs, not physical appearance. We must also get rid of the expectations that people will eventually do us wrong or that they're out to get us. How likely are you to find love if you believe everyone you meet is devious? None, the focus on betrayal paints that reality of your love life. It suppresses your attention to the devoted.

We downplay our thoughts as if they do not influence the way we see when that's where it starts. Nobody will understand you unless you let go and express yourself. Holding back will never create successful relations. We all know how scary it can be to open up. But what really holds you back from initiating that convo? We may fear their reaction a lot of times. It's still critical to express yourself because their reaction could tell you everything you need to know. Once again, communication is essential. It is the only guide that helps portray the love we have for one another. It's continuous.

A woman may know you love her, but she still wants to hear it. Consistent communication is the only way we can get a precise idea of how someone else sees things. The need for reassurance may be so critical to people because of the power in perception and how it could quickly leave your significant another feeling differently. Many people express themselves only for their feelings to be downplayed. It is essential to understand that communication isn't one-sided. If someone isn't willing to listen and sympathize with you, your attempts at communicating won't adhere to them.

I think when it comes to falling in love, a lot of times we don't appreciate the feeling until it has a tragic ending. Is it because we don't see the extent to which we value something until it is taken away from us? It's that desire to have more, even when you already have it all that can fool you into never taking the time to value what you already have. Or maybe we as humans are behaving irrationally to think we could ever satisfy another human in every way. Ultimately you should value your peace so much that you always take responsibility for your happiness.

As a result, other people will only complement something you've already established and prioritized within. You'll also become more comfortable with the way you feel to where other people's advice can be helpful, but only to an extent. Sure, we can take advice and learn from others' mistakes, but it is something surreal about experiencing it for yourself firsthand that hits you hard. While we naturally may become a bit cold-hearted after these life lessons, the right way to learn from them is to find peace.

Something interesting to me is how we have this perception that people's actions always reveal how they feel. Think about different times in your life where you held back on doing things, whether because you were afraid of the potential outcome or because you didn't want to look weak. Depending on our attitude towards others can determine how empathetic or prideful we may become. Actions don't always represent how you feel. We all like to believe actions show how we truly feel, but that isn't always the case.

I can honestly say in the past I did things that weren't me. Things that didn't portray the love I wanted to show deep down. Things that a "sorry" can't fix. You may say my actions showed how I felt, but they did the complete opposite. In a lot of cases, it was because of pride. Pride only becomes greater than love if you are ok with losing someone you love. Losing a loved one isn't worth playing the pride game. Especially since you don't find love, love finds you.

Real love in my eyes happens so naturally, and so uniquely that you'd spend a lifetime searching for another connection that brings you that feeling. That is if you are hooking up for that real connection and not just for the image. It's not something you find every day. So take heed to the value in someone who cares about you and is genuine with their motives.

Assure that you extend love unconditionally to avoid the constant stress that comes with always feeling like people are out to get you. The feeling we get when we do things for others, knowing how much they needed it, or only because it makes us feel great is power. I didn't extend this love to the world with expectations. I did it for me and my own gratifying experience.

Lack of Expression

One thing I've come to learn about love is how critical the authentic expression of it is. It's so easy to begin entertaining thoughts that could keep you from spreading love, even if it's genuinely what you may want to do. Those times in my life where I may have been thinking of someone and didn't call are essentially meaningless.

If we never act on our natural tendencies to want to care for others, or even check up on them from time to time, that love never happened. At least not from the person who would be the receiver of this love. Nobody can read your mind. I think it'd be nice if people could know how we feel and act accordingly without you speaking, but that isn't realistic. That's why it's easy for people to assume you may not care, or form their conclusions about your behavior. You didn't act on what you wanted to do deep down.

I've heard many stories of people who may want to call

their significant other after a conflict but didn't. A lot of times, we may find ourselves in situations where we want to feel loved before spreading it. If two people have this attitude, then many times, they may go a while without speaking or may never speak again. Simply because you both were afraid to be the initiator or first one to give in.

Most people do this not to appear weak or desperate. This may be necessary in some cases. People can quickly begin to get used to the love you give, and for some reason, humans don't a lot of times realize the things they have until they're gone. Most often then not it's simply pride. We think we are tough and durable with this pride when it shows how much we lack true peace with longevity. Often the people who don't believe in terms of looking weak or desperate are not only the most influential people but the ones that are usually remembered and successful. You can't be afraid to admit when you're wrong or when you need help or when you have something to say. Closed mounts don't get fed. We're all human and nobody is perfect.

Start recognizing the times you may have wanted to say something, or do anything but didn't because you begin to think of the worst scenarios. "Oh, they don't care. "Oh, they're probably busy." "They're probably not interested." When we are always thinking of the good things that could happen, the feelings that are created is what creates possibility. Think of the power you hold when you are consistently vibrating high. You can completely change someone's day or life. We walk past people every day on the brink of suicide and depression hidden with smiles and jokes.

Just remember everybody is dealing with perception at any given moment. When you come to this more enlightening perspective of your daily interactions, you won't become so prideful or hateful to others. It's as if you no longer become the prideful protector over who appreciates the love you give. Honestly, if the love you wish to spread is genuine, then there would be no pride or expectations of what you should get in return associated with this.

If the love you give to others isn't given back, then we should remove ourselves, but with no need to hate. The reason the love we may want to give others a lot of time can go unexpressed is because of how much we value being appreciated. Thinking back on times when I didn't feel appreciated brought the worst feeling. It's a feeling that will make you saddened by the fact they don't see your effort or value. And as you'll realize throughout this book, people see what they want. If they want to see good in you they will. If they're going to see the bad in you, surely they'll find something to scoff at. A good manager will make his employees feel appreciated because they know they'll work harder. A wise spouse will show appreciation to the person he loves because usually, that love will be given back times two. Often people want to feel loved and appreciated.

I must acknowledge the fact that I'm an introvert. This is probably why all of the content in this book just exploded out of me. It was all being kept inside. It's not to say I'm not good at interacting or casual conversation. I feel more comfortable alone most times because of how sensitive I am to other people's energy. If I sense something inauthentic based on my observation skills, I may tend to avoid you. I've always enjoyed the inner stimulations as opposed to the external. I'm sure it has made some people feel like I may not care. I apologize to the people who may question my love for them. I still think about my best friend from 3rd grade, Darion. I still think about my grandma often, even though I don't call or visit as much as I should. I still think of Qui and Bubba. I still think of my cousins often and imagine us living life amazingly. I think about the love I want to give deep down and wonder what makes me hold back on it sometimes. Maybe I want to feel like people care for me as well. Maybe I understand that you can't please everyone.

There are two significant character traits we all must acknowledge about ourselves. These two attitudes will determine how you handle rejection or people's reactions. The first character trait is people who I call avoiders. Many people don't bother putting themselves in situations where they might even have a slim chance of being rejected. They may get anxiety when showing or talking about their creations. They may not be quick to ask others for things because they hate asking people for anything. But they may tend to help others and have a hard time telling people no. These types of people subconsciously avoid any situation that leaves them looking like they need anything from anybody.

Then you have seekers. These people seek opportunities

to take advantage of others. Their attitude is set on getting what they want even at the risk of rejection. These are people who have no problem with it at all. They don't mind asking you for a ride, pitching a sale, or 20 bucks. If you say no they may go on about their day without thinking twice to the next person. They never look too deep into people who tell them no. These are things we can identify in our character to help become more aware of ourselves. Many of us may have never been taught or given true love, so we don't even know the right ways to go about expressing it. It's all a learning experience that we must try to understand by first attempting to understand ourselves.

My Love Experience

Yes, I once fell in love. I've never voiced or wrote down how I felt. I guess this is the right time. I still love her from afar. We haven't spoken in a while now. I still think about her from time to time. I wonder what she did on her birthday. I wonder how often she wonders about me. You don't meet women like her every day. I always felt like we were meant to be. The first night I met her was in a parking lot in a location I won't reveal. When she got out of her car, man, I couldn't believe how beautiful she was. A physical connection, but soon nothing compared to the mental connection. She was so intelligent, her heart was so big, and she didn't know how beautiful she was. Love is what we see in people. What I saw in her was something incredible, things that she didn't even see.

I can now see why people don't truly understand the connection between two people in love. Advice from other people is good only to a certain point. They may speak from their experience when, in your case, it could be completely different. Know how you feel. Only you will have to live with your decisions. When I saw her, I saw perfection in her imperfections. I saw myself. Well, a girl version of me.

My biggest regrets were not making her feel like she was worthy of admiration. I remember staring at her while she would be getting ready in the bathroom, thinking about how lucky I am. She would always offer to pay for dinner or at least half. She worked hard for everything she had. I wish I could have given her the world. She was my best friend. Sometimes I would think to myself that God had to have given you to me. Or maybe he placed you in my life for only a particular time, for a specific purpose. Or maybe this outcome was a lesson for the hearts I've broken in the past. No matter how I chose to perceive this conclusion, my love for her is undeniable.

How we let it get to the point of breaking up is disappointing. Not expressing myself to her enough caused her to believe I had become careless. She knew I loved her, but I had gotten away from the little things that mattered the most. Carelessness was never the case. Despite how it ended I've learned a lot. I've become a better man. That experience will help any relationships I'll have in the future.

Sometimes I hate how vivid my memories of us are. Now that it's over, I compare who I am today to who I was before. It ended because I got too comfortable. I didn't listen enough to change. Ok, and I admit, I didn't think another guy could take my girl. If I were being realistic though, I would realize that she wasn't happy. It's as if my own perception was blurred at that moment. When someone isn't happy, you leave the opportunity for other guys to fill that space.

Throughout our relationship, she was committed. I had my encounters with other women occasionally, I'm sure she had her encounters with guys. I was still finding myself, she was still finding herself, but I always knew what girl had my heart. Whenever she'd say, "I love you," and I'd say, "I love you too," she would follow up by saying, "I Know." She knew I had fallen in love with her.

There's so much to say about us. I'm having difficulty expressing the vibe we once had. After all, nobody knows that feeling and connection except you and that person. People on the outside looking in have no idea of how authentic the love two people have for one another is. They just see a couple. Whenever I find myself reflecting about us, I think about becoming the man she saw potential in. I think about becoming rich or famous only to wonder if it'll leave her with regrets. Then I still don't see the vengeance, only how disappointing it is that she isn't by my side.

Funny how I'm able to acknowledge these things now. Oh, how easy it is to give out advice, but fail to apply it to your own love life. Funny how I have no desire to find anything to blame her for. At this moment, I'm too busy putting myself in her shoes. Besides, nothing good comes out of pointing out others' flaws and ignoring your imperfections. She gave effort, she forgave me when I did wrong, and she wanted to grow with me.

After it was over, I would meet other women, I'd even find peace in being alone, but it didn't matter. This girl would always be someone I'd remember. I realized how impactful the experience I had with her was, and there was no going back. She would always mean something to me. I can't blame her for wanting more because she honestly deserved better. Had she not left me I don't know if I would've ever transitioned into the person I am today.

I look back at myself and feel disappointed that I overlooked the stress she was going through. Especially because I would've done anything for her. Maybe that's why I care so much about mental health now. It hurts to acknowledge these things. It hurts to let go of my pride enough to put this in writing. Though I miss that chapter in my life, I don't know if things could ever be the same. Two beings could connect powerfully, and it still doesn't mean they'll spend the rest of their lives together, but they may provide life lessons to each other that last a lifetime.

It feels weird writing about her. My thoughts are scattered, I could write the rest of this chapter about her, and there will still be so much left unsaid. She's usually just in my thoughts. Not sure what even compelled me to express these feelings. Maybe guilt or the relief I get by putting it all in the open. Maybe because I wouldn't be writing this book without her. I still remember the day I went and bought my first book after splitting. I've never been the same since. It's as if she knew she had to let me go in order for me to become the person I am today. She saw things in me that I was too stubborn to realize about myself. Beyond our relationship, I can say she was my best friend, and I think that's what hurt the most.

I stumbled upon a couple of letters she once wrote to me. I was amazed at how she felt about me at one point. It was tough to read. Whenever I think about her, the bad times never catch my attention. It was all the good times we had.

"Anytime away from you is too much time. I'm usually not so easily attached. This is not me. But then again, I'm not myself lately. I'm so interested in the person that you are, but more importantly, the person that I am when I'm in your arms, in your presence. I hope that you smile when you think of me, miss me just a little when I'm not in your arms, in your presence."

She wanted to give me my space, afraid that I would one day lose the desire to be in her presence. She just wanted to know I would never leave her or find interest in someone else.

"I said I'd give you back your space, didn't want to be a bother. I didn't want to take up the room that I left you to miss me, use up all the space that you would have had to desire to hug and kiss me. But what happens when my desires increase and yours remain unchanged? I'm left in the middle of the night trying to catch the smell of your scent that's nearly faded into my pillowcases. I said I'd fall back and let you breathe. Give you a bit of time to do what you want, do what you need. But there goes my desire, increasing and shit again. Making it difficult for me to keep my word. Trying to be strong enough to let you miss me. Taking back space, I left open for you to kiss me. Damn the time that moves too slowly. Damn my desire to want to let you know, that I already miss you."

She was beautiful in so many ways I thought I could easily explain. As I reflect on these letters I once considered throwing away, I see more than I ever understood.

We all have experienced love letters in relationships. The feeling was mutual, but I don't think it was ever expressed enough. The way she feels in the letter can easily be said to how I felt when she left.

The Love for Knowledge

When she left, a part of me did too. I had to fill that happiness with something else. Something that this time couldn't be taken away. I replaced her with knowledge. Knowledge of self, the world, and the way I was feeling. A lot of times, the pain we go through is what we need to change or create passion. Maybe I wanted to show myself, and whoever is reading that, I'm not afraid to let go of pride. I'm not afraid to feel like an idiot. I'm not afraid to make an example out of myself.

I had gotten so caught up in the wrong things. It's like losing her helped me find myself. Or at least the part of me that left with her. I thank her for helping me see. Sometimes it takes the most life-changing events to change our perceptions forever. I'll never treat or see the love the same way. I'll go about doing some things differently if love ever strikes again. I must stay true to myself. It feels better being honest and real than being in denial. I wish I could've been a better man to her. I can't continue to lie about the way I feel about anything. I never intended to find love, but it always seems to find you when you least expect.

I would always tell her I just want you to be happy. I never concluded that that could mean her being with another guy. I couldn't even picture her with another guy. Yea, it would be easy to get another girl. It's not something I do for the image, though. It would have to be a deeper connection. Pretending like you don't care can fool others, but not you. I live with the fact that it is over. It doesn't make me coldhearted. It doesn't make me see any other woman as unfaithful or matchless for me. Everybody has a story about their experience with love. I'm glad I was able to feel this despite the way it ended. There are stunning women everywhere, still, I'll never meet anybody quite like her. Whether she feels the same about me is irrelevant now, I guess.

There are many different people who talk about sex transmutation. I had never heard of this before and the concept was basically saying that a woman is one of the primary reasons for any man's success. When we talk about love, sex, and purpose, there's always a woman that was usually the motivation behind it. Man has always been in an effort to please women. If you were to destroy the sex glands in an animal or man, there wouldn't be much action at all. This says a lot. In fact, I never looked at it this way.

The sex energy that comes from a natural attraction to women can be used by men to create success in their own life. Not by having sex, but by using that brain stimulation to transfer that energy into whatever goals they have for themselves. The man who masters this becomes a genius. The brain is all about stimulation. Love, music, desire for money, alcohol, and autosuggestion are examples. That's what gets us going.

The highest form of vibration is the desire for sex. A man may knowingly or unknowingly take action based on the subconscious desire to please women. This hit me hard. I started thinking about how I picked up on the habit of reading, creating a blog, writing this book, AFTER my experience with her. The experience of love changed my life. It doesn't mean that man doesn't do things for his fulfillment or can't function without women. It's simply acknowledging how you can use energy in creative ways.

Love or Hate?

Many of us have hate and guilt in our hearts. These are things that can hold us back in life. The fact that I can acknowledge things without any hate attached to them shows how much I've mentally grown. We all can come to this level of acceptance. I don't feel weak for basically sounding like another guy who lost his girl. I feel like a man for acknowledging my mistakes and moving on from them. It starts by finding peace within yourself.

Where does the hate come from? It comes from attachment and your ego fooling you into thinking the world revolves around you. Be happy for people even when their decisions don't match yours. If they're pleased with what they're doing, then you should be happy for them. A lot of times the anger that gets built up is from us not getting our way and that isn't how life works. What is for you will be, and what isn't won't. Now feel the freeness that comes with that perspective.

The success and failures no longer matter anymore because I'll always receive the things I need when the time is right. While we are all quick to judge other people, we're also ready to say how misunderstood we are. I'm sure you feel that anyone who dislikes you doesn't honestly know you. I know I feel this way. I'm the coolest guy, any hate towards me has got to be from a misguided perception. Yet, from someone else's perspective, my actions could have come off as disrespectful.

When we feel like somebody has betrayed us, it can potentially ruin it for everybody. We take it out on others trying to prevent ourselves from being taken advantage of again. You're only hurting yourself.

Napoleon Hill says in his book Think and Grow Rich, "There should be no disappointment over love, and there would be none if people understood the difference between the emotions of love and sex. The major difference is that love is spiritual, while sex is biological. No experience, which touches the human heart with a spiritual force, can be possibly harmful, except through ignorance, or jealousy. Love is, without question, life's greatest experience."

I once heard someone state that Buddha was not a Buddhist, Jesus was not a Christian, Muhammed was not a Muslim. They were teachers who taught love. It is critical to understand the deeper underlying meanings of any religions we follow. How we as humans always seem to overlook the bigger picture and create conflict in between the smaller differences perplexes me. Those smaller differences are the perspectives that make us unique to the very preferences of our favorite color.

When you think about it, there is no fun in any of us being exactly alike. Can you even imagine? Everyone doing the same thing, thinking the same way, and not embracing creation isn't something any of us want. Yet, we fight with one another over our differences in perspective. Love is all we have. Love is always the answer. If you've formed a feeling of hatred or jealousy for someone else, there is some reflection there about ones' attitudes and perception of themselves.

Takes one to know one

The depths of our perception toward people tend to be directly associated with how we see ourselves. Most times, people give their deep subconscious feelings about things when they feel it doesn't have any personal ties to their character. If you pay attention, though, what we see in others is all a reflection of how we have decided to make sense of situations and others. The conclusions we've come to either have been created from the fact we have seen it before or because that's what you would do.

To some extent, it takes one to know one, right? If you see yourself as a moral person, more than likely, you'll see that in others before you see traits of someone crooked. It isn't to say you will overlook visible signs of someone who is. Yet, we've all had an experience with someone who shows signs of bad character, but we tell our selves differently, hindering our ability to see. Then, finally, it is too late.

We always think we are so sure of ourselves and what we see. When we look in the past, though, we always wish we could go back. Undoubtedly, we all can recall moments where we thought wrong. The art of perception is influential when we channel it towards peace and not hating each other. We can choose to see the good or the bad qualities in other people. Don't be the person always looking to seek the flaws in others. We all have those. Something rarely done is seeing the beauty in others.

Often the expression of this to people may come off as surprising. They may have not known or seen this beauty in themselves. The energy that generates from a simple compliment can reverse a mood. You can tell a woman how beautiful she is, and it could make her day. Other times it may not mean much to her because she's heard it so many times. Pointing out something more specific about people that they may not have thought anyone noticed is a genuine compliment.

Many people do a lot of great things or show high character that rarely gets acknowledged. Being able to point out things about people that may be subtle, but significant is powerful. This creates a fulfilling sensation for anyone to be viewed in ways that go beyond pointing out what they can't do, or what they're not. People are always pointing out flaws, even their flawed characteristics. We focus on the bad so much it ends up being all we see in others and ourselves. It can make you overlook some advanced skills you have naturally and could profit from.

Create a balance to where you don't see too much good that you overlook the bad, and where you don't see too much wrong, to where you can't see the good nature in others. When we talk about love, we often have a view in our head of what we see in them potentially, that idea of who they can become. Well, love is acceptance for who they are naturally. I might not like the things a family member does, but that doesn't mean I still don't love them. That is because your love for people isn't based on your idea of the potential they have to be. It is based on the acceptance of who they are naturally.

There are certain things about us that won't ever change. Yes, overtime time, we can change and mature. And ignoring harmful characteristics of others isn't the message I'm intending to send. We all know a change in perspective can make someone stop selling drugs, or stop cheating, or live a more promising life. And in times, we all need a mentor in a sense. Somebody who tells us what we aren't doing right. Somebody that stays on us and points out what character flaws we may need to try and fix to better our overall selves. The critical point here is not to become too consumed in projecting your attitude or personal desires on others.

Do you ever notice how some babies are born more calm and quiet than others? Then some babies may be more active and loud. As I briefly stated in the introduction of the book, our genes and behavior are already being influenced in the womb. Still, some things carry over to adulthood, which explains the phenomenon associated with who we are naturally. Deep down we are still who we are. We must not get too consumed in all the bad qualities in others when we all make mistakes to the day that we die. Allow people to be themselves instead of pushing our own beliefs and values onto them as if our values are always the same.

Balanced Love

The same way we can quickly point out a flaw; we should be able to point out a list of things you love about them as well. Imagine if we all caught each other while we did something right. We don't necessarily need acknowledgment for doing something we are supposed to do. But the boost in confidence when hearing these things is very appreciated.

When you speak about positive vibes, don't always think others are the ones who should give it, you should be radiating it at a high level as well. People should become more happy, confident, and loving when you're in their presence. We all like to be acknowledged for our good deeds. It makes us feel good, even when it is what we're supposed to do. Someone who does good deeds and someone who does unethical acts can both have underlying intentions of wanting love and acceptance.

Know that random compliment can make someone's day. They will feed off that energy and benefit from it. Know that when we spread love, it becomes contagious in the same ways hating and condemning do. So whenever one is more dominant than the other, which one is being expressed more? We end up hating and judging only to become sensitive when we become the victims of it. Many people like to state how much they don't care about others. I'd agree that reflecting on what people may think of you is pointless, but the things we care about still show in subtle ways, even when we consciously try to convince ourselves otherwise.

The strongest people are able to love knowing that nobody is perfect. The most influential people see perfection in people's imperfections. They see what we can overcome when we turn to love. They know that is where all the power and strength lies. I once heard a rapper, J Cole, on the radio, speaking about happiness and love. He was saying that chasing money, women, and material things is comparable to a drug. You never have enough. You're always seeking more and more.

When the things you love are money, women, cars, clothes, etc. When is it ever enough? It never is. Our happiness and love will never be satisfied this way. We'll always be chasing after something that has no end. When we define our love and appreciate the things we have now, we are showing love for what is. Instead of overlooking this our whole life we should wake up every day conscious of all the things we should be thankful for. We should know what happiness and love really mean.

Our happiness should never be vaguely defined as something never genuinely attainable. Define your happiness, look around you and see all the things you should appreciate. Your friends, family, house, clothes, water, even the fact that you're breathing at this moment. When we talk about love and happiness, nobody ever defines or talks about what our perception of that is. When we have the right perception of it, we realize we already have it.

The Psychopath

There have been books written about the science of evilness. When we analyze the childhood experiences of others, we can usually begin to understand why some people are indeed evil. Think about the amount of love and nourishment a baby needs upon being born. Now think about the number of children who may have been neglected or even harassed. This may traumatize many people as they mature into adulthood.

While we all grow older and become responsible for ourselves, we usually still are operating from a belief system instilled in our youth. Many people don't know how to handle these emotions and may take it out on themselves or the world. What state of mind must someone evil consistently be in to be vile? After all, the amount of energy it takes to stay mad is hard. It's not a natural way to feel, and you may have experienced this yourself many times.

Even when there may be times when we're extremely mad, staying mad for a long period of time is draining. In order for people to do this, they may have years of anger built up. Their perception of the world may be as if everyone is out to get them. So they are always instinctively hurting others before they get hurt. Just like any particular habit, it can become something we do without thinking. In their mind, certain areas of their brain may be stimulating the reward centers from this behavior. This will make them act in similar ways again to receive this dopamine. I guess this is why many villains have this evil laugh associated with their bad deeds.

The average person may be somewhat poor at using their cognitive abilities for genuine empathy. We may be sympathetic to people, but to really feel the troubles others may be going through is a more powerful and skillful task. Some people naturally have these abilities, which makes them helpful when giving advice. It may even give themselves anxiety because of all the things they notice that the average person overlooks. The psychopath rarely ever uses these abilities. The neurons responsible for doing this are more often than not weak and rarely ever creating any synapses.

When we wonder why some leaders could care less about the number of innocent people who starve every day or die in wars, they lack empathy. This shows in the way they treat themselves. To be this type of person is to be unnatural. To keep a frequency so low that it feels you with hate consistently is to harm yourself more than anyone else. Even when you're the only one who knows about something terrible you've done, it will still eat at your conscience. Why would these people be so careless? Because they desire to love. The love they never got from others, or their family is something that fuels this urge.

When we are dealing with emotions, the way in which we choose to use this energy is consequential, as I'll explain in a later chapter. Not only that, many people have a disregard for anybody else beyond their family. Many of us don't realize that when we look at others, beyond our family, we'll still see a reflection of ourselves. This isn't saying evil people are like you. It's saying we're all a reflection of some emotion, which creates our perception and forms our approach to life.

Many people will admit that they've entertained thoughts of suicide, murder, or thoughts leading to depression. They may have not allowed themselves to actually follow through and do things they may consciously know they'll regret. Usually, we as people understand how temporary these feelings can be, which is why we are told to calm down or count to ten. If we are unstable and entertain these thoughts for too long when these particular emotions arise, then we could easily do something vile. This is why we must learn how to understand ourselves deeply. Empathize with yourself, combat those emotions, and as you become more aware, you'll overcome the trauma that was preventing you from becoming peaceful.

When we realize it is our emotions causing us to perceive life in specific ways, we'll see why people's approaches in life may differ while subtly desiring the same things. The only cure to evilness or anything that may be detrimental to us mentally is to begin to expand our awareness of the real cause.

To be completely oblivious to your emotions, perception, and energy is disastrous. You'll be emotionally unstable and never fully take control of your life, which is sad because you have a gift of consciousness unique to any other living entity on this earth. No matter how bad our mental attitude is, it can be reconstructed. While there may not be many institutions designed to help the average person escape bad beliefs, hopefully, this book will be a start. As I've become more and more aware, I look at the world in a way in which I thought I could never understand or articulate. Evilness is a result of the power of the mind. We can use our mind to go places you'd never think, or we can use it to self destruct under our conceptual illusions.

CHAPTER 3

Group Think

Contagious Energy

"The energy of the mind is the essence of life." - Aristotle

The things humans can accomplish when they're working together is infinite. It's the most powerful force in the universe. Without millions of single atoms vibrating together at once, we wouldn't have a material world or the illusion of having a solid body. When you zoom in on an atom, it is recognized as a physical particle. This is essentially what we're all made of. When you zoom in on these particles, you will see electrons and protons, but what are they made of? The realization that these physical particles are nothing more than a spinning force field of energy is incredible.

It'll make you look at everything around you differently. Everything is interconnected, and we're all broadcasting energy in ways we don't realize. Great things are formed in unity. Whether it be ants floating on water by holding each other together, creating a land base or humans working together to manifest beautiful creations all over the world, the unified effort does wonder.

This realization leaves me zealous to discover how humans can constructively adjoin our generalized goals without destructing over miscellaneous passions or perspectives. Much of our reactions are instinctively instilled to the point we lose the ability to see beyond them. When you realize your impulsive reactions are mostly based on personal experience, education, and close-mindedness, you will begin to use that awareness to take a more understanding approach.

Humans naturally have a good sense of energy. It could be someone's facial expression, shady humor, or even dry conversation that could tell you everything you need to know about someone's vibe. The vibe is short for vibrations that can go very high and very low. Humans have such a great sense of these vibrational frequencies we've been able to identify and name them to describe our any given mood. We all have these intuitive powers that some people are in tune with, and others may overlook it.

The more you become aware of how energy works, the more powerful you become. As your sense of others' energy becomes heightened, you'll start understanding how it can psychologically and inexplicably create miraculous results. Energy transfer is a mental state we become succumbed too unconsciously unless thoroughly aware of how to counterpunch the energy. Instead of becoming influenced by it, you manipulate others into a good mood without their realization.

It works the same way when we suddenly feel down when people come to us being negative. It can be done by bringing up a specific subject, showcasing high energy, joking, or even by giving a motivational speech. It can also cause people to fall in line due to the limited creative opinions and one-sided beliefs. Most people become influenced by the type of energy they're around. People who understand energy understand that in these most trying moments when the majority are hanging their heads, they see how this energy begins to spread throughout the group.

Notice how you feel when you're around certain people. Is there energy uplifting or draining? Do you feel happy around them or discouraged? The true essence of energy is sporadic and spontaneous in a sense. Our moods can shift rather conflictingly and the immensity of causes for stimulation not only vary but are fairly unpredictable. Realizing the nature of the mind can leave us on an emotional rollercoaster, due to the inability of our inner soul to differentiate from what is real and fake, is life-changing awareness.

The same way we react to a scary movie is the same way we react to undesirable scenarios playing in our heads. Real or fake, we react as if it has happened. It is the time we spend reflecting in our heads that make us lose sight of reality, and the irony of it all is how it is perplexingly intertwined with our subjective suppositions. So, in a sense, what we think IS what we end up seeing in the world. The more we focus on anything, the more vivid it becomes. People have a hard time grasping the fact that this is happening in their heads before their consciousness of it. Feeding your mind good thoughts will help replace those negative instinctive thoughts to more uplifting ones.

These thoughts, where do they come from? If you've ever meditated, you may have gotten frustrated at some point, attempting to keep your mind from wandering off. I would sit calmly and sometimes be thrown off by the randomness of my thoughts. I would say to myself. "What made me think of that?" Ultimately it brought me to a more enlightened perspective about how we can become impulsive to figments of our imagination.

The purpose of this chapter is to demonstrate the many ways we can direct energy productively. When I ponder on how it'd be possible to create a consensus that results in a better relationship culture to culture and race to race, it makes me realize how everyone has to face the personal battles that create the attitudes they possess.

As I mentioned in chapter one, the reasons why you may treat certain people better or worse than others can be vast. To become more aware of your personal biases and realize how others easily construct their own as well will make you handle situations better. Ultimately, when you control your reactions to events or people, you become the prize. It can be something as simple as the wrong comment or doubt others may show in you that could easily piss you off.

The mentality you need is one that pauses and takes into consideration how most people don't know enough about you to make the claims they do. If they understood this, they wouldn't be so quick to speak on people as if they genuinely do know. Everyone is valuable to life in some way. We can choose to focus on those things or focus on the things that we don't like. This makes the difference in us as people using each other to ascend intellectually or descend destructively. This type of wisdom and mindset is centered around individual self-control. So in order to truly even think about better communication and relations around the world, we must practice the self-control we have regarding our personal daily lives and thoughts.

Understand that you will have good thoughts and bad thoughts by nature, but you aren't those thoughts, you are a reflection of your reactions to them. Reflecting on the wrong things can cause you to have poor self-control and judgment. Practice shifting your focus during temptations or negative feelings until you've gained enough awareness and strength to think this way automatically. Even kids naturally know the consequences of where their attention lies.

The Marshmallow

A good example of this is a popular test that was done to kids dealing with marshmallows. The kids were offered a marshmallow but were told if they could wait 15 more minutes, then they would receive two. During that 15 minute wait, some kids ate the marshmallow, and some didn't. Those same kids grew up to become more successful than the kids who couldn't overcome the temptation. It was noted how the kids who were able to wait found some way to distract themselves instead of concentrating on the marshmallow.

Those moments when you may feel tempted to procrastinate, or cheat on your diet, reflect on the feeling of you accomplishing. It is critical to understand how a shift in focus, or attention, can relieve any unwanted feelings you may be having. It always feels better when you finish your homework compared to when you choose to blow it off. Putting things to the side may appear to be the easiest thing to do, but it only creates subtle anxiety. In the back of your mind, you'll always know you have some unfinished business that'll eventually catch up to you. You can only run from your problems for so long before you'll eventually have to face them.

The difference is in the short and long term pleasure. For us to establish some basis of self-control, we must learn how to push aside our short term pleasures for a more blissful future experience. Based upon my own personal observations of my own feelings I've realized the true control is what we choose to entertain.

It's as if whatever we tend to reflect on for an extended period of time only enhances the sense of it being real. Before we know it, we've lowered or raised our vibrations to that mental state, which can stay for as long as we continue to reflect. In that split second, when your emotions kick in and despite you consciously being able to understand what's happening, it can be tough to calm yourself down. Think of a moment when you've been extremely nervous, angry, hurt, or fearful. It may have been hard to calm yourself down because some regions of our brain can shut down that rational control thinking.

Fight or Flight causes a reaction from your body to pump more blood to certain areas. Your body is essentially preparing itself to react strictly on its instincts. You don't have to think about how to run when in danger or fight when being attacked. You may even sort of blank out or not feel anything until after your adrenalin goes back to normal. Your instincts kick in to keep you safe, so it's beyond our conscious ability to control it completely. Yet, with awareness and practice, anyone can develop a more efficient thinking pattern that'll create an ability to become at more peace with life.

It's as if you've learned how to tame your emotions or calm that monkey mind, which is a popularly used metaphor for our restless thoughts. It is all in those few seconds when we feel that anxiety comes along that we quickly shift our reflection of thought on more favorable outcomes, at least ones that make us feel content. Any scenario can be turned into a positive perspective that can lead you to feel a lot better. It's up to you to realize this and know in those moments you have control. Anger and frustration are natural emotions. If you didn't know how it felt to feel bad, you wouldn't appreciate how it feels to be happy. When we understand this, we'll use these emotions to empower us in accomplishing our goals as opposed to using that energy to do destructive things.

Directing Energy

Whenever there may come a time when you are frustrated remind yourself what is happening to you. Sometimes showing anger can be useful. It shows the desire, passion, and powerful energy that can be used as fuel to achieve anything. How will you direct this energy though? This reminds me of this scene in the movie Remember the Titans. Denzel Washington stared at his team after they got into a huge scuffle during camp. He scoffed at them saying, "You look like a bunch of fifth-grade sissies after a catfight! You got anger, that's good you're gonna need it, you got aggression that's even better you're gonna need that too. But any little two-year-old child can throw a fit! Football is about controlling that anger, harnessing that aggression into a team effort to achieve perfection!"

Denzel realized the power in them uniting as a group. And while he was explicitly emphasizing football, it is just as critical to understanding how this pertains to life as well. He also realized how we could use the feelings and energy we have built up in a more consciously controlling way. Use whatever energy or desire you have to complete any goals you have set out for yourself. It can be small or big.

All we really want in life is to feel at peace. While we would like to wait until we have millions of dollars or the perfect relationship, or our dream house, to feel completely blissful, we have that choice of serenity every day in the way we choose to see and think. If you genuinely want to be happy, you have to practice the skill of thinking like someone who is. Then it will show in the way we treat one another and ourselves. Direct any bad energy into something that ends up benefiting you in some way.

Escaping bad energy

One of the most complicated things to do in life is to escape bad energy. Many people can't just get up and leave the negative environment they live in. Bad energy can be anywhere, which is to say it's unavoidable. You can eventually remove yourself and maneuver through it, uplifting those who may be vibrating lower, and become unmoved by people who may try to bring you down. It will take a lot of awareness to reach this level, and even then life will present creative challenges that will continuously test your faith in the universe and yourself. Sometimes people end up better off taking the risk of escaping bad energy by any means. When you trust yourself and are ready to take that leap of faith, it is at some point necessary. At the same time, we don't want to make any decisions without thinking it through and end up in a worst position.

It can be hard to escape the toxic family or friends. The reason it's so important to is because you'll never experience what life has to offer if you're never around people who are committed to blissful experiences. Hanging with people who have no hopes, dreams, or ambitions won't help you in any way.

For example, say you meet a new friend. You never been outside of your state and never been on a plane before. You and your new friend become best buds and end up hanging out more and more. Before you know it, your new friend has convinced you to get a passport and come with them across the country.

All of this happened because of this new energy you are around. The things that can happen when we are around different people can land you in positions you never thought you'd be. Going places and mingling can create new friends and opportunities for you. Sometimes all it takes is for you to introduce yourself, and that could lead to a friendship that lasts for years. To escape bad energy practice doing spontaneous things and being around people you've never met before.

You've mastered this particular power of escaping bad energy when even when you're in the midst of it, you maintain the same frame of mind. This is essentially you not allowing other people's feelings to project the way you feel. Remain happy even when those around appear miserable. You don't have to sink into that way of thinking when you understand it is really a result of how they perceive things.

Be that person that doesn't allow others to feel sorry for themselves. Encourage and uplift people. State how possible the things they think are impossible are. Make them reevaluate their own energy. This will make you secure in the sense that you now control the vibe instead of allowing others to change it.

There's nothing wrong with protecting your energy if

it can't be escaped. Telling people no or preferring to spend time alone is never a bad thing. Self-care is something that should always be prioritized. Never let others drain you of your energy, most of it should be reserved for you and whatever makes you peaceful.

Realize that if you have good intentions that your presence is valuable no matter where you are. If people don't appreciate that remove yourself and they will then see. Like-minded people usually attract the same type of people. So negative people seem to enjoy each other's company.

Some people even like it when you maybe mean. It may gain the respect of others when you show no sympathy or are ruthless in regards to the things you say or how you treat people. In some cases, this is necessary. People tend to act according to the things you tolerate. Some people also tend to take kindness for weakness.

It's never a bad thing to show aggression or emotions when needed. Never attempt to be a rude person for the sake of respect or the ego, though. Never get in the habit of stooping to people's level, most things people say aren't even worth your energy. This won't get you far in life, and it will come back to bite you at some point. The things people say rarely are ever critically thought out. They may say things backed behind emotion or simply because that's the first thing that came to their mind.

Think of a time when someone said something that made you feel disrespected. You may have reacted or reflected on it at a later time allowing it to bother you. Meanwhile, they went on about their day and may have never thought twice about it. Small talk and the opinions thrown around amid any midday casual conversations can reveal a lot about people. At the same time, trying to decipher everything people say or do can make you create problems that aren't even there.

Sometimes men may even treat women in a way that comes off as mean or careless, and some women like it. It makes them feel as if you are not only dominant but not intimidated. A lot of women are used to being called intimidating or hard to approach, so to be on the opposite end of that can be exciting. This is a turn on because they sense you have your mind. The way you treat them isn't any different because they are more or less attractive.

They may be used to guys treating them nicely, but your energy is as if they're a regular person who presents them with a challenge. Energy never lies, those signs could sometimes lead to an abusive relationship that you may now want to escape. Stay focused on the way people make you feel and act accordingly.

There are certain times when people don't realize how their words or actions may come off. Never be afraid to say something that needs to be said, especially when it's throwing your energy off. Always be honest and try to give opinions when they are wanted. People will come to you about many things when they know you will tell them your honest opinion.

Assure that you take yourself seriously and stand by your beliefs when they are aligned the right way. People will respect the fact you know who you are and aren't phased by doubters. Once again, life isn't about letting people walk over you or turning the other cheek. It is being conscious of your emotions at all times and having a purpose in the way you direct your energy. Mastering yourself is about being in control at all times.

Absorbing Energy

Humans can absorb energy from one another, and whether it happens knowingly or not, you could find yourself at the same vibration as whoever you are around. Imagine working around funny, emotionally intelligent, and helping people. Work wouldn't seem so bad, but it's the constant type of energy that you're around that makes the job draining.

I used to think white-collar jobs were better than blue-collar jobs until I had an office job and was just as miserable. Someone could have a way more physically demanding job and be happier and energized than someone who works in a corporate office around bad energy. Many jobs are easy, but the management and character of the people can be so poor, it eventually becomes overwhelming. People spend 40 or more hours a week working almost every day. If you are spending 8 hours a day around a group that brings your vibrations down, it is never worth sticking around.

We should be encouraging different ideas and uplifting one another. That is what a real team does. So if we were to begin to constructively analyze and implement a strategic way for us to diminish groupthink, the first step is understanding psychological safety and taking an understanding approach. Still, many other factors play a part in the way we treat one another. The things that form our culture, what becomes popular, and what doesn't, isn't something you can predict.

When it comes to being loved and appreciated, it can influence actions rooted in validation. Our perception of how people see us plays a part in how we may carry ourselves at any given moment as well. While you may be quick to feel as if you're always yourself and above the influence, it can be subtle things overlooked by you consciously.

You may have taken that 3rd shot of Tequila to prove you can hang when you are a light drinker. We see millions of kids influenced by music to the point they are taking drugs at an irresponsible level just because. It's also not a coincidence that many of our parents at some point during our childhood, have asked us, "If your friend jumped off a bridge, would you do it too?" The immediate reaction by us is of mixed feelings. On one side we get the point, on the other side, it may be a possibility depending on the circumstances, so..possibly.

Peer pressure is real and the passiveness about it makes us overlook the transition to conformity. Sometimes what drives us so hard to be great or even do things we don't want to is because of the number of people who may have doubted our abilities. In some cases, the feeling of having something to prove or needing certain things to fit in can make people conform in inauthentic ways.

One reason the energy you give is so important is

because people always tend to react to how others treat them. Meaning if you give them good vibes, they'll return the favor and vice versa. The way people may feel about themselves can drastically change by a simple compliment you made. Now their perception of you may be of someone they want to hang around or talk to more.

If you give people negative energy, they'll usually avoid you or treat you in similar ways. This isn't always the case, but when we do give this good energy, and others don't appreciate it, don't feel bad. Realize they may be unaware of energy and the way that it manifests and creates peace and opportunities. They may be miserable or could not be in the mood to be kind. Either way, it is a reflection of their own problems, not yours. This shouldn't affect your mood in the slightest. If you hold the door open for someone and they don't say thank you, oh well. I did that because I'm a good person, and that is all. Nipsey Hussle once said, "I still show love when I feel hate." This is a powerful state of mind that puts you at a level of awareness that not many people ever reach.

The Ego's Energy

Your ego is associated with who people think you are. Your character is who you are when nobody's watching. Many people's egos are easily bruised, and all it takes is being embarrassed, wrong, or misunderstood. This can cause us to act out of character. If we remained composed in many cases our egos wouldn't take over causing an unwanted illusion of reality. It's what makes us feel as if the world is crashing down like our life is that bad.

Your ego will exaggerate circumstances, which is why when we are engaged in it to a great extent, our reactions are over the top. When we are aware of this we understand how to tap into a state of mind that reminds you of your worth despite anyone who may doubt or discredit you, mentally you'd never be phased. An example of how our ego can cause us to do things out of character is everywhere at any given moment. The arguments, the lies people tell, the big words people use, or even the things we buy all represent the ego and lengths we will go to assure it's portrayed in a way that gains people's respect.

Men may take pics with money, women may take a pic of their ass. Everyone can respect someone who is getting money, right? Everyone appreciates a nice ass I suppose. What are we trying to prove to one another? While many of us may state how much we don't care what others think, it is naïve to underestimate any impressions made on the subconscious mind and the extent to which it influenced us. It's critical to understand that there is an infinite amount of reasons someone may look at you a certain way. It is enough to overwhelm you and make you feel silly for worrying or focusing on something with no realistic way to go about receiving consistent clarification.

Sure, showing off money could potentially impress some women, but some women don't like that. The same goes for men. Some may like and enjoy that ass pic, but other men may see it as a bad look. As much as we try to go out of our way to do things to attract the opposite sex, some people will find you appealing for being you. We then won't even have to spend energy doing things to impress them because we attracted them by being who we are naturally. This doesn't mean everyone who posts pics is doing it for some attention despite it a lot of times being the case. Sometimes people do things for them and them only. From that perspective, I encourage people to do anything that uplifts them.

Think about a time when you were frustrated and took that anger out on someone else. Think about how it most times immediately made their energy drop. This can be a ripple effect, and it is happening in a multitude of ways. You may have felt some regret for the way you treated other people after calming down. One of the toughest things to do is overcome anger in the heat of the moment.

The only way to keep from becoming triggered in the first place is to always have a powerful sense of your feelings and understand the bigger picture at all times. It's inevitable that these feelings at some point will arise. When you're mad or have let your ego get to you, immediately remind yourself of all the great things you've done or are working towards. Remind yourself how blessed you are to be alive, and being mad or prideful at this moment isn't worth a second of your life.

Think about all the things that make you happy until you've regained your true natural frequency and state of mind. This is extremely powerful knowledge to acquire and implement. People's lives have ended because of their inability to use this level of awareness. The more you work at it the better you will get.

Many times we may go out of our way to protect our ego while it may conflictingly actually create low self-esteem. Think about how a lot of people may be afraid to ask questions in class. Their quick assessment is that people will think they're not smart. In that same sense, someone could easily look at you and be impressed that you were paying attention enough to engage, which to them is a sign of intelligence.

You'd be surprised how many people don't ask questions or don't act period because of how they think others may react. You'd also be surprised how many people aren't paying attention in class or have questions too but don't ask. When we remove those thoughts or at least direct them to a more uplifting perspective that creates confidence or courage, we are becoming our true selves.

The basis of our character isn't influenced by anything besides the way in which we direct it. Meaning if I'm happy I'll be smiling. If I have a question in class, I'll ask. If I feel like giving someone a compliment, I'll give them one. If I want to start a random conversation with a stranger, I'll do it. Being free from worrying, "What they might think" can land you in amazing places and meeting great people.

The person we have envisioned as appealing to others is what we'll align our characteristics and symbolic materials with. Keep in mind this a lot of times is at a very subtle level. If you had a job interview, you would conduct yourself differently than if you were around your peers. The way you sit in the chair, word articulation, clothes, overall posture, and demeanor will be of someone worthy of a job. I don't blame anyone for this. It is wise to know what behavioral traits to show in the right scenarios subliminally.

The way we perceive ourselves will inspire us to be the class clown or the one who sits in the back hoping not to be noticed. It makes some people leaders. It makes some people followers. Essentially the conveyance of any type of expression within any group is a mere reflection of how you feel about yourself. These rationalities are formed on the basis of one's attempt to be likable.

While adjusting our behavior sometimes can be good, we don't want to become an inauthentic version of ourselves. We want to have a good interview, but we don't want to lose who we are. We want the interviewer to sense comfort, honesty, and high self-esteem as well. Don't get caught up in trying to come off as a perfect candidate, relax, and be yourself. Even when it comes to writing a book, editing is essential, but not if it takes away the uniqueness and voice of the author.

Many people are afraid of speaking in interviews or large crowds in general. This is only because of how we become overly self-conscious in moments when we'd do fine if we'd just relax. We begin to think too hard about how to do things our brain is already hardwired for. That could be presenting your paper in class, which is simply a summarized elaboration of research. If we were explaining this to a friend, it would roll off our tongues naturally. In front of a crowd, anxiety builds up from us focusing on scenarios we don't want to happen. If I'm worried about my appearance, if I mess up or what the crowd may think about me, I'll be distracted and may stutter or freeze up.

It's important to be comfortable with who you are in any setting. When we are comfortable everything flows the way we want it too. That's because we're at our natural state. It frees our minds enough to focus on the present moment allowing us to perform at our highest potential. We must realize that people shouldn't make us nervous. There's nothing to be afraid of when meeting new people or speaking in crowds.

Always remember it isn't you that is hurt, it is your ego. When you let it go, life's obstacles and distractions become comical in a sense. You'll realize people say things to try and get to you, people will do things to try and appeal to you, people will do things completely unaware of their ego being in the way. You'll no longer be caught into the ego trap, you'll appreciate your mindfulness and awareness. You'll realize that is all it is, and with that power, you'll master yourself.

From some people's perspective, the ego can be a good thing. The ego is almost comparable to a role an actor may have to play. There's a particular type of state of mind that many actors have to get into to fully become that character. You can use your ego to act in ways that are aligned with who you want to be, even if you haven't quite reached the level you're striving for. Just never let your ego get the best of you.

Flow

Maneuver through life smoothly, embracing everything you may face at any given moment. Tune out any and everything distracting you from what you want and who you are. This state of relaxation or being at ease will create significant opportunities for you. It will also diminish the chances of you subliminally becoming too caught up in your reputation or what others may think of you.

Have you ever been so focused you lose track of time? Many people call this flow, and while we're in it, we become extremely productive. That is the "in the zone" feeling we get while concentrating on one thing. We lose our sense of time and are so in the present moment. It's as if the real power in it is the fact that we are entirely removed from our thoughts. When you spend too much time thinking, you miss out on a lot of information that could help you with whatever you're doing.

I've noticed how the best results come when we're genuinely focused and using as much information to our advantage as it happens. This will always give you the ability to make great decisions. This is comparable to when we just let things go. It is then when it seems as if everything happens at the right time.

Have you ever been in an argument and later on thought of something you should've said? You've simply calmed down enough to make more sense of the situation as opposed to when you were mad. After all, if you were calm, you all may have come to better rational conclusions instead of being left even more confused afterward. There are moments alone when you could be expressing things to yourself, and it was articulated perfectly and wonder why it doesn't flow that naturally when it matters the most. It's because we aren't comfortable. Comfort is a clear sign of peacefulness and can be easily sensed.

Think about what we may accomplish if we had this mindset every day of every moment. Becoming aware of this is a power you can use to do things many people who are unaware of become a victim too. The reason it's easy to feed into what others may think of us is because of our psychological need to be loved and accepted. Today people may call it social validation or even clout. It turns people into attention cravers acting upon those typical characteristics, trends, or materials that make us feel and appear more appealing.

You don't have to be like everyone else to fit it in. The people who set trends and gain a lot of respect from others are the ones who don't conform or worry about what's cool to do. So instead of seeking validation based on the wrong things, we, be. The universe will then bring the people and things we want to us naturally.

There are places we want to be or things we want to accomplish and when the people or opportunity is near our subconscious mind senses it. It may be an urge to speak to someone or to drive to a specific place. While in a peaceful state and comfortable, we don't let anxiety keep us from trusting ourselves. We are, in a sense, in sync with nature and the possibilities within it. Once we've escaped the maze of trying to be perceived as perfect and just let if flow, groupthink can be directed to a more valuable thing and not a diminishing one.

Teamwork

I've often been curious about our behavior within groups. Why do some groups succeed so well? Why do some groups fail despite having the potential? What is that feeling that we get when we're around certain people? You may feel shy, irritated, happy, successful, inspired, sad, superior, inferior, or even funny depending on who you are around. Our feelings and actions displayed within groups erratically coincide with any underlying personal perceptions of ourselves, fears, and subtle conformities. When our feelings are aligned as a group, everything is easy, it flows, and the energy in sync is enchanting. Creating uplifting, honest, and sincerity within a group allows for the belief in one another to reach vibrations ascending that of the norm.

Charles Duhigg (who is the author of "Smarter Faster Better: The Secrets of being Productive in Life and Business") found some vital information that gives us insight into how groups can become successful or fail. To create the fulfilling results we want from group activity, we must understand the power of our own choices. The things that make projects, jobs, or anything group related boring and unproductive is our inability to take initiative. To max out the full potential of the group, everyone must feel a sense of control. When we genuinely feel like we have an essential role within a group, and our ideas are appreciated, it instills trust.

This psychologically, for some reason, also gives us motivation, which, according to the studies, is considered a skill like reading or writing. People seem to be more excited to play a game that allowed them to choose and have control as opposed to it being computer-generated results, even when the outcomes were the same. When too many people are trying to be the leader or make demands, it causes confusion. It makes certain people within the group less confident about their abilities when there's constant criticism of their creative side.

The results of things like this are what can cause Groupthink. If the chemistry is off then the energy can be draining for anybody. Groups who show a lack of open-mindedness probably aren't productive despite the talent. A high IQ doesn't mean a team will perform at a high level at all. It was discovered that balance was vital, meaning everyone's ideas were considered. It also is essential to note that each successful group had an above-average sense of emotional intelligence.

Being able to identify someone who is angry, sad, serious, etc. is a great skill to possess. It shows how much the group sympathizes with one another. If there's something wrong with one of us, then there's something wrong with all of us. Groups who achieve beyond the norm usually show some signs of psychological safety. This is simply the way people are treated within the group. How much do they trust one another? Do they feel comfortable enough to speak out and say how they feel? All this plays a part in the overall productiveness of any team. We a lot of times are on the wrong page whenever things aren't going the way we need them to. Pay attention to the energy that you feel and learn how to channel it productively.

What is groupthink?

You ask people why they wake up and do the same things everyone else is doing and they don't know why. They may say well everybody else is doing it. This is only proof of how we must escape this conforming behavior to reach inner peace. We fool ourselves into thinking life is more peaceful when we are always cooperating or never questioning when, in reality, it makes us feel mentally caged.

It's easier to go with the flow rather than disagree and be stereotyped or even demonized for thinking any differently. School, our parents, and society have conditioned our beliefs to the point we are crazy even to question certain things. This can have a damaging effect on how we feel sometimes. There's no wonder many people feel like nobody understands them. Being different and thinking for yourself isn't truly embraced and often overlooked to the popular way of doing things.

The term often used to describe the natural psychological behavior is Groupthink. Many people have great ideas, they often wonder about things that may seem crazy to others. It's easy to get stuck in a manipulated perception of life. When we have escaped that mental maze, we realize how everything we ever wanted was always attainable.

Groupthink is the practice of thinking or making decisions as a group in a way that discourages creativity or individual responsibility. How often do we participate in groupthink? If you've ever hesitated or felt discouraged about your ideas it may be because of this. Many of our beliefs have started within groups and lack the ideas or opinions of others, which leads to irrational actions and nobody comfortable enough to object. These opinions could have prevented wars, deaths, debt, a programmed society, etc.

If you don't think you've subconsciously engaged in groupthink you may want to think again. There are countless things we do as a group or society that make no sense but are still going on today because of groupthink. Not enough people question popular opinions because they don't want to be the one person who causes conflict, which, of course, means we don't "fit in."

In this world today, being your authentic self takes courage and a realization that just because everyone is doing it, doesn't make it right. Many may not agree with you even at times when you're being sensible, that doesn't make you wrong. Just because there lies tradition doesn't mean it will be a logical thing to do 20 years later when the circumstances have changed. Who though has the courage to speak against the people making these decisions? Obviously, they think their way of thinking is the only way of thinking. Look at these examples of groupthink that may bring memories of you being in similar situations

1. **The illusion of invulnerability** – Many great leaders speak in a vague creative way giving the illusion that the actions taking place are 100 percent right and vital.
2. **Collective rationalization** – People within the group will always create their own twisted theories despite taking a more rational look at what they've decided to do. This leads to ignoring warnings and has a history of consequences. How many times have you heard there were plenty of warnings about what was going to happen on Sep 11th? Or even Pearl Harbor, where senior officers did not take warnings from Washington D.C seriously about a potential invasion.
3. **Inherent Morality** – The group assumes that everything they are doing is ethical and beneficial but when speaking on worldly issues it is more so only beneficial to the group.
4. **Stereotyping** – Anyone who creates conflict with the beliefs of the group is demonized and they create a negative image on those who try to oppose their beliefs. This only keeps them from rationally addressing objections to their decisions. This is character assassination and the reason why people are afraid of speaking up.
5. **Direct pressure to conform** – People a lot of times don't act unless they feel pressured to or

obligated to. In this case, people are pressured to agree with the ideas and not question.

6. **Self-Censorship** – Willingly removing oneself from any conflict by not speaking on their objections and unpopular opinions.
7. **Misapprehension of Unity** – Often, leaders take silence as acceptance when nobody voices their true feelings on the matter.
8. **Mind Protectors** – You also have the people who participate 100 percent no matter how stupid of an idea it is they play their role.

Keep this in mind, and it won't be long before you see how you begin to stand out from others. It won't be forced; it will only be because of how you've embraced your mind and thoughts.

The Power of Groupthink

Groupthink is the most powerful source of humanity's greatest accomplishments. It is the same energy that makes a college football team like Alabama consistently great, and an NFL team like the Browns willing to do anything to escape the mentality of being unworthy.

When there is nobody around that will question beliefs or decisions to whereas a group they all think more critically, it will usually cause destruction. You may have heard that if you were to hang around four millionaires long enough, you'd eventually become the 5th. The way our levels of understanding are enhanced through interaction as opposed to just reading or hearing about things hits the subconscious deeper. Our ways of thinking, habits, values, perceptions, slang, and even diet can be modified depending on who we're consistently around. There are a vast number of ways we can construct logical reasoning as to why we behave differently depending on who we're around.

It's shameful how we can allow groupthink to override our common sense. Concepts of evolution or agendas can leave humanity infallible to any wrongdoings. Everyone else that objects to these ways of thinking is deemed as crazy. To think it all derived from a simple thought, a proposal, an unquestioned suggestion is astonishing. We get caught up in philosophies that we support or believe wholeheartedly, never acknowledging that it all begins from a popular perspective. I can give a wide range of examples dealing with groupthink that has caused wars, defined racial backgrounds, and unethical corporate decisions.

I once stumbled upon a book called, "This Idea Must Die". The entire book is about different scientists, philosophers, and advanced concepts. They all have either conducted studies or created theories that challenge a lot of popular beliefs. Things like Geometry, Calculus, Artificial Intelligence, Science, Essentialism, Culture, Race, and many more subjects were debunked. This book made me realize that the very things we believe today are still being questioned. This opened my eyes to something beyond the book itself. Despite the things we believe that aren't totally accurate, people need something to believe in. There are consequences to some of these common beliefs though.

For example, the alleged science behind race has created a way of thinking that still defines us today. Race cannot be scientifically defined, and it was eventually denounced in the 20th century. Mainly because of racial scientists and their bias attitude towards natural selection, natural melanin to climate change, and philosophies of human potential.

The first people to create a geographic grouping of humans as "races" were Immanuel Kant and David Hume. They were two popular philosophers in the 19th century whose concepts have created an irrational assessment of people based on skin complexion. In 1775, Kant wrote about human diversity, he says, "There was never a civilized nation of any complexion other than white." Nina Jablonski is a big critic of this philosophy that seemed to have derived from a lack of real thought and evidence. She said, "There were four "races" characterized by skin color, hair form, cranial shape, and other anatomical features, and also by their capacity for morality. And they were arranged hierarchically, with only the European race, in his estimations being capable of self-improvement."

All of the things we believe as truly begin from a thought, a suggestion whose popularity enhanced the prevalent view of humanity. The characterization basically rejected the acceptance of non-Europeans, especially African Americans who were portrayed with a servitude fate. Not surprising that slavery undoubtedly was the backbone of economic growth in America. It at this point is a deception and a belief system that has crippled our perception of one another.

Conforming

Conforming is easy to do because we learn a lot of things from people by simply doing what they do. Knowing how to embrace our creativity at times instead of thinking the typical way, or taking action the way it has always been done is critical. We must tap back into our inner child. We must become more in touch with our imagination. When we haven't created a definite purpose for our life, we only end up living the life that someone else has created. We conform to the way of life or ideas by others when we can do this ourselves.

We can all consciously comprehend this but it's deeper than that. You've been conditioned from the moment of birth. This means to see the change you have to tap into the deeper part of your feelings.

Another reason it's easy to fall into this trap is that once we've been around something potentially influencing for a while, we eventually partake in it. A great example of this can be seen in how men sometimes become criminals. Men may at first despise the crime they experience as they grow older.

After a while, they may become comfortable within the very dangers they initially took caution to. They in a sense have begun to tolerate it or subconsciously accept it for what it is. If they continue to be surrounded by this influence, they will eventually embrace and become inclined to participate in it. This is a law!

This makes sense when we look at black neighborhoods and wonder why there is violence within the communities. People already are at odds, they already have a desire to survive, drugs are purposely thrown into the communities, and good jobs may be scarce. It's an easy plan to keep men locked up. More importantly, it is a successfully planned illusion of influence that is continuous.

Simply put, that instinct of consistent thought will eventually be accepted and translated into your physical reality. When we understand this, we can see why it is so hard to come out of this illusion, unless we reprogram ourselves to believe in something else. Don't be that person who has accepted a thought simply because you've heard it a hundred times.

These things happen outside of our awareness unless we understand the critical psychological laws behind how our mind works. It can get so severe that we don't even know why we continue to do things knowing the consequences. Even when it comes to other people's thinking, it's easy to look at them foolish for not thinking the way that we do. On the outside looking in it, all seems so senseless. When we experience this thought, it is an entirely different perspective that is formed.

It's almost as if we develop the number of neuron connections necessary to be able to understand why they do what they do, or say what they say. Which is to say, our mind can adapt to any environmental setting. If you hang around people that you in sense respect or are influenced by to some extent, it may not be long before you become a reflection of them. I've noticed this with how people speak. We adapt to the sounding out of words or slang from city to city, state to state, and country to country. The way they talk has become a thing.

When others aren't from a certain area people can immediately tell. Either by the way, they talk or by the way, they carry themselves. After months of hanging around this new crowd, they eventually will begin to sound like them and behave like them. There may be a few distinguishing characteristics still even after years. One thing that is clear here, though, is that we become who we hang around the most.

That's why people say they can tell a lot about you by simply seeing who your friends are. It's because, to some extent, you all rub off on each other knowingly and unconsciously. A woman tends to take on the lingo of the guy she's in a relationship with. The guy tends to form different values based upon the ones his girl has, which has rubbed off on him.

It is a natural phenomenon that is simply the different connections building based on the things we are experiencing. So that's why you have a hard time relating to people you've never spent much time around. You don't get them, and they don't get you. The more time that is spent around them will give you more and more understanding of why they are who they are.

Beyond groupthink, we must have a sense of individuality that won't always align with any group. We must conclude that our way of life extends beyond it. I'm pretty sure none of these things come to mind at the moment. Try and remember this information and be mindful of how you can use it to your advantage throughout life.

Paralleling your relations, success, and journey to self-actualization is the goal. With relations, your approach is everything. Become more willing to listen and understand. With success, trust in yourself and know you can create anything. Be confident, you have a gift which is your mind. With self-actualization, know this will bring you the peace and happiness that we are all in search of. So many people are depressed with life, if we can reprogram ourselves, over time we will find consistent blissfulness.

Self Actualization

We all have a psychological desire to belong and to be accepted by others. We all enjoy the feeling of being accepted or fitting in. In fact, when we look at any basic self-actualization chart you'll see this. It starts with our physiological needs, like food, water, and sleep. Next would be our need for safety. Things like our health, property, family, and employment are examples.

Next would be the need to be loved and desired. We want some sense of connection with everyone. This psychological need can backfire in ways we don't even realize. The things people do to receive this stimulation go beyond understanding. Someone could commit a crime to receive the attention or respect he may subconsciously be desiring from others. It isn't a logical way to go about satisfying this desire, but it happens.

When you realize how important this is to us, there's no surprise people are willing to accept irrational beliefs to avoid being excluded from fitting in. We want to feel loved and desired; this is natural, and we should have no shame if we have these feelings. We must realize that too much reliance on this love from others can be detrimental. People's love for you will come and go, never become saddened or frustrated if you feel like you aren't appreciated enough.

A lot of great people are overlooked sometimes, it doesn't take away from how great you are. Be bold and stand up for what you believe in. The people who gravitate and the people who descend from us only represent the different levels of vibrations and energy at any given moment. This stage is challenging because we must stay true to ourselves despite our natural need to feel loved. It can make us question ourselves or feel discouraged. This is where we learn to maintain a consistent mental state despite lacking the support.

The next psychological need on the chart is self-esteem, which includes confidence, achievement, and the need to be a unique individual. Then, of course, we have self-actualization. When we reach this stage, we have reached the true spiritual identity within. We have experienced a purpose. We are creative, moral, and have reached our inner potential.

The conflict with wanting to belong can confuse us

on our journey to becoming our true selves. When we are creating and accepting who we are, the respect from others will eventually come. We must not accept groupthink just to give us that falsified feeling of fitting in. We must explore beyond to become who we are meant to be.

A popular quote Nipsey Hussle lived by is, "The reasonable man adapts himself to the world, the unreasonable ones persist in trying to adapt the world to himself." This isn't to say we persist in not reasoning with other people. It's saying when we are pure and wise; we persist in pushing our beliefs and creations until they've become appreciated and influential, even if it happens after we are gone. Many may not see or appreciate the great things you do now, but perception has a way of handling that in time.

CHAPTER 4

Stimuli

I feel good

When you think of stimulation, you may quickly find this synonymous with anything we find pleasurable, exciting, fun, or even scary. Whatever it is that may get your blood pumping to where you're uncontrollably excited can be described as stimulation. Without stimulation, we wouldn't have any desire to act on anything. So the more you pay attention to those things that get you going, the more you can use it to manipulate how you feel at any given moment.

Think about the endless amount of life quotes or things that make you instantly happy. Those life quotes are designed to keep your mind in the right perspective despite any troubling times you may experience. It could be a person, food, that ice cream you have waiting at home, your future, or anything that makes you smile. You will begin to understand the impact your thoughts have on your feelings and how you can identify the most powerful ones, the ones that can change your mood instantaneously.

It's no wonder we have those times where we are sad and can't explain why. We have those moments when we're just extremely happy and can't give anybody an explanation for this particular mood. It's incredibly subtle, but the realization of this can help you overcome the negative things that keep you away from blissfulness.

Even if you have to make a list of the things that make you happy and repeat them every day, it will help. Remember, sometimes, we can be one decision away from doing something that could change our life forever, depending on what state of mind we're in. It could leave you wealthy or even in prison. We need to realize that when we're not feeling good, it is up to us to take responsibility for our health. Most times, it may be problems we have created in our heads.

Even in situations when things may not be going your way, allowing yourself to feel down is only making it worse for you. There is always something out there that can change your mood or make you feel better. You may not always get the results you wanted, but a lot of times opportunities still come. To doubt the universe's potential to bring you anything you desire is to question your very existence. Many people may give themselves rewards after accomplishing something or use any obstacles as motivation. You can do this in many other ways as well when we've begun to identify things we find pleasurable or exciting.

Instead of creating a skillful way of shifting your thoughts to an enlightening perspective, we tend to cling to things that release dopamine but aren't the best habits. Drugs, alcohol, gambling, overeating, shopping, and many more bad habits are created because of the false sense of relief it gives us. Our brain is releasing reward chemicals because it makes us feel good. What makes us feel good about things is our perception of its pleasure. There are things you've done in the past that were once pleasurable, but you may look at those past experiences in disgust now.

In a sense, those bad habits help us cope with our problems, but never completely resolve the real issues. Many of the problems we have are continuous because we never go directly to the source of the problem. We find things that can temporarily make them go away. If I wanted to go to the direct source of my problems, I would begin to be more attentive to my thoughts.

Stimulation is tricky because our senses are always coming into contact with the objective world. Consciously removing ourselves from places or things that stimulate us but don't help us grow is critical. Yet, we're bound to run into temptations, so consciously understand how you can direct these stimulations logically. Many of us that may procrastinate or form any habit that we don't necessarily want have fallen short of creating stimulating emotions that overpower the original one. It can make you realize how essential self-control is in life.

What is Stimuli?.

Stimuli is an essential part of seeing and the energy we have to do pretty much anything. According to google, **stimuli is a thing or event that evokes a specific functional reaction in an organ or tissue. Or a thing that rouses activity or energy in someone or something; a spur or incentive. Stimuli can be visual, auditory (sound), tactile (touch), olfactory (smell), or gustatory (taste).**

Since we're dealing with the perception, I will focus in detail with the eye and how it produces a specific reaction based upon the light rays. Then I will go in detail about how stimulation through the senses gets the brain going and gives us the energy to do things. It all appears to be subjective pleasures that decide what chemicals are released through the brain and cause happiness or sadness. It influences behavior and creates habits in our everyday life. It is the source of all action since it happens in our brains first.

When we talk about the eye and how we even have the ability to see, it starts with the physical stimuli of light rays that through an extremely fast process, turn this into electrical and chemical signals. Then our brain makes sense of this information, which forms physical images. Most animals rely more on smell and hearing which a lot of times is more advanced than humans. Humans have a very complex and advanced visual system compared to other animals. You'd be surprised to know that the human eye is one of the most complicated structures on earth. Our visual capabilities are possible through three significant layers.

The Sclera is the outer white area of the eye. It protects and supports the shape of the eye. Conjunctiva is the clear mucous that helps lubricate the eye. This includes the cornea, which is the outer layer that protects the pupil. This is the color of the eye that most people see. When people have brown or blue eyes, they are looking at the cornea.

The Choroid is a thin layer of tissue, the part of the eye that is in between the sclera and the retina. It is packed with blood vessels that carry oxygen to the retina. The choroid, which is also known as choroidea or choroid, is located toward the rear of the eye. Immediately you can see how multiple parts of the eye play a role in its overall function. Without each area playing its part, we have no vision. Which is comparable to the brain and how one dysfunctional area can diminish our overall conscious abilities as well.

The Retina is the part of the eye that pieces images together and includes cones and rods. This layer is also at the back of the eye and is sensitive to light. It is the most critical part of converting that light through nerve impulses which form visual images. Damage to this area of the brain can cause blindness. When the retina forms a picture through the focused light, the brain is left to decide what the picture is. It is at this point where we begin to make sense of the objects in our physical reality. From then on, we know that is a tree, or that is a car, as well as the colors associated with them. When the brain makes sense of these images it is stored through a process called neuroplasticity. This is the electric connections or synapses that make consciousness possible through stimulation.

The Pupil is said to be the window to the soul. It can give off information where no words are needed to describe the mental state. The pupils dilate for many reasons. The more we are exposed to light or focused on an object can make our pupils shrink. If you were in the dark, your pupils would expand to capture as much light as possible. In other instances, our pupils can dilate as we gather information or try and work out a problem. Psychologist Daniel Kahneman conducted a study that accurately presented the pupils increasing in size, depending on the difficulty of the task at hand. Our eyes become dilated when we're interested in what someone is saying as well as when we're sexually aroused. Pupils can dilate when we're on drugs or even when we're mad. It seems to me that whatever images or things that tamper and spark stimulation with the mind will show in the pupil through dilation. To make sense of this, it appears that the eyes are expanding in a natural reaction to observe one's surroundings at a more increased rate.

When I take in this information about the eye it makes me think about ideas and visualization. It is well known that anything we create was visualized in our minds first. As we grow up we have a basic understanding of the physical objects in our reality. With the connections going on in our heads, ideas are formed through our ability to create synapses with weaker or other stronger neuron impulses. When this happens, we are using the things we know and combining them with other neurons that end up forming something new. This would be considered an idea to us.

Just think we have billions of these neurons, each providing some form of information. Ideas and your potential are endless if you're able to realize there is nothing about you that is mediocre. If you're able to tap into these connections to form creative ideas, you're using the gift of consciousness. Somewhere in your head, your mind has the answer to how to do anything. We just have to learn how to direct our inner mind so that we attract it to us. The beauty in perception is vast and incredible. Even the physical makeup of how we're able to see is magical.

Mirage?

This isn't even half of the information that deals with the eyes and perception. There have been entire books written on just the eye, enough information to cover the rest of this book. This necessary information that I provided was to give you an idea of how many factors play a part in our ability to see and create.

Anyone can look more into this by a simple search on the internet. Keep in mind this is just one of the senses. It's so detailed and complicated that there are still tons of questions that are formed as we try and make sense of how we see. One reason why is because of how, to an extent, our minds can assume what things are sometimes.

Psychologist Richard Gregory has his opinions on perception. He says, "The eye receives a lot of information, but by the time it reaches the brain, much of it is lost." Based on past experiences, the brain makes sense of what it is seeing.

The brain is actively shaping our perception of reality from our environment, combined with past experiences and stored information. This explains why we don't always recall memories accurately. It, of course, always seems as if we do, but most times, we don't. That's because our brain dug up some information from the past to make sense of it. When we recall something from the past, we are remembering the last time we remembered it. This makes the memory more and more inaccurate each time. Our brains can play tricks on us! What does this say about history, and how it may have been conveyed?

Hundreds of studies have been conducted that test the accuracy of people's memories, and they usually fail despite their confidence in how vividly they claim to remember. At any given moment, wherever our focus is will determine how we remember specific events. It gets deep since we can confuse things we've seen weeks ago with things we've seen days ago.

We don't notice everything, it is impossible, so relying on a witness despite their confidence in what they saw is unfortunately unreliable. Daniel C. Bennet who is the author of Consciousness Explained talks about memory contamination. He writes how flashes of people or things we see over time can be combined, creating something that we thought was accurate. When people say life is an illusion, the in-depth theories of thought, memories, and subjective perceptions support it.

Think about how even your expectations can make you falsely perceive things that are happening when they're not. Have you ever been expecting a message and felt your phone vibrate, check your phone, only to see no message? Think about how at any given moment, the things you are focusing on are the only things that matter. Many studies have been done with people giving them specific instructions to either look for a certain color or thing. Most of the people become so focused on that particular thing. They don't notice how much other things are going on in the same area. As I stated earlier in the book, we as humans can't pay attention to everything, even when you feel you're skillful at your observations.

The ways we can go about describing how we make sense of things at any given moment are endless. Have you ever noticed that when you're in a new house, you hear weird noises, then after a while, you become used to these sounds to the point you may not even notice them anymore? Or what about when you've cooked something and after a while no longer smell it while someone who may visit hours later can smell it as if you've just finished? Our senses are very powerful in many subtle ways. Depending on how we uniquely make sense of the external and internal nature of life will determine our perceptions or reactions at any given moment. I realize how it goes beyond our control, yet with this understanding, we may reach a different level of consciousness that changes the way we see and feel about ourselves, each other, and the world.

I've read different books and studies about human consciousness, the senses, and perception which often leave me speechless or confused. There are so many intricate parts of the body. There are many things to consider when trying to explain our abilities and where they come from. It caused me to form my own subjective theories of life, which are no different than any scientist or philosopher was known to man.

The Matrix

I think as much as we try to make sense of life, it may be reasonably simple. When we are born, we take in all this information and make subjective sense of the world. Our brains at a young age are extremely active because it is storing tons of information. If our brain and mind are a direct reflection of the activity going on in our head, then we have a false sense of everything. If our brains are continually changing with experiences, then our memories, sense of self, and perception are regularly being overridden.

It just always appears as if we are in control or accurate when it comes to everything. In reality, we aren't. We are simply the result or expression of whatever neuron connections that have built up in our head. We are whatever our brain has made sense of. This illusion of life is a battle of your brain playing tricks on you and you playing tricks on your mind.

You are who you believe you are. The world is what you believe it is. It is said that the subconscious mind can't differentiate from what is real and what is fake. How more evident is it that we form our own subjective opinions about life? These connections going on in our head and the ones we show the most attention to create life. With that being said, allowing your mind to take in new information is the key to endless growth. The more you understand this matrix, the more you will use it to your advantage.

The combination of things that stimulate us play a big factor in our accomplishments in life. Think about how far someone will go in life when they feed off the stimulation of accomplishing something. Maybe now you can see how there are people who can become obsessed with their goals. Whenever you see people who may work endlessly or perform in amazing ways, it is all some form of stimulation that fuels them. Acknowledge the things that stimulate you and use them to your advantage.

Perceptual Pleasures

What is it that makes us stimulated by the things we experience anyway? It is our perception of the pleasurable experience that makes it fun or horrific. After all, I think we can all agree that some things may be boring to us, and quite stimulating to others. This generally speaks to all the senses and even something that goes beyond them. It's important to note that an engaging or blissful activity can be described as stimulating regardless of the impact it has on the physical senses.

What makes us like food or candy where our eyes instantly widen? When it comes to our preferences, it can date back to when we were in the womb. When it comes to certain foods or even music, we tend to enjoy those same things when we are born. If you were raised eating certain things and you try something new, it may have a similar flavor to other foods you enjoy if you instantly like it.

In other cases, it is our idea of the things that are good and bad before they happen to us that make us stimulated. The good and bad determine the chemicals released in the brain. The events in our life we mark as pleasurable can be the total opposite for other people. Think about how pain can be pleasurable to people.

If the brain is releasing dopamine during this experience, you will enjoy it. Some people enjoy the pain of tattoos or the pain during sexual intercourse with whips. Others, not so much. The point is, stimulation is subjective as well.

We all can recall numerous occasions where we look at others in disbelief because of their random fetishes or habits that we could never partake in. Or we simply just don't see how there is any pleasure associated with the activity. Stimulation can be something so subtle it's no wonder why people wonder what makes us like it so much. A lot of times that person couldn't even tell you. They just like it. Our perceptions of things and the stimulation they provide the brain can be based on a combination of things.

Pretty Privilege?

Many attractive people can manipulate others into getting their way because of how appealing they are. It shows how powerful perception can be for people who can't see beyond physical appearance. It's as if it really can put people in some trans to where that person's beauty leaves them mesmerized. We all know the power in sex appeal and lust. The combination creates billions of dollars in its respective industries, and it's because of the very natural urge to mate.

These people may be able to get away with doing things other people can't and may find more success than others simply because of how appealing they are. In some instances, they may even come off as smarter. People who aren't considered attractive sometimes are dismissed or treated wrongly as if it defines their level of intelligence. The power in perception shows how this still doesn't mean someone who may be considered generally unattractive can't find great fortune, success, or love. To the right person, they may very well be the perfect fit.

Think about attraction and what it really means to you. Our first thought is to assume that when we like someone, we put physical attraction first. I firmly believe we don't know what exactly can make us attracted to anyone. We all have the illusion of having types, but do we? A woman may be attracted to a man for several reasons beyond his physical appearance. It could be his nice car. She may love cars herself. To see him in one of her favorite cars may have made him attractive. It could be his ability to make her laugh. He's essentially making her feel good. Which makes her subconsciously more attracted to him.

Now take into consideration a physically attractive guy or girl. How many times have we met someone physically attractive and come to find out their personality is either boring or rude? The experience makes you perceive that person in a different way. It is amazing how easily our perspectives can change.

Nobody knows what jokes you find funnier than others. Nobody knows why he or she personality sticks out to you, or why you gave him a chance despite having other options. It could be underlying stimulations. It could be you seen him with an attractive girl. It could be because he has kids. It could be because he favors someone you once were in love with. It could be his cologne. Nobody knows, not even you most times.

How often have you heard the line, "I don't know what it is about her she's just different." Women or men may hate to hear this because they want a more detailed reason, but the stimulations are so vast. All we know is that the mind goes crazy whenever you're around. Nobody has a type. It is all subtle cues that cause these stimulations.

When I see other women, yes, physical attraction may be the first thing I notice, but I see attractive women all the time. Every so often it is that one girl I must pursue, I don't know what exactly it is about them that makes them so appealing. It is something deeper that we often can't explain.

Stimulation can override physical appearances because that's just how strong it is. It is the true engine of action once aroused. Stimulation is the gas that gets us going like a vehicle. Try to get in tune with your stimulations. Try and become aware of them. I once heard someone say, "I was never a morning person until I started doing what I loved." When we don't have the energy to do things, what does that say about the stimulation involved?

Do what stimulates you because that's what will create the best results in your life. Life is about stimulation, that's the only time we really put enough energy into something to ever make a difference. Even at times when we are doing something we don't feel like doing, thinking of the result of this work will stimulate us to keep going. Use this energy constantly. It can become a dominant force in your life if one has become aware of how to use it.

Brainwaves

Many people don't realize how their present state of mind is directly associated with the brain waves in their heads. Even more intriguing is the science behind how we can entrain the brain through repetition. The advancement of technology over the last 100 years makes this possible with binaural beats, but the awareness of this dates back to ancient tribes. It was used for healing, guidance, stress relief, and pain relief. Whenever you are sleeping, engaging in conversation, focusing hard, or having a bright idea, there is naturally a specific type of frequency stimulating the brain.

To manipulate these brainwaves into the state of mind we desire, use binaural beats to cause a physiological response based on perception. For example, when we play two tones of different frequencies with headphones in our ear at the same time, the difference between the frequencies will create brainwaves at the same rate of Hertz.

If the two frequencies happen to have 300Hz going into the left ear and 305Hz going into the right ear, the brain will make a new frequency at 5Hz. In order to understand what type of state of mind you'd like to be in, you will have to understand the differences of each brainwave. These are methods that may enhance your perceptual experience, but I personally find the natural thoughts we have as an overriding factor.

Delta waves operate at the lowest level of frequency which is about 0-4Hz. When your brain is releasing frequencies at this level, you are likely sleeping. Many people use this mental state for deep sleep and healing. Other possible reactions to using binaural beats at this frequency can result in pain relief, anti-aging, and access to the unconscious mind.

Theta waves operate at the second-lowest level which is about 4-8Hz. In this state naturally, you might be meditating or extremely relaxed. This state of mind or frequency brings peace and creativity when tapped into. If you were looking to be at your most relaxed state while trying to create whether that be writing, art, music, etc. This would be a great frequency to reach.

Alpha waves operate at a level of 8-14Hz. This frequency is more associated with how active we are. If you're engaging with others and want to maintain a positive flow like the state of mind this is the frequency to be at. Problem solving, creativity, accelerated learning, and a generally relaxed focus will be your state of mind in this frequency.

Beta waves operate at a level starting at around 14-40Hz. We are usually participating in activities that have our full focus when in this state of mind. We could be playing sports, making a presentation, or having a very enlightening conversation with someone. This state of mind generates a lot of energy and action. It's a frequency that is a result of high-level cognition and analytical thinking.

Gamma waves are the highest forms of brain waves operating at 40Hz or higher. This frequency is the result of sudden memory recall and peak awareness. This usually results in the moments when out of nowhere you have this bright idea and you just know what you have to do. Your brain in this state is processing information at a very high level.

Hemispheric Brain Synchronization

While binaural beats often are used to create a particular state of mind, it should also be noted how it generally helps the brain function more synchronized. We all have heard of the left vs. right brain comparisons and how too much of either side creates an imbalance. When we are balanced within our emotions and logic, we can maneuver through circumstances in a state of mind that gives us the best results. This is because of hemispheric brain synchronization.

The concept behind this is similar to how movies like Limitless present a pill that allows us to unlock full access to our minds. Being able to pull information from our subconscious minds and use our brains to the fullest potential is a desire humans have. We all know deep down that we have the capabilities to do great things, we simply haven't trained our mind in the right way. A healthier brain is no different than a healthier body from eating well and working out.

Neurostimulation and brain entrainment through meditation in a way guides your nervous system into its most optimal form. This information can very well change the way you look at mental health. I've never heard of this before until I stumbled upon a video that emphasized how significant this information is.

Binaural beats were first discovered in 1839 by a man named Heinrich Wilhelm Dove. He was a Prussian physicist and meteorologist. In 1973, a man named

Doctor Gerald Oster made this information more popular in his paper "Auditory beats in the brain".

Frequencies

The more aware we become of our feelings, the more willingly and effortlessly we'll be able to direct them to the frequencies we desire. The higher the frequency we give off, the better we feel. When you realize that these high vibrations are the only way to create a better life for you, you'll be more protective of these feelings.

Below is a list of particular emotions that are represented by numbers to illustrate the power of each one. As you read each one, try to become familiar with them, and how it is affecting you based on those numbers. Understand how the frequencies that we have are similar to a radios frequency. Whenever you change the channels on a radio, you're changing the wavelength it emits. In fact, these invisible waves have been theorized to potentially cause harm to us as well. With all the technology and us constantly being around these electromagnetic fields, many have become concerned about our ability to adapt to it over time. Everything has a frequency, some matters frequency never changes, and some matter does. We as humans have the ability to alter our frequency (knowingly or unknowingly) and it'll dictate how we experience life.

Think of your emotions as channels like a radio. To learn the secret to life, you have to understand how often people's emotions can transcend up and down throughout your typical day. Depending on the particular emotions you entertain will determine your energy that day. Those emotions are directed by how you tune in to your perspective of life at any given moment. That's why some people can work endlessly, and some people may never have the energy to do anything. Understanding what drives you to take action are the emotions that will attract new things in your life. People will like and dislike whatever it is you do depending on their frequency. Whether good or bad things are happening to you right now, understanding frequencies will benefit you eventually.

There's this concept of ultimate consciousness that gives a visual scale that represents the different types of vibrations we experience depending on the kind of emotion. Pay attention to the type of emotion and frequency number below and think about how often you have these feelings.

Enlightenment 700+ – This is essentially the goal of us all. To reach and grow to a level where we have, in a sense, mastered ourselves. We've reached a high level of understanding about the ups and downs of life and have embraced it all. The good and bad times all represent an opportunity to better ourselves. We've learned how to commit to our desires and goals and are conscious of how to allow them to form in our reality. We've gained enough emotional intelligence to handle the nature of others' emotions and perceptions. The way we carry ourselves and see life is now consistently stuck in a frame of mind that brings us actualizations and reframes from any destructive attempts at manipulation.

Peace 600 – When we have a peaceful feeling, we've gained acceptance towards the things that may weigh us down. To make peace with the things that have hurt you in the past is the most powerful thing we can do. We could never reach a state of peace if we didn't let go of emotions that keep our frequency low. Remember that despite what others may do to you it only matters when you allow it to hurt you. Remind yourself that whatever actions people take is always on the basis of whatever state of mind they're in. Whether they intended to hurt you or not, instinctively begin to smile and realize my peace will always be a bigger priority.

Joy 540 – Having joy is such a great emotion to experience. It's as if everything in your life is perfect in those moments. It's not something you could ever fake. Many people cheat themselves of joy because they're stressing themselves most of their lives trying to get to a certain point of success in order to then feel joy. The wise know that this is an illusion we entertain that confuses us of what joy is. Joy isn't anything in the past or future. Joy is in this moment, you're very next breath is joy. I just thought about how we can cry tears of joy. It truly is a beautiful feeling that is internal.

Love 500 – Love is such a powerful and critical frequency. The intense emotion of love can turn to hate when we feel betrayed. A lot of us allow love to hurt us. We must realize that's not true love by definition. The idea of love is rarely consistent when we've been done wrong by someone we love. If your love for that person is real, they cannot hurt you, because if your love for them is wanting them to be happy, then in any of those moments when they've crossed you, you'll still wish them the best. To love someone even when they don't love themselves or do things we don't condone is higher wisdom. Especially since we now don't allow our love to feel neglected or unappreciated. Sometimes we are lessons for other people's growth. The things they may do to you is a result of inner issues they've not dealt with. While we're quick to get offended, realize that isn't true love.

Reason 400 – In order to grow, we must be able to critically analyze situations. The importance of this shows how we feel based on the conclusions we've come to. Showing reason in situations will keep you from showing signs of being emotionally unstable. It will show in pressure moments by your poise. It will show in your ability to bring others to better quality conclusions as well. There's always a bigger picture or a more reasonable way to go about handling life's troubles. When we're unwilling to reason, we've created a flaw that will only hurt us in the end. We'll stick by our bad decisions and beliefs because we don't want to think logically. If you can learn to reason, you can learn to love, have joy, and peace as well.

Acceptance 350 – It's extremely hard to have to accept certain things in life. Yet, as hard as it can be, it is the gateway to your happiness. Most of the things that cause our sadness are things we don't want to accept. One day we will all pass away, at least from this dimension. If someone close to you passed away, a common problem is people not wanting to accept that they're gone. There will be no healing until one has accepted reality for what it is. It is possible to gain acceptance and still mourn your loved ones. The difference is the feeling, and that feeling is everything. Gaining acceptance in other areas in life that go outside of our control is wisdom. The more we deny, the more we only hurt ourselves and lower our frequency.

Willingness 310 – To be willing is to be open to possibilities. In life, not much is attainable or genuinely understood if we're not willing to put in the effort, sacrifice, and focus on doing things that we consciously know are for the advancement of our health and collective human experience. For my peace and a better world, I'm willing to do anything. And if we're unwilling, the possibility of reaching a level of higher consciousness is doubtful.

Neutrality 250 – Our bodies naturally give off a frequency even in its most neutral state. To just be, not forcing anything or reacting to anything is to be healthy. Even the earth has a natural frequency as well. Learning how to not react to everything can be beneficial. Everything doesn't need a reaction. Sometimes we are better off not trying to make sense of everything or arguing amongst our peers. Sometimes being neutral is necessary. Let things be what they are. To be neutral is not always to feel the need to change or force anything. It's not to say we are emotionless. We are unmoved. Understanding everything doesn't need a reaction can be healthy.

Courage 200 – Being courageous in a sense, is a reflection of the power in one's thoughts. It takes strong beliefs and faith to be courageous. The fear people have keeps them from showing fortitude in life that could make a difference in their circumstances. Sometimes in order to reach the true power you behold, you'll have to be brave enough to stand tall in those moments when you're outnumbered. The energy and attitude you display despite the doubters or critics is the essence of courage. Without courage, we are too weak to ever instill the methodologies we believe in. This is simply maintaining your frequency when challenged by nonbelievers.

Pride 175 – Pride can be a good thing or a bad thing. It is only an issue when we don't know when to utilize it and when to reframe from it. To be proud of yourself or anything is essential. There's nothing wrong with this. The only problem is when we lose respect for others because we put our standards and accomplishments above theirs. Sometimes when dealing with people we love or care about, we may end up losing them despite keeping our pride. The feeling is one that leaves us feeling proud for not standing down but ultimately defeated in a sense that you weren't strong enough to let go of your pride.

Anger 150 – Know that whenever you have a feeling of anger, your vibrations are low. This is why people go on to do things they usually regret in this mental state. Anger is a lack of understanding. It is also a part of life. It comes down to how we decide to direct this energy. Wisdom is knowing I can use this anger as motivation. Wisdom is knowing this anger is derived from a flawed perception. The feeling of anger should immediately make us reevaluate ourselves and energy.

Desire 125 – As you begin to see how the frequency scale is dropping, it is essential to understand this doesn't take away the power in the feeling. It just refers to the frequency of the emotion. Desire is one of the most powerful feelings, so powerful it can fuel us to do anything. When our desire for something is very strong, we could potentially do immoral things to satisfy it. This is why desire is so low on the chart. People's desires can actually be more harmful than good when we don't direct them the right way. Our desires can keep us living in an illusion. We can lose sight of the true purpose of enlightenment. Never misguide your desires in ways that will hurt you or other people. Never let your desire outweigh your reasoning. Guide your desires in ways that will benefit you in life and spirit. Remember that our desires are all perceptions of what will bring us peace. Assure you align your desires properly because we can easily become misguided.

Fear 100 – Fear is an extremely low vibrational feeling. So low it almost completely shapes your reality in a way that leaves you with anxiety. To be in fear is to feel unsafe as if to be in a constant mental state of wanting to escape or defend oneself. There are many emotions that can triumph this fear feeling. Desire, anger, pride, reason, all can make you overcome fear. This is why having fear is such a weak emotion. It holds you back in ways that are dramatized. If you are ever in a fearful state, immediately shift your frequency by reminding yourself of the power you possess at all times.

Grief 75 – At times in life there may be tragic events that occur which is inevitable. Grief is a frequency that is extremely low as it is synonymous with misery. There are moments when we may help but enter this state. The most important thing to realize is as much as it hurts, there is a way to heal and cope with the inevitable. It is possible to turn this grief into a feeling that leaves you extraordinarily peaceful or even a better person.

Apathy 50 – To be in a frequency feeling of apathy is to, in a sense, be close to lifeless. When consciousness leaves us dispassionate about anything, we've somehow disconnected from the gift of life. When you may procrastinate, think about how low you are vibrating. Now think about the rejuvenating feeling you get from when you accomplish anything or work towards something. We are made to manifest our desires and thoughts. When we have become doubtful, resulting in a lack of motivation, the frequency leaves us lacking in many areas of life. Naturally, we all have this will to live, love, and be loved. Never lose your enthusiasm to chase your dreams; that's the engine that drives you to them.

Guilt 30 – To have guilt is to feel disappointment in oneself. Guilt is a feeling that is strong and low in frequency because of how a lot of times we knew better. These are the times we are wrong, and we have no way of defending ourselves. We're just wrong. Acknowledge your wrongdoings and mean it. Don't beat yourself up though. Never get into a habit of continually blaming yourself. You'll remain at an extremely low frequency, which will only lower your confidence to achieve. And when you face any obstacles, you'll see them as failures. If your intentions were good don't take the mistakes you may make to heart. And don't make the same mistakes twice.

Shame 20 – To feel shame is to be embarrassed by

one's existence. I remember reading old literature wherein moments of tragedy. The shame was enough to make a man pluck his eyes out. When we speak of guilt and shame it's no wonder many people may commit suicide in these mental states. No matter what it is, you may have done, never sink to this low of vibration to where you feel unworthy as a human. We all have things we are guilty of. We all have things we ought to be ashamed of for saying or doing. None of us is above or below one another, only in the conceptual sense of frequencies. If you ever feel shameful, take heed to what you may have done and vow never to do it again.

It's important to note that these feelings all adjust our perception in different ways. Our natural senses are the right guides of our perception and aren't limited to the five senses. We can sense embarrassment, loneliness, jealousy, anger, shyness, and many other things when we pay attention and are in tune with energy.

Whether it be our natural senses like touch, sight, hearing, smell, and taste or the ones that give us a sense of accomplishment, connection, love, hate, or validation, it all creates a particular feeling. These feelings give us a particular state of mind at the moment. It can leave us feeling on top of the world or on the bottom.

Senses simply provide data for perception. Sometimes that sensory data isn't correct because the information we may use on our own leaves us forming bad conclusions. What we are attempting to do with this information is become more aware of the causes of certain emotions so we can begin consciously directing them. If you're unaware, you're liable to act out in unstable ways, thinking the world or other people are causing your problems when it's always you.

Emotions must be expressed. In some way, sexual energy, the need for attention, love, success, or money, all must be expressed. The energy we put in to conforming and disguising our authentic self is draining. The times we strive for purity and fall short to our flaws only arise from those inconsistencies in our thought process at times. We all have experiences and inner demons we must let go of. We must not try to hide them or suppress them. We must deal with them, or the urge for it to come out will only become worse. It will come out in ways disguised, so we don't look envious, hateful, desperate, insecure, etc.

It is common for people not to know how to go about dealing with their emotions. It causes hypocrisy. When people lash out and show a side of them that is a form of bad vibrations, we must examine their behavior for what it is. At any given moment when you look into the world, you'll see how everyone is in different states of mind. It'll make you become advanced at dealing with your emotions and others. This is the start of you using the power of your mind in a way you may have never thought you could control.

CHAPTER 5

Have You Ever?

What guides our behavior?

A lot of times the gift of perception or consciousness itself leaves me mesmerized. The way we inevitably have these dispositions that form our lifestyle goes beyond our acknowledgment individually. It's the reason the things we partake in as a society overrule a lot of logic. A behaviorist may not care for the mental aspect of theorizing behavior, but even objectively, the things societies collectively do environmentally speaks volumes. For whatever traditional reason you can think of to explain why we celebrate certain holidays, eat certain foods, or even play certain games, it is all a reflection of a society's collective disposition.

While there will always be small groups or individuals who have seen life beyond the manipulative narratives, rarely do they have the platform to affect real change. The few who have been are a lot of times demonized, killed, or participating in the manipulation posed as an activist. Real change comes when the people, for the most part, have collectively decided.

The problem is everyone doesn't come together just off of logic itself. There is always some leader pushing an agenda. They are able to tap into their emotions, which is the real generator of action. The goal is to make you feel a certain way and your actions will follow. This is the reason why people can be led to do great things or participate in horrible things. You see it all the time in movies and throughout history.

In the movie I Robot, Will Smith had to consistently fight to convince people that the robots couldn't be trusted. He was seen as crazy at first, and the people who created the robots had convinced themselves that a robot takeover wasn't possible. Instead of considering his opinion and thinking rationally they became too engulfed in their ego and desire to accomplish their goals. Ultimately, ignorance was almost the price of humanity being wiped out.

The way Hitler was able to convince millions of people to follow his agenda must be noted. Nobody may have ever felt threatened or entitled to do the things they did without a clear motive, or someone to direct their perceptions in that way. I think we all understand the power within a message, especially to those who need direction, the people who need something to believe in. The people need someone to help them understand the power of themselves, not use it against them.

In which way do speakers sway their perception of

the situation to make you angry, jealous, happy, sad, or even thankful? Becoming aware of this is so hard because the power of perception, it's true essence lies, so in the present moment, we usually do act before we think. Truly thinking and analyzing a situation takes more than a few seconds. If you've reacted to the first one or are in a hypnotic state while listening to anything, you've become accepting of that information.

I once stumbled across the ending of the movie, "A Bug's Life". It had been so long since I've seen that movie I might've been a little kid the last time I recall watching it. Much of the movie, the ant's duties were centered around always collecting food for the grasshoppers. They feared them. Toward the end, they had rigged up a plan to scare the grasshoppers away by creating a fake bird. The plan was working until the fake bird caught on fire, and the project failed.

Upon realizing the fake plan, the leader of the grasshoppers yelled out, "Who's plan was this?!" A small and stepped forward and said, "It was me." Then he begins to be beaten by the grasshopper in front of everyone. The act of courage isn't something the grasshoppers wanted so they used him as an example to instill fear in the rest. The grasshopper yelled, "Where do you get the guts to do this to me?" The ant answered, "You were going to squish the queen." The grasshopper responded by saying, "I hate when someone ruins the ending. You piece of dirt. No, I'm wrong you're lower than dirt, you're an ant."

This was an attempt to make the ant feel worthless, inferior, and powerless. The grasshopper continued, "Let this be a lesson to all you ants, ideas are very dangerous things, you are mindless soil shoving losers put on this earth to serve us!" All of a sudden, the severely beaten ant begin to mumble something. "You're wrong, Hopper." He slowly rises despite his bruises and stands up. "Ants are not meant to serve grasshoppers. I've seen these ants do great things, and year after year, they somehow manage to pick the food for themselves and you. So..so who's the weaker species? Ants don't serve grasshoppers! It is YOU that NEEDS US!"

Hopper had been walking closer and closer to the ant by this time. Surely this was true but may cost him his life. Then suddenly, the grasshopper heard mumbling by all the ants. They begin to realize all of the fear was shading their reasoning. Because had they been thinking clearly, they would see how much they outnumbered the grasshoppers. The talking had begun to get louder as the ant finally said, "We're a lot stronger than you say we are...., and you know it, don't you?" As you may have guessed or known, the ants fought off the grasshoppers. A simple, confident claim or proposal can paint a picture in a civilians mind that doesn't even exist. Yet, if it exists in one's thoughts, that's all that matters.

Psychological Warfare

Psychological understanding may have been a tool for power long before any of us was born. When we speak of power in any sense, we are talking about the mind. The mind is the one who decides what power is and who is the true holder of it. If you have my mind you have my power. Whether we're discussing Hitler, slavery, marketing, the million man march, or even Martin Luther King Jr's speech, one thing they all have in common is a strong emotion that brought about particular outcomes.

The same way we analyze our habits individually and understand how it creates a particular lifestyle for us is the same concept culturally. It's easy to overlook our behaviors. This is the reason we sometimes can't believe we ever participated in certain things or were ever attracted to certain people. When we understand the power in our emotions, we see how it is always directing our perception.

One of the simplest ways we experience this is those times when we are hungry or tired. Whatever we may be trying to do in this mental state can appear worse than what it really is. We may easily become irritated, or our concentration becomes poor. It's as if there's a constant battle with how we feel. If other people's energetic fields are not pulling you, then you're being swayed by their wordplay in the midst of trying to dissect your feelings and emotions that can leave you confused.

The only way to go about coping with these natural causes is to use our imagination. After all your imagination can be the cause for your misery why not use it to bring you consistent harmony? We must always be in tune with our feelings and making efforts to make sure we are in the right mind frame.

The superior race, the war for land, the chase for wealth, the desire for power, the history of our true selves, the truth about UFO's, and the endless information used to sway you in any which way is all overwhelmingly perplexing. And as much as we choose which beliefs we wholeheartedly believe, it still leaves a question that we often leave to conspiracy. We may drive ourselves crazy trying to figure it all out in the midst of all the propaganda. It's all designed to keep you confused.

Life is more simple than complicated. Don't overwhelm yourself trying to understand something that's ultimately defined by how you decide to see. I now see how it can cause complete madness or dysfunction. Have you noticed how divided people are? Whether by religions, race or financially there's always something pushing your ego into feeling as if one person is better than the other.

People will look to subtly flex the fact they have money, privilege, or even that they went to church. The feeling we get when our ego makes us feel better than someone else can be harmful to you. That's the whole agenda behind conquering and dividing. The more the people argue and push their ego against each other, the less they are focused on the people who are actually the true cause of their sorrow. They're the reason you feel as if you need all these things to be accepted in the world.

Having the best clothes, cars, or other materials is cool to have personally. Most people get these things only because they're motivated to show it off to others. This can bring the wrong type of attention to you. There is no need to try and impress people who only measure your value according to the materials you have. It goes way deeper than that.

I read a story of a girl in college who got wired millions of dollars from her dad, who illegally allowed goods to pass through the border untaxed. She eventually got caught because of all the cars, traveling, and money she would post. You could downright just say that she wasn't smart. But it speaks to something more powerful than the logical thing to do, which was lay low. It was the need to show others how lavishly she was living.

We want others to see us living our best life. We want to be great. Many times we go about doing this in the wrong ways. Just live your life smile and have fun. People will love the fact that you know how to live life peacefully and carefree. It could even make others jealous without you even flexing materials. They may be depressed often and wonder how someone can be so joyous. That alone speaks to how positive energy triumphs anything money can buy.

Your attention is worth billions of dollars, so choose wisely what you consciously decide to focus on. Remember people want your mind. They want your perception. It's all psychological warfare. After a while, you'll see the game for what it is. You'll notice the tactics used to create emotional reactions from people. You'll see how all it takes is for them to create a problem that many people despise and then give a solution to this problem which is what their true intent was. They first had to create a problem that would make people angry where they would want something done about it. It's been working for decades and maybe even centuries.

This works on a global level and even works in sporting

games. Think about what the purpose of talking trash in a game is. You're trying to get your opponent focused on you and not the game. You're attempting to distract them to keep them from prospering. I remember Jalen Rose giving his statements on the game that Kobe Bryant dropped 81 points. "He never talked trash." Kobe was so focused on this game that he even described it as a blurry memory. In a pickup game trash talk is mostly harmless. When the intent is to misguide millions of people in a way that leaves them harmed mentally or physically, it is deceit.

Unexpected Events

As we wake every day it's easy to get consumed in the things we did yesterday. Many get caught up in such a routine that it does appear as if we're doing the same thing every day. Never get caught up living life in a cycle. Every day is an adventure with limitless opportunities. You never know what will happen that moment you get out of bed.

It's easy to stray away from this realization, but we must keep this in mind. This way we will never take a second of our life for granted. You may win a million off a scratch-off today, a meteor may hit earth today and end our existence. When you keep these things in mind, it makes you so appreciative and in tune with your life that it will create a different attitude.

Many people have regrets about the way they treated

people or things they had in the past that they took advantage of. If we reminded ourselves of what we have and how easily it could be all gone, we'd never be caught having regrets because there was never a time that we devalued what we had.

Think about the synchronizations that happen to you every day. There was an interesting statement I once read regarding synchronizations. "Has something random ever happened in your favor and you sit and think, "Damn I had to snooze two times, get cut off in traffic, pick this exact parking spot, and stay in the car an extra 3 minutes just to walk in the building and bump into this opportunity that changed my life"."

Over the course of my life the women I may have met, the jobs I've come across, the friends I've made, or any other opportunities were merely by chance. When we seem to be focused on living spontaneously and just doing whatever feels uplifting, the opportunities will arise in ways we couldn't have even predicted. None of this would be possible to work for you if you don't trust the nature of life and energy.

Take heed to the people you pass every day and may never see again. For some reason, it was always crazy to me how we see people every day for the last time. Every day we never know who we will meet or what may happen. At any given time, life, the present moment should be appreciated. I remember times in my life when I proclaimed to be "bored." That is disrespectful to the gift of consciousness.

The mere essence of your next breath should you give

chills. We should never be in a state of mind that makes us bored. There's no such thing or time for that. Not when you have an infinite amount of things you could be doing to entertain you or benefit you in some way.

When you begin to appreciate every second of life, you begin to truly live. Sometimes it may take a near-death experience for people to never live the same way. I once read a book where the author explained how he had been in a wreck so bad he didn't understand how he was still alive. From that moment on everything about him changed. His lifestyle and love for life never went unappreciated. Sometimes age or even a question from our kids can make us reevaluate everything we've been too passive to acknowledge ourselves.

But why mom?

It was a Sunday evening, and as usual, Lisa was washing the dishes preparing for another week of work. Her 4-year-old son Devin who had been nagging her all evening once again, found his way into the kitchen. "Hey there beautiful boy," she said. He gave a little giggle and kept playing with his ball. "It's almost time for bed little man!" The boy jumped up as if she said, "Ice Cream!"

He was a good boy, and the fact he got excited about bedtime was a perk after a long day of cleaning. All of a sudden, he stopped bouncing the ball. "Mommy", he said. She looked down at the boy and could tell his mood had changed. "Where is daddy?" He asked. Lisa knew where this was going. Her son was a curious boy. He'd often wonder about things and ask questions until he was satisfied with the answers.

To her, this was a little unusual, but this is primarily what many kids thought process is like at a young age. Childhood is the most critical time of our life. The strongest beliefs we end up having start from the type of answers we get from the people we trust the most growing up. Lisa knew this and one thing she didn't want to do was take away Devins's sense of imagination and curiosity. Once those things are gone, there's no more hope. Like many people who've become adults, the things we were told no to, the dreams we had that were scoffed continuously at, and the ideas we expressed that were looked down on as if not possible all determined where he'd go in life.

As she looked down at him, she finally said, "Daddy had to go to work, honey, he'll be back in a few weeks." The boy looked more concerned after this, he made a slight frown and then asked, "But why, mom?" The mom answered, "Dad is protecting our country in the Army son, sometimes they are away for a while because they have duties to attend to." The boy stood there, still looking a bit confused and asked, "But why, mom?"

She was instinctively getting a little frustrated and was about to send him off to bed, as she looked down at him, she noticed his big watery eyes, his runny nose, and a bag of Cheeze Itz about to be stuffed in his mouth. She wiped his nose and could tell he was concerned about why his Dad was going to be gone so long. So she said ok, I'll play along. Son, that's a part of life. If we didn't have an army, we wouldn't have the protection we needed or peace of mind. Bad things could happen, so daddy goes to protect us. He is a hero.

The boy sat there for a second as if he finally understood, and then finally asked, "Why can't everybody get along so daddy can come home?" She laughed and said, "It doesn't work that way, honey, people don't agree on everything, and it causes wars and harmful things to happen. The boy, at this point, was aggravated that people couldn't get along so he could see his dad. Well, at least that's what he concluded to about all of this. "But..but ma. Isn't there enough food, water, and land for everybody to be happy? Why do we have wars? She patiently replied, "Because son, some people want power and are greedy, they want it all, and sometimes a lot of people get the short end of the stick. We also have an army to protect us from bad people."

The boy sat there again as if he was somehow actually processing this information and trying to make sense of it. Lisa thought this'd be the end of his quest to find out why. He looked down at his bag of chips and seen there were only a couple left, and stretched his hand out to her. She smiled and ate a couple of crackers, then said, "thank you, son." "See mom, I shared with you I'm not greedy!" She laughed again and said, "no, you're not."

The boy noticed something about his mom at that moment, her smile. He realized he hadn't seen her do it quite often. And as you may have guessed he immediately wanted to know why. "Mom, why don't you smile more?"

The boy asked. The mom said, "I'm smiling more now because of you baby boy." The boy smiled back and she finally sent him off to bed. After her little talk with Devin, she began to feel differently and wonder more about life. It's almost as if the curious little girl she used to come out.

The things she was passive towards or didn't quite understand begin to create a powerful urge that was stimulated by her son. Why did the world have wars? Why did her husband have to leave for such a long time fighting and harming people for money and power? Was sharing really as easy as her son made it seem? Do humans really get caught up in the wrong things that harm the world and each other? Why don't I smile as often as I used to? Why had she been pretending like everything was ok?

This could've easily been a mid-life crisis, but this was something more spiritual. Lisa felt as if she had lost her sense of self and appreciation for everything. She begins to have flashbacks to her as a teen when she used to be so passionate about her artwork. She remembers after college when all of her dreams slowly seemed out of reach. Things happen, responsibilities, and an unexpected pregnancy created a shift in her life that she wasn't necessarily upset about, it was just as if she had forgotten who she was. The artwork she used to create used to be so amazing and deep. She went back and found all of her work in the basement.

Tears begin to run down as she realized how different her life was supposed to turn out. Not only that she realized how there hadn't been any excitement in her life. She'd been doing the same things every day. This was a realization that she'd been so caught up in a way of thinking, it caused her reality to reflect it. The moment she started seeing differently, she started feeling differently. This caused her to take action differently. The things she used to be fearful of didn't scare her. The people that used to bring her down now didn't shift her confidence. The opportunities that she was accustomed to overlooking, she saw them. Lisa was indeed a new woman.

There are plenty of things that we can use to help guide our energy into becoming who we desire to be. In this case, it was an unexpected reaction to a simple conversation with a kid. Our sensitive perceptions, even with awareness, have much power in the way we quickly react to anything at any given moment. Sometimes many people get into conflicts with others who may have doubted them. That energy can be used to push you to do great things. It could be the spark you needed to finish that book, painting, business idea, poem, or website.

Use this energy wisely because it can be used to do tremendous or harmful things. We must value that desire that moves us when we have it because most of us have no true control over our motivation. We just feel motivated sometimes and other times we don't. It's all constructed in the way you've consistently decided to see. Yet we also sometimes fall short of being perfect (because we're not) and react to certain situations based on our state of mind.

This causes flawed perceptions which can cause bad reactions and create bad habits that first happen mentally, then transitions physically. You can have a habit of thinking a certain way, and it will cause you to react the same way continuously. The "shift" in mentality can happen at any moment. Sometimes it may not last long, and sometimes it may last forever.

Think about a moment when you had an epiphany that may have given you chills. This overwhelming sensation can bring you to a realization that you may have been overlooking. It's truly the essence of life. The point is if you're aware of how our desires, stimulations, and reactions are the reason we create anything, you'd understand how money and everything is just energy. It also will give you a powerful feeling of appreciation for everything.

The time and effort people put in to write books, build things, invent things, graduate, work out, etc all come from desire. A feeling that only is gifted to those who are in the right mind frame, or are put in a situation where they have no choice but to use this power. You can't force yourself to put effort into something you don't want to do. You have to want it and you have to consistently remind yourself. This is simply a way of keeping you in the right state of mind to where your habits get you on the right track.

None of this is easy or completely controllable. I'm willing to accept the fact much of the coincidences, perfect timing, and synchronicities we experience may be beyond our understanding. One thing we can do is become more gratified than we've ever been for the gift of life. The challenge, mysterious nature, and abundance flows around, and through us all in ways, we can see physically, and in ways beyond the naked eye. The feeling, though, that feeling describes everything.

Since I've pretty much let down the barrier to my inner thoughts, I've decided to take it a step further. I want to go deeper. I want to reveal things that I didn't know could be put into words. It seems that despite the differences we focus on, we as people can relate to a lot. Self-disclosure feels amazing. Holding in all your inner thoughts and feelings can distract you from living. It can hold you back from becoming the best version of yourself.

I think humans have many of the same thoughts and desires. The more they are expressed, the better you understand yourself. The better we understand each other. I'm now reminiscing about the collective experiences we all have gone through. While we have unique experiences as well, there are many things we can all say we've been through. It's quite amazing how connected we all really are.

Have you ever?

Have you ever gazed at something and felt an indescribable feeling? A feeling that is filled with wonder, hope, and desire combined in one? There's this big tree outside my apartment window. During the spring, I noticed how beautiful the flowers growing on the tree was.

During the summer, I would also gaze at this tree randomly late at night. The wind blowing the leaves, the nature behind it all. I would keep staring, not knowing exactly why the feeling attached to this simple tree was so stunning. During the fall, the leaves would turn brown. Until finally, winter came and all was left were the branches.

It's easy to overlook nature as if it's the norm when every day we witness something amazing. From the moon to this big fireball (sun) keeping us alive. Have you ever stared at a beautiful picture, admiring the scene? It may be a picture of a sun rising over the beach, a forest, or a city. You begin to picture yourself lying back, sipping your favorite beverage, enjoying life. Then, reality hits, you have work in the morning.

Some people may love their job, and some may hate it. A lot of times beyond those rationalizations, the purpose I speak of goes beyond the American way. It is something more fulfilling and purposeful for us as humans that I'm trying to express.

It is hard for me not to wonder what purpose we have that goes beyond working all week. Especially when this world is abundant. The only things that make us feel as if we need money are our collective beliefs in that system. We get excited about the weekend that we spend dreading having to go back to do it all over again.

Have you ever told yourself that this isn't life? If you have, there is something you may feel is missing. Have you ever stopped and thought to yourself, what are we doing? Or maybe it's what we are not doing. I once saw someone post on social media, "What's the craziest thing you ever did for money?" Many people responded, saying,

"Worked 40 hours a week." It's as if they know how crazy it is, but don't know any other options.

Have you ever bought a car and strangely noticed that car more and more? You may have never noticed how often you saw that car until you bought it for yourself. Imagine that car being a negative thought. You'd see this everywhere while ignoring the positive thoughts that are also there. Our minds can't take in everything in the world. It would take too much work. So the things you give attention to will be the things you notice more and more.

Have you ever thought about something different? You may snap back into the "real" world after a while because of how imaginative your thoughts become. You may feel like those thoughts are just that, thoughts. The very depths of life and all creations are only possible because of what we can see in the mind. It then becomes our reality. I know your mind can take you on endless journeys. Some that may seem impossible, but everything you see today derived from a thought.

The people we admire the most today stepped out of ordinary thought. They became more intact with their imagination, even when people called them crazy. It never discouraged them from embracing their own powers of perception. That imagination created curiosity, that curiosity created discoveries. Discoveries created new ways of thinking. The world you see today hasn't always been this way.

To be naïve enough to think life as we see it today is the only way to is insanity. I can imagine money, cars, and clothes and a lot of times I do. Then there are times when I imagine a world completely different from what we live today. These changes come naturally with evolution, but it doesn't stop me from basking in this thought as if me seeing a better world in my life is possible. Maybe I'll only be a piece to the process of this change, a step stool to a new way of thinking.

I sit back and ask myself what am I in search of in this life. And although money, happiness, and love vaguely sound correct, something that more accurately describes this is a purpose. I want to know and really feel my purpose on this earth. We all feel something within us that deserves praise, something that tells us when we are settling, or when we aren't doing something that makes us feel purposeful. There are unique things about you that come so naturally and effortlessly. You don't even realize it is a gift. We all have a purpose, but you'll never find it until you acknowledge yourself worthy of a purpose or gift. Trust yourself, believe in yourself.

Have you ever woken up crying from a dream? Has anyone ever told you that you were smiling in your dream? Have you ever woken up heart racing from a nightmare? Just think, something we experience through our thoughts appears so real we awake reacting. Remember those dreams that are so blissful it makes you try and go back to sleep to finish it? We can make these dreams a reality for us. It is all in the vision. It is all in the amount of focus and desire to make it come true that makes it happen for us. That desire drives you to overcome any fear or doubt. That desire creates faith that it will come true.

Have you ever thought of other cultures and how their way of life is totally different than ours? There are tribes that practice polyandry. A woman having multiple husbands isn't something we may think is natural. Throughout history, though there have been ancient civilizations that have put this to practice. It is a way of life created to make life easier. We've heard of many other cultures and their different beliefs. Still, we hold the same value and perception of what is morally right based upon the way of life we have grown accustomed to. If they were to be shown the same things from birth, they would too.

Have you ever thought about why we enforce a belief or way of life on others when we continuously see it is all created within the beauty of perception? Have you ever been on a road trip at night and just stared into the sky? I've done this before, and I randomly saw a shooting star. It gave me chills.

Being attacked by terrorists strikes fear in our hearts because of the possibility of being invaded. Wars date back to as far as any of us can remember. Have you ever asked yourself what is the true purpose of it all? Why are we killing each other? Why do atomic bombs threaten our very existence? This reminds me of a quote by Martin Luther King. "We have learned to fly the air like birds and swim the sea like fish, but we have not learned the simple art of living together as brothers." Wow, can you even imagine? People, humans getting along? There might be a greater chance that aliens get us first.

Have you ever thought of life forms that go beyond earth in the cosmos where it is said to have unlimited galaxies formed? Have you ever wondered what it's like to see the earth from the moon? Have you ever realized that everything we have believed in has some conspiracy attached to it? What makes it a conspiracy is the number of objective questions that simply can't be answered. That's what leaves it up for debate. I guess then it is left up to whether you believe in it or not

I once read a quote from an astronaut named Frank Borman. He commanded Apollo 8, and it was the first mission to circumnavigate the moon. The most interesting thing to me wasn't the actual mission. It was the realizations he came to due to the change in scenery. "The view of the earth from the moon fascinated me- a small disk, 240,000 miles away. It was hard to believe that little thing held so many problems, so many frustrations. Raging nationalistic interests, famines, wars. Pestilence doesn't show from that distance." The perception had changed simply from a different view. One brought himself to the conclusion that we are precisely that, one. It made him question all of the things we get caught up in that destroy the earth and each other.

All of the things we do on earth seemed pointless when you see the bigger picture of life. It may take a different experience or event to change the way you see, but it is always possible. Have you ever been called crazy? That is a word often used for people who don't know the true art and beauty in perspective. The people who don't see beyond what they perceive think everybody is crazy. People who have conformed to the most popular beliefs have been conditioned. It is well known that we often believe something is right or wrong depending upon how many people are in support.

Studies have been conducted where kids were given a problem. Certain kids were told to pick the wrong answer and kids that weren't were studied to see if they would pick the same wrong answer. Many of them chose the same wrong answer simply because everyone else did. Now that's crazy. Thinking for yourself might leave you looking crazy or even condemned, but you may be right.

The truth is, anything that has ever become a widespread belief started from someone who thought for themselves. When you limit your thoughts, you close the barrier to what is possible. You can't even see something that may be clear in your face when you've already told yourself it's not there. You'd be surprised at how many opportunities present themselves in front of us, but we never take advantage because we haven't trained ourselves to see.

Have you ever wondered what your life would be like if you were born in another part of the world? It's not like we chose which life we wanted or if we knew life existed until we were born. What if you were born white? What if you were born black or Asian as opposed to the race you are now? You'd be fighting for the same rights as the people you see as different than you now.

Have you ever thought about energy and how it never dies? It is said that immediately after death your body mass drops as if your soul literally left your body. If death isn't real and is seen as more of a transformation, did we choose the life we have? We ask questions and dismiss the unseen as if it means it's not there. For years scientists never saw black matter until finding some proof that there is some invisible coating that is keeping galaxies together. Maybe it isn't meant for us to see the unseen, perhaps we were just meant to feel it. It isn't surprising to know that most things about the answer of life remain unknown or go beyond our understanding.

Maybe the answer to life is always within ourselves and the things we create which speak to the beauty of it all. Have you ever been thinking of someone and then they happen to call you? Could we be communicating in ways that speak to the power of our energy and thoughts? Have you ever realized that we're stardust? We are the very stars and the unexplainable phenomena we gasp at in the sky. We are marvels of the universe with the power to transcend inexplicable events in our life. Have you ever wondered what God is? If we were made in his image doesn't that make us Gods?

Have you ever had a deep conversation with someone? Aren't those the best feelings? Knowing that someone thinks about the things you do. Knowing someone feels and understands the deeper thoughts you may have never considered being open about is amazing. Knowing you're not alone is great. You're never alone. Have you ever realized that as much as we are striving for more, people are praying for the things we already have?

CHAPTER 6

We Are All Hypocrites

Hypocrisy

Admit it, you've said something before and later had a change of heart. You've looked down on someone for doing something you've done before. You've believed in something moral, but have done things that don't quite match up with that belief. It's ok. We've all done it. Hypocrisy is something we've all been guilty of. That is because we are all human beings. It is because perception is that powerful. We have strong beliefs about certain things only for them to be turned around on us in different scenarios, which can sometimes lead to contradictions.

If someone were to make a statement with a different choice of words, you might agree with what they say, even if there was initial disagreement. You may at some point in your life have found yourself rooting for the villain because of his charm, humor, carelessness, or passion. It truly shows the power of words. "It's not what you say, it's how you say it" that can make a huge difference in the way people see it. Someone with great wordplay can become skilled at directing people's perceptions to bring them the things they desire.

The vastness in perspective can make us question why we feel strongly about particular situations, but we could careless in other situations. We believe strongly about certain things with no consistency, and it shows when it is presented in other illustrations. This leaves room for hypocrisy.

People have religious beliefs and yet, don't practice the simple methods that it promotes. If the average person did, then all religions would love each other and respect each other, not kill or judge. One of the biggest reasons the world is so split today is because of religions. It's not the religion itself, because religions encourage peace and prosperity. It is the thought of someone else's alternate perception of the way the world is, that causes people to act in ways their religions don't even condone. I don't mean to say that you're a liar or live a fake life 24/7. I'm not saying that you don't practice most things that you preach. I'm saying that in certain times in life we have fooled ourselves into thinking we believe things should be done a certain way, but become passive under different circumstances.

It truly hurts to even face the fact that I've done this, but it is true. As I mentioned in chapter 1, acknowledging these types of things makes you more powerful than someone consistently in denial. Just examine yourself and others, and you'll see how often this may happen. In fact, it appears to be endless.

Many of the things people argue about are biases that have blatantly exposed double standards, contradictions, or hypocrisy. So everyone is calling out each other's flawed conclusions. Sometimes it isn't necessarily flawed thinking, but the perspective is too limited. This means if more experiences and scenarios were brought to your attention, you might consider expanding or even changing the conclusions you previously came to.

People will say, "Free John" after they've been locked up. Unless they're sure of their innocence, it is hypocritical to want them free if they've committed an actual crime. Then again, depending on what they may be locked up for will determine if people perceive them innocent, not the laws which are supposed to be constructed to convey good and bad deeds.

One of the biggest examples of this is how we see people who've done time or are still in prison from marijuana laws, and people creating cannabis businesses simultaneously. People have gone to prison, fighting for things that may have been the right thing to do at that moment. You may see marijuana sellers on the street as drug dealers when there is not much difference except our perception that makes us perceive them a criminal as opposed to an entrepreneur.

Now, if someone committed a terrible crime and people still wish them free, it only speaks to how much people only care about their own experiences. Imagine if someone did that same crime to someone you cared for, you would be angered and wish they got the jail time they deserved. Imagine when we mistreat others how we would react if someone treated our children or family the same way. We'd be angered. It seems as if we have a complete disregard for anyone else and what happens to them, as long as it isn't us or someone we care for.

I see it on social media all the time. Every day people are calling other people out about what they say. They may have expressed anger over someone's preference but marked it as hate. Funny thing is we all can go back and read some of our old tweets and laugh because of how ignorant they may have been. Or because we are surprised at how we expressed ourselves. This makes some people uncomfortable because now we see ourselves from another angle. Then it may be common in other areas of gossip but doesn't get the same reaction. It is ironic that we don't think about how others may feel when we say or do things. But we can express ourselves and call out any wrongdoings when we are the victims of the same treatment.

Imagine riding the passenger side with your kids or with your friends and yelling at them for texting while driving. Despite how much you may do it, you don't like it when others do it. Think about how much people preach how much they care about the world but have littered multiple times in their life. Think about how people say, "I have black friends." Or, "My husband is black." To come off as someone who doesn't judge off skin tone. Yet, clinch their purse whenever a random black person walks by them. Many people know that when planning a trip most of the people who committed initially won't end up going. Everyone has been caught in a situation when you said you were going to attend an event, but felt a bit discouraged when the time came for whatever reason.

The average person may tell you they hate gossip, but that doesn't stop them from spreading and participating in it despite hating when they end up the topic of discussion. We as Americans love technology and privileges that come with living here. Have we thought about who slaves in warehouses in other countries to make this possible? Have we ever realized that as much as we upgrade our cell phones, there are people, including kids who have died in other countries, to make this possible? Cobalt is a medal that is used to make batteries for some of the top brands in technology. Developing countries risk their lives searching underground for these metals to feed their families.

Most of us couldn't even tell you the new features of the phone, let alone if we use them. We mostly use the basic functions of it. That isn't what makes us continuously buy it. It is a fact that we have the latest product. It makes us feel better than the next person. I'm sure nobody would be in support of this. Especially if we preach all day about the murders taking place in our own country.

Have we thought about the private prisons that pay inmates small amounts of change an hour to produce a vast number of products only to have still trouble finding jobs after serving time? You may feel sorry for the millions of Muslims who, after September 11th, are wrongly accused or profiled, but get nervous when you see one on the same flight as you. How often do you get road rage when someone is driving slow, yet scorn upon someone who's riding too close behind you when you're in no hurry? People who have cheated in the past will look at others as if they are the worst people in the world when someone else does it. If you've done it in the past how much can we judge someone else? How much do we respect people for being honest yet still get mad when we hear the truth? How many times in our life have we lied about something?

No wonder we're good at giving others great advice, but can't seem to take our own. We all have a considerable amount of respectability towards people's privacy, right? That doesn't stop people from going through their boyfriend or girlfriend's phone. That doesn't stop the government from illegally spying on everyone for years. Monitoring calls, storing emails, quite frankly all of the above. You may be able to recall yourself eavesdropping at some point in the past as well. We complain about the government, environments, and communities yet don't form any real collective efforts to make any real change.

We see people who get caught doing things that are against the law all the time. It doesn't mean people of the law don't break the same laws. It is a matter of who gets caught, who didn't, and who created them. I see it in the world every day. You may be resentful toward millionaires but have never made any attempts to try and become financially literate to prosper yourself potentially. You may scoff at the rich not paying taxes, but if you learned the rules and loopholes, you could do it too. You may hate that there are billionaires, but if you came across that amount of money wouldn't be committed to changing the world either. If you were in a position of power you'd probably do anything to maintain it as well. It's only wrong when we're at a disadvantage.

If they were to wipe out debt and start fresh there will be people who eventually will go broke and become in debt again. The money gap may very well eventually become distributed unevenly again. It takes a society who is committed to creating laws that prevent things like this from happening, but life is fair game. I know there are a lot of good people in the world, some who would do the right things if given the opportunity. There are philanthropy and donations that have helped people throughout the world. Still, greed and fear hold a lot of power because of how it controls our lives and decisions.

The things people hate one day and then suddenly like when they see it under different circumstances is very telling. Many people don't offer their support until they see other people who've given it. Think about the people others bash or talk down on, but are at a pause when the situation is turned around on them. Or even the constant debates that are caused by a continuous shift in perception.

We as people think we know what we want and how we feel, and then something changes. Now that I really focus on perception, I see how often this happens among people. I see why it appears to be an endless journey of who is right and who is wrong. I see why we are at war with ourselves. I see why we may contradict ourselves. We want people to see the world the way we do, not knowing if our perception of it will even stay the same. This happens naturally as our present desires, moods, and perspectives change. With the knowledge of this though we must strive to be better human beings. Even the very principles of the way this country strives to live up to fall short sometimes.

Oh say can you see, by the dawn's early light, What so proudly we hailed at the twilight's last gleaming,
Whose broad stripes and bright stars, through the perilous fight,
O'er the ramparts we watched, were so gallantly streaming?
And the rockets' red glare, the bombs bursting in air,
Gave proof through the night that our flag was still there.
Oh say, does that star-spangled banner yet wave
O'er the land of the free and the home of the brave?

Many people have held their hearts up to the flag and recited this poem. I know that there are millions of people who have a lot of pride associated with this flag and the words that define what America is supposed to represent. I also know that we don't always see these words being enforced throughout the country. Not when I see videos of a little boy crying holding his mom, who is about to be deported out of the country. I wouldn't wish that on anyone. Not when I see cop after cop goes unpunished for killings of people like Philando Castile.

It has become so apparent that Bernie Sanders says,

"Our criminal justice system is profoundly broken and has failed African Americans over and over again." Not when I see a guy like Colin Kaepernick end up jobless for taking a knee during the pledge. Not because he wants to disrespect the flag of the country, but because he wants to see those words be lived up to in reality. Those words are deeply enriched in patriotism and history. Yet, we've never seen those words fully portrayed in this country. Coach Popovich said in an interview how patriotic Kaepernick's actions were while you have other people who see his actions disrespectful. You can see how a different take easily can make someone a hero or a villain. Unless these words are covered in vagueness, they are supposed to represent everyone in America.

It seems as if we are all consciously moral enough to understand what America is supposed to be, or even the world. Yet, we fall short of the very commitments and beliefs we praise when it comes to people who aren't like us. This all comes from a lack of understanding of others and ourselves. We all must look in the mirror at some point.

Despite the things that misrepresent the meanings of those words, I know there are still good moral citizens in America, no matter what color you are. We have pride though. When our emotions get involved, we lack the mental toughness to see the bigger picture. If Hypocrisy is someone who professes certain beliefs but fails to live up to them, I've done it, you've done it, we've all done it.

Until we can all admit that, we'll all continue to live in denial. We'll continue to pretend like we see no wrongdoings. We'll continue to get offended. How often are we quick to judge yet are forcefully opposed to being judged? We don't even realize how wrong we are sometimes because our initial reactions aren't to see things beyond just one perspective.

With that being said, I can see why someone may get offended if someone takes a knee during the pledge. They could easily come off as disrespectful. I can see why someone would kneel during the pledge when you see murder after murder and injustice after injustice. I can see how we may become too emotionally caught up to only see one side. I can see why being a hypocrite is simply being human. The more we acknowledge this, the better humans we will become. Hypocrisy is often acted upon blindly or subconsciously. All of this information will help you evaluate situations in a more advanced way. A mature way, that if can become a common skill, will elevate human intelligence.

Contradictions

Contradictions are everywhere. We can easily spot it when others have done it, but can never catch ourselves for some reason. The reason we react so differently to certain things is because of the infinite number of subconscious cues happening at any moment. Here's a twisted analogy of how our minds play tricks on us. At any given moment, the timing of what you do can produce different results.

If you approach a woman/man while they're in a good

mood, there is a good chance they will give you some good conversation. You might even get the number, and vice versa. Yet, if their mood is unwelcoming, you may conclude that that person is uninterested. In reality, they could not have been feeling well. They could have had a significant other. You could have reminded him/her of someone in the past that he/she doesn't like. You may even allow your confidence to drop because of how that person made you feel. It seems natural to think this way. I mean, they could of honestly just not have been interested. In reality, the reasons for anybody acting in a particular way are determined by their present mental state. That's why at some point in everybody's life we contradict ourselves. Onc day we feel this way; the next day, we may change our mind.

The point is, we put too much thought into certain situations that have an unlimited number of outcomes tied to the behavior. We rarely realize this on either end. It's not surprising that we always choose the negative outcomes. That attitude could make you hesitate to speak to others in the future. It could prevent you from meeting great people. We are naturally biased, and the most subliminal cues can be the defining perception of somebody who has made a good impression or a bad one. As irrational as that is, it's even more interesting than first impressions seem to last even after we may have misjudged someone's character. As much as we like to go with our gut feeling, the generalizations can hinder your ability to see beyond what you truly want to see. We must notice how much our perception can change. We deem someone as bad or guilty but can create an excuse for someone we find likable in an instant.

Character is the only form of judgment. We usually judge immediately through stereotypes which is your brain's natural instincts. When we begin to gain more knowledge of this, false narratives won't sway our opinions and reactions as easily. Everyone has their mind and character based on experiences.

To really get a feel of how often you may contradict yourself pay attention to the things you say and do. Try and live up to your word and mean what you say. It'll make you think before you speak on situations or maybe not say anything at all. If we want to be taken seriously, then we have to be willing to take ourselves seriously. While nobody is perfect, effort stands out and is appreciated.

Double Standards

Double standards and stereotypes are the reason it is more likely a black man will be shot or convicted of a crime he may be innocent of. Or the reason someone from a better-ranking college may get the job over someone from a smaller college. It can be the reason someone with no college education is deemed unqualified altogether. We all have held someone to a certain standard or judged them for a specific way that they look.

We can't avoid our subjective selves no matter how logical we think we are being. The more we are convinced we are entirely rational, the more irrational we seem to be. There was a study done on judges and their rulings throughout the day. They noticed that the judge's rulings were a bit more sympathetic in the hours right after lunch. And a lot harsher right before. This gave a clear insight into how, when we are hungry, sleepy, or frustrated, how we lose conscious ability to concentrate on what we're doing.

The judge may have become more careless as his stomach growled and didn't give a fair judgment. Depending on the mood of the judge can mean jail time or a lucky day for someone who has been convicted. It alters your perception at that moment. We all know this feeling. When you are hungry, it's hard to concentrate on doing anything.

Our attitude toward things can change and be completely different if we were full or feeling happy. Nothing gives a more explicit example than our perception of the world on a day to day basis. Some days you wake up feeling completely shitty. Other days we wake up feeling on top of the world. I don't understand what exactly causes this. I do know it is our perceptions, though, that makes us feel this way.

Emotional responses like this happen in everyday life. Imagine if we took the time to see how irrational we are being. The result of this is endless conflicts. Hopefully, this makes you more aware of the cycle we get caught in. If you pay more attention, you too will notice how often this happens. It truly is something we overlook and don't pay attention to.

Show more accountability toward yourself and the

natural mistakes and misjudgments you make. Maybe it'll keep you from only seeing other people's double standards and focusing more on your own. When we talk about this being a cycle, it reminds me of the saying, "What goes around comes back around." Is this popular quote simply saying we're all behaving in irrational ways that eventually hit us based on cosmic laws?

This to me in a sense explains how karma works. When you think of karma, you may immediately think of something happening to you because of what you did in the past. Karma is usually associated with a negative deed of some sort, that eventually comes back to haunt you. The actual definition of karma is the **sum of a person's actions in this and previous states of existence, viewed as deciding their fate in future existences.**

So karma can actually date back to previous lifetimes that we have no memory of. Wow, to think whatever you may be going through in life has some connection with past lifetimes is interesting. Karma is action. Every action that we take place in has some sort of consequence. This can be good or bad. Karma closely resembles the laws of cause and effect.

Every action determines your life in the future, as well as our personality traits that can indicate how we may have acted in the past. Some even say karma isn't external. Meaning if I rob you, the consequences of going to jail would be external. But the suffering and guilt, which is internal, is the karma. There are even considered to be different stages of karma as well.

What is more important is what we have control

of in the present. Despite whatever you may be going through, living, or thinking in an offensive manner is only a reflection of your future fate. Living virtuously is like planting the seeds of your future reality. If we plant an apple seed, there will only be apples that can grow from this tree, there aren't any other possible scenarios. No plums, berries, or bananas can grow from a tree that wasn't planted with this fate. What goes around comes around. Whenever you are seeking revenge or feeding into your ego, you are only selfish. You are only planning your fate.

When you take all of this information in, you really should strive to be pure in your intentions. We should really take more caution about how we think and react. We should think about the things we've done, and try to see every situation from many different perspectives. That is the only way to broaden your understanding. I guess thinking before you speak really is critical.

It's easy to react without thinking. Many of us have a hard time even remembering all the things we may have reacted to irrationally in the past. It truly speaks to the nature of human beings and how conflict is created every day. Maybe we can't see past our embedded natural makeup of the mind, but we can become more intelligent in how we go about living and treating others.

We are only living and reacting to our experiences and present moods. We are only a reflection of evolution and our ancestors. We aren't perfect, but if we can become more aware, we'll understand this. We'll see that we all have more in common than we think. We're all one consciousness. With more understanding, maybe, just maybe, we'll learn to communicate, sympathize, and treat each other better.

Indecision

Many times in life, we can become indecisive about what we want out of life. It can make us frustrated with ourselves. It can cause us to consciously state what we want, but it's deeper than that. We really just want many things that we don't have. The desire is increased when we are prevented from getting it. We can become hypocrites when we get it and then don't feel the same after.

While we all may expect people to take us seriously when we give our opinions that we all think are valuable, sometimes you can't even take yourself seriously. This reminds me of the countless amount of times I've heard, "I changed my mind". What was the true cause of this? It's the shift in perception which becomes interchangeable, pending the new experience, moods, or information. This only speaks to the importance of being open-minded. You'll look foolish in a lot of scenarios if you never take the time to understand how hypocritical you can be.

Indecisiveness can be caused by being overwhelmed with too many options you like. People often change majors in college multiple times because of the many different routes there are to take. Many times I find myself thinking about what I want to eat longer than I should when really I just can't decide. All of these things can happen simply because of how we over-analyze situations.

This can be a good thing when you take into consideration that making quick decisions without thinking them through can be costly. Yet, being indecisive is a bit different once you realize you're no longer just critically thinking, you just simply can't decide. It's, in a way, a very enlightening time of reflection because you begin to realize how all of the decisions we make no matter how small create some impact on our life. The vivid reflection of these potential decisions is vast, unpredictable, and imaginative. Many may become overwhelmed by this, causing anxiety or lack of focus.

It goes to show you just how infinite the wonders of the mind go when we are in our thoughts. The things you want out of life will come faster to you when you know what it is you want, although depending on what it is, it may still require some patience. One must be truly honest with themselves, and in tune with their feelings to trust, they're making the right choices in life. Once you truly decide what it is that you want, that's when it will all start coming together.

Many times in life I've been too hesitant or indecisive. If you can't make a choice and stick by it, you'll never align your behavior long enough to see those choices manifest. The hardest part is actually deciding what it is we want out of life. We have to get in touch with our true selves and figure out what makes us happy.

Saying money, traveling, and friends are too vague. Look deep and think about what happiness means to you and decide what you're willing to do to create that happiness. The more I write and get closer to finishing this book, the more I get this overwhelmingly joyous feeling. As if I have a purpose in life centered around doing something I love. The more I acknowledge and create these feelings, the more it'll show in the objective world. It will also create keystone habits in other areas of your life. Yet, none of this would have happened had I never actually decided to do it.

This attitude can extend to the type of people we value vs the people we overlook. We think we want people who appear to be valued in society, at least to us. Many people don't want a man/woman that everybody has had, they want a man/woman that everybody else wishes they had. The feeling of having something exclusive makes us feel good when it comes to people and even materials.

Have you ever thought about why many times the people you crush on don't have that same energy for you? Many times the fact that we know that person doesn't desire us makes us desire them more. Yet, the people who may be crazy over us don't catch our interest as much. Is this because it's too easy? Is it the challenge or the thought of not being able to have something that excites us that triumphs above everything? Why are gifts that are harder to get better than gifts you could get anywhere?

It's the exclusivity feeling we get when we show others these things knowing how hard it may have been to attain it. All of this should make us more knowledgeable about how to prevent our desires from confusing us. Many times it's nothing more than lust. Everybody thinks they know exactly what they want when it's not that simple. It's evident in the times that we still may feel like something is missing after getting it. Genuinely seek to understand yourself to find out what uplifts you so that indecisiveness won't get the best of your potential blissful experiences.

Crabs in a bucket

Many times we may get offended by how other races treat us. What about how we treat ourselves? If you get offended when other races look down on you but won't support your kind, that's hypocritical. If you're black and look at other black people who are trying to prosper in life and see their work as less valuable, then you are a part of the problem. I remember a lot of black actors coming out and saying Tyler Perry was the first person to pay them what they're truly worth. I've even seen videos of kids who are shown white dolls verse black dolls and have already been conditioned into thinking the lighter toys were prettier. Many people don't realize how the whole crabs in a bucket mentality are rooted in so much confusion and insecurities.

People don't want to see others doing better than them so nobody ever prospers to the point they can help others. They may pull each other down or flex on each other instead of having enough love in their heart to wanna see their kind be great. What does that say about how we feel about ourselves deep down? There isn't one way to make it. Many people have different skills that could support a career. Our support for one another is essentially what makes money flow. It's the engine for a prosperous society or community.

Even if I may "make it out" with a great career, a big house, and a family, am I satisfied? Will I be fine with seeing my race never prosper or even humanity? Would I wake up every day completely passive toward others or even the world simply because "I'm good"?

I often ask myself these questions to gain an understanding of what it truly is I want in life. Where would my satisfaction or contentment completely kick in? That desire that has taken over me is hard to describe even after all these words. It goes beyond any personal accomplishments I may receive. It's a desire to be free.

When I write I feel as if I'm freeing my mind. It's a desire for understanding. When I truly seek understanding I feel as if I've mastered ignorance. It's a desire for a purpose. When I feel purposeful, I get chills from the sensation of knowing who I am and I'm in a sense synchronized with nature. Beyond the illusions and conflict, I want us all to stop thinking we have to be this way. I want the human race to master themselves, which I think is the ultimate test of our true intelligence. I want to be a part of something that could be appreciated for lifetimes.

Many have been taught how inferior their race is that they're still dealing with perceptions of them being unworthy. Even if they consciously acknowledge the power they truly possess, it is something inside still being battled, preventing them from ever tapping into that energy. We can see how a particular race could have all the power within them but don't utilize it because of how past traumatic experiences have been. To me, it still shows subtly in different ways. I notice how enriched their souls are in how they still laugh and joke through the pain. I notice it in the style and humor they naturally possess. I'm in love with it, but it doesn't shy away from my accountability. We can't be afraid of change in any aspect of life, no matter who you are.

We must strive to instill and inspire one another. The constant bashing and blaming is only keeping those crabs in the same bucket. It's all frustrating and it's all mental. When we begin to truly appreciate each other we will immediately see the collective power in that energy. I love you black woman, I love you, black man. Hell, if you're reading this, I'm genuinely inspired by the essence of what makes you who are. Your strength is immeasurable, and when you put your mind to what you want, you will have the world.

The Finesser

Cory was as slick as they come. He could steal from people without them even knowing. He may even help you look for those same items he confiscated. He was funny, which was good because it usually distracted people from his true motives. He was good at pinpointing people's character and using it to his advantage. He'd use people that he knew were too nice to tell him no for random favors. He often lied to people so much sometimes he'd convince himself it was true. It all became a game for him.

Much of what he learned came from his dad. He sold drugs and was a real street wiz. He taught Cory everything he knew. Whether it was selling drugs, telling a good joke, how to fight, lie, spit game, or use people in general, it was all he knew. The art of finessing was in his blood. His dad once told him, "Everybody has a desire for something, and everybody has weaknesses. You can achieve anything you want if you can identify these things."

Cory would never forget those statements. More so because his dad was killed by an enemy he had gotten over on, or finessed. For some reason, this motivated Cory to take what his dad taught him and go further than what he got the opportunity too. Cory would often contradict himself a lot. He could care less, though, as long as it got him what he wanted. He sold drugs and stole from people, but at an above-average level. He would rarely get caught. He took heed to his dad's mistakes and tried to be more discrete and aware of his surroundings.

Cory never knew how it felt to be compassionate. He always had this mindset that people were out to get him, so he would have to get them first. He made a lot of money but barely had any friends. His mom would try to give him talks about his mindset, but Cory was far too consumed in his dad's persona. Cory always had a plan to get over on people whether it be skipping a line, stealing, or business. He'd been cheating his way through college as well. He knew some smart kids that liked weed, and as you may have guessed, it worked out.

One day as he was leaving campus, he noticed this gorgeous young woman walking to class. Cory never hesitated to speak to people. One thing about him is he knew how powerful first impressions were. He would always have a good warm-up line or particular subject to shift their focus in the way that he chose. It worked about 90% of the time. As he eyed her down, planning his approach, she spotted him looking at her and immediately asked, "What do you want?"

This girl had never seen him before and he wondered what made her sense that he wanted something so easily. Cory knew he was great at looking uninterested, or as if he minded his own business. But she noticed him first. It threw him off because it wasn't what he expected, but he quickly regained his confidence and began spitting his typical lines at her that usually worked on 80% of women according to his statistics. But even after some small talk and telling his best joke, she didn't budge.

This had never happened to Cory before. She would eventually continue walking to class, and Cory was left empty-handed without a number. For some reason, this increased his desire for her. Cory always got what he wanted. He did it in ways that were never by force but by finesse. When it came down to it, he knew there was a true art to it. He was good at making people feel as if he'd got them a great deal, or that his products were the best.

It was no different when it came to how he marketed himself to women. There were plenty of other women

Cory could've talked to, I mean she was only one girl. None, however, made him intimidated as she did for some reason. Was it her beauty or the fact she sensed things about him nobody else could quite read? It was on his mind for the rest of the day.

Weeks had gone by and he still hadn't seen her after that day. He even went out of his way to go to the library and study, but his true intent was to run into her again, hopefully. One day he finally saw her at a basketball game. He wasted no time confronting her. She immediately recognized him and gave out a small chuckle before he said anything. She was with all of her friends, but Cory didn't care. He spoke to them and then continued to use his humorous lines to win her over.

This time she seemed a bit more open to him as if he had become a familiar friend, or maybe she still took him for a joke. He didn't care, plus her friends laughed at some of the jokes. His boldness and willingness to get rejected in front of them made her friends like him. She finally told him her name which was Layla. She eventually gave him her number with a look on her face that came off as if she may be possibly regretting this.

Layla was a smart girl. She knew how to keep guys interest because her mom taught her about boys at a young age. Many women would always be jealous of her because of the attention she got. Something that was even more baffling to other women is how she did it effortlessly. It was as if men saw her as a grand prize that not many can say they won. Layla knew guys that didn't get what they want only increased their desire. She would play hard to get but give them small signs that made them feel as if they had a slight chance.

This was a normal thing for her, and depending on how much she liked that particular person would determine how much she'd take advantage of them. She knew even a wiz like Cory couldn't escape her mesmerizing figure and enchanting spirit. This left him open in ways that were usually guarded. They would text and talk on the phone after they met the second time. Cory tried not to bother her too much, and Layla would continue to play it cool.

Her mom always got her way with men, and that's because she understood what men wanted. This allowed her to always flourish and that gained Layla's admiration. It was almost as if her mom passed down laws for men that stuck with her. They eventually went out, and it wasn't long before they connected. Cory never told her about his lifestyle or the fact he knew so many things about finessing. In fact finessing her never crossed his mind, well, only once.

One night she got a little too drunk at a party and he took care of her. He thought she was a cool down to earth person and didn't take advantage of her by stealing or trying to have sex. For some reason, she had his respect. Plus he didn't want her to judge him and mess his chances up. She didn't seem like the type to be enthused about that bad boy type of stuff. He'd play the college boy role more until he felt more comfortable.

When he looked in her eyes, he felt a way he never had before. It was as if she helped discover another side of him he didn't know existed. Most guys Layla came across never really fascinated her, but Cory was quite different, and over time, she started valuing his attention and style. Cory was still a true finesse at heart except when it came to her.

Layla was still always one step ahead of everybody, but Cory sometimes would make her feel like she didn't always have to be. She respected his grind and wisdom and didn't mind following his lead, which was surprising to her. They would talk for months and many people knew they had a thing for each other. Layla was close to graduating, and Cory never brought up what she was going to do after.

The next time he met up with her, he planned on having a serious talk about their future. He was thinking about getting serious with her. Cory always played out many scenarios in his head and thought about the possibility of her leaving him. He would quickly dismiss these thoughts that became natural for him. He was thinking like his dad again. Cory supported her the day she graduated and they had plans to celebrate more afterward. She told him to meet her at a hotel where she was having a party later on. Cory didn't like parties, but this was a special occasion so that he would attend.

As he left his room and was on the way there, Cory had this weird feeling. For some reason, he was nervous, but couldn't figure out why. Would her parents be there? Was he deep down nervous about asking her to marry him? Was there something fishy going on that his senses were trying to make him realize?

He ignored them all and continued driving to the

hotel. When he got there, the parking lot looks pretty empty. He checked in at the front desk for the room, and the management pointed out that this room was vacant. He immediately felt this sick feeling in his stomach, something was up. He called her phone, and there was no answer. Now he was worried. He figured she may have just been busy taking pics or around family. He went back to campus; maybe she'd be there.

When he got there, he stopped by his room for a second to get the flowers he left. When he opened the door, everything was gone. His tv, his shoes, and most importantly, his secret stash of money he got from finessing. Cory let out a small chuckle as if he was in disbelief. He began to put two and two together and started to realize he had been finessed.

He would later find out Layla had moved that same night and knew some guys he had got over on in the past. So she helped them get him away from his room. All of a sudden, Cory started backtracking and realized all the opportunities he had to finesse her. He could've hit and quit after she finally gave in. He could've taken her credit cards from her purse that night she got drunk but took care of her. He could've insisted that they stayed and drive to the hotel together and plotted his revenge when he had that weird feeling…but he didn't. He actually had good intentions and this time for the first time it happened to him.

While he usually may have started plotting for revenge, it did something different to him. It made him realize how inconsiderate he'd been throughout his life to other people. Seeing all of his things gone was the worst feeling he had felt in his life besides when his dad died. From that moment on Cory never looked to get over on people anymore, it disgusted him. He could've just easily charged it to the game and started hustling over, but this time was different. He was truly humbled in a way that made him more of a man than he ever thought he was. He walked back outside and stared at the sky while sitting on the back of his car. He wondered what Layla was doing and how she could've done that to him.

Layla was riding in the backseat by this time halfway across the country, traveling to a job she never told Cory she got. As nightfall hit, she looked up at the sky gazing. A tear fell, she knew she actually had feelings, Cory. She knew he had never experienced what she had done to him and knew it was necessary. It was as if they were speaking to each other in a way that went beyond confrontation. It was as if the stars told them both everything they needed to know.

Cory would eventually finish school himself, and the passion he once had to lie, steal, and get over on people had left. He remembered being a kid and how much he loved writing. His dad never told him to stop, but he did distract him in ways that made him prioritize writing last. He had almost completely forgotten he even once loved to do it. He had revived that passion and started writing a script for a movie he was looking to produce. There were some investors who came across his writing and wanted to bring it to life.

Cory had found a passion that benefitted him.

Unquestionably if he hadn't, he didn't even believe he would be alive. Now he was headed to LA to help produce a film. The plot and storyline were ones that could potentially be a big hit because of how unique and different it was. The investors would contact him and ask him what should they call the film. Cory smirked and said, The Finesser.

Many times we don't truly see how our life is wholly comprised of our thoughts. We will think our actions that we have made sense of are always right despite the people we may hurt. Many people in power don't feel guilty when millions of people die in war, starve from hunger, or are homeless. They've created this perception of it all being beneficial, which is a good thing to them. It isn't truly understood until the tables are turned. Then those same people want sympathy when the roles are reversed. Cory never took into consideration the way people felt until he was put into that situation.

The purpose of this story was to show how we truly can get confused about who we are. We can go about doing things the wrong way which is why there is eventually some sort of unwanted outcome. Those outcomes are simply events that reveal everything you need to know about your approach to life and what you may need to change. Not in the material sense, but rather your character.

There are prideful ways, bad perceptions, and fear that we must release before we could ever truly evolve. Cory would have never reached another level had he not looked himself in the mirror. He would have still been taking the same approach that may have left him hurt or dead. Take the time to study yourself. Pay attention to your moods and feelings. Seek to understand the deeper side of you. This is the gateway to your freedom and happiness.

CHAPTER 7

Past, Present, and Future

"Life is only available in the present moment. If you abandon the present moment you cannot live the moments of your daily life deeply." Thich Nhat Hanh

"The secret of health for both mind and body is not to mourn for the past, worry about the future, or anticipate troubles, but to live in the present moment wisely and earnestly." ~Buddha

"When you are here and now, sitting totally, not jumping ahead, the miracle has happened. To be in the moment is the miracle." ~Osho

Overthinking

It is important to be in the present moment. If we do take the time to reflect, it must be a vision of us in a better situation. It shouldn't be something that keeps us at a low vibration. We can't go back in the past, but we spend more time reflecting on it rather than taking advantage of the present moment. We can't predict the future, and even when we plan for it, it usually doesn't go exactly as planned. Either way, we're spending time in our heads instead of realizing this moment is all we have. It's so easy to become consumed in thought, I mean, after all, we have thousands of them a day. A problem often shared amongst people is the amount of time they spend overthinking.

So many scenarios are being played in our head, and it's usually the negative ones that we end up entertaining. Before we know it, we feel bad. Remember, thoughts convert to feelings; feelings convert to energy in motion. The action based on that energy is the force creating what becomes our reality. The mind naturally is creating synapses with any neurons near it. That's why you can be thinking of one thing, and next thing you know, you're thinking about something random and off-topic. We are battling the natural brain activity to create a more peaceful present state.

The mind feeds off repetition. Gaining mental strength comes with continually reminding yourself of what is happening. Meditation is also a powerful activity to partake in. While meditating, you will notice how your mind starts to think about random things. It is important to bring your attention back to your breathing or the present moment. It can get frustrating, but you become better at it over time. The whole point is to stop your mind from being so uncontrolled.

We go about our days reacting uncontrollably to all these thoughts, that's why meditation is a great way to form more peace in your life. MRI scans of the brain before and after meditation show less activity in the brain, which means a healthier mind and body for you. If we can't go in the past and the future is determined by what we do today, then a reflection of the past or future can be counterproductive.

Life is short, but would it seem short if we lived every moment doing what we loved to do? Or even creating what we want to create? You come to realize living in the moment is truly living. Stop taking life so seriously. Enjoy it. Ask yourself what makes you get out of the bed each morning and find a way to make that something you do every day. Sure, people get out of bed every day for a check and to pay bills, but life is deeper than that. You must realize there's a gift that you have that's meant to help others while simultaneously fulfilling your spirit. Once you find it, it will more than likely turn into something profitable. More importantly, you will feel free and at peace with yourself. You will get a lot more things done living this way. You will be a lot happier.

When we are thinking of the past we normally are having feelings of regret or nostalgia. When we are thinking of the future, we, at times, are filled with doubt, worry, and even excitement. How far will we go in life if we spent more time at that moment acting on our goals and desires instead of worrying about bad outcomes? We would go very far. You're capable of this, but you must consistently remind yourself that this very moment is all that matters.

The best thing you can do is take control over how you think. Notice when your thoughts don't adhere to the way you want to feel and channel them in a different direction. When you become mindful of how easily your thoughts can drift away, the more control you will have of directing your mind in the way that benefits you. Nobody wants to be an impulsive being, reacting to every provoking thought. Can you imagine the levels of anxiety on a day to day basis? Well, you'd be surprised how many people experience this and don't know why. It is because they are unaware of what is happening inside their head.

The amount of peace and tranquility that comes with the knowledge of this will do wonders for you in your life. You will get to the point where even when times become troubling you're calm. You're never panicking or showing signs of intense worry because you know all that stems from how we are creating those situations in our head. It's crazy how we can think of dreams and believe they aren't possible, but think of ourselves in negative cases and react as if it has happened.

Become aware of the importance of your health and the realization of what you can accomplish when you do this. Focus on what you can do right now. This moment truly is a present. So treat it as if it is a gift. Notice how when you do bring your attention to what's happening now, there are no worries. There is no regret. There is only consciousness. There is only peace. There is only the sound of your breath, so you're ok. As much as we create all these horrific scenarios in our head that make us feel down, you're still here. You've overcome it. Take control over your mind, don't let it control you. Master the art of the present moment.

Overworking

Why do some people work so much? Obviously, bills won't pay themselves and everyone likes money, but can it be something deeper? A lot of people stay busy as a way to distract themselves. It can keep people from having to think about things that may be bothering them. We may quickly become bored or sad when we aren't doing anything work-related or entertaining.

This is that awkward moment in life where you are free from distractions and don't realize this is an opportunity to get in touch with a side of yourself you rarely make time for. You can become so consumed in working that it's now something you use to avoid reflecting on your life or searching for something more fulfilling. We can run from things in the most subtle ways even when it is ourselves. A lot of people only feel ok when they're always busy, and that's a problem. It appears to be a good way to cope with those more in-depth emotions, but they've only been temporarily blocked.

It is also worth noting how there's this rule that if you're not working endlessly, then you are lazy. We have become conditioned to believe working five or even six days a week, with one vacation a year is typical. The time spent off is us dreading having to go back, but we have to do what we have to do. Our belief in having to work hard to make money can make us overlook opportunities to make money passively.

Subtle Stress

I once read a statement made by someone on social media that made me realize how mental stress can be. "If you're reading this release your shoulders from your ears, unclench your jaw, and remove your tongue from the roof of your mouth. We physically tend to hold on to stress in the least visible ways." As I read that and followed the instructions, I realized how tense I was. It made me calmer, and more in the present moment. Sometimes the best thing we can do is relax.

Many times we never give our bodies this sensation because there's always something that is keeping us on edge. It can be the source of other problems like lack of quality sleep, or energy. Learning how to calm yourself down and be in the moment will bring you more peace and happiness. Oddly the universe usually brings us what we want once we let it go. When you make claims to what you want and no longer stress about how it will manifest, it comes in ways you least expected them too. When you become in tune with life, you're in a sense, never in a hurry.

Time, after all, is a man-made concept. The universe is always on time. You'll eat your food more slowly instead of eating so fast. You'll have more patience for things that may have normally irritated you so easily. You'll become more understanding before lashing out at people so often. You'll master the game of perspective.

One of the big reasons people fast is to bring themselves to a point where their mind must overpower their senses. We state how we could never eat certain foods or drink particular drinks, but what if there were no other options, and you were on the brink of starvation? Never overlook any meal or drink that quenches your thirst. Many people struggle for these basic things to survive around the world. Every day we are faced with a choice. We can either choose to endlessly have emotions of worry or choose to focus on what's going right. It's easier to build off the momentum of efficient thoughts. It helps you put more effort into your goals. This is why many wise speakers regularly promote positive thinking.

It is important to also exercise your willpower. You can mentally relieve yourself of specific emotions and feelings only by consciously shifting your attitude. You can shift your entire energy by continuously focusing on the right things.

Buddhism

Growing up, I had the opportunity to experience going to the mosque as well as the church. When I think about religion it always draws me back to a bigger picture. Most religions story is somewhat relatable to other religions. Islam and Christianity have more similarities than differences if anybody ever cared to study the two.

The only differences in most religions are the names, different practices or rituals. The amount of hate people have for other religions only shows how serious you take your own. Truly following the teachings of any religion will preach love. So why is our approach to others the opposite? We get caught up in the specific religion that we tend to think is better than others or the only way of thinking. That's when it becomes a problem.

The way we believe life was created, whether by God or the Big Bang theory, has its consequences. It's all a matter of how we have decided to see life. The need for something to believe in is important to people. Once they've been convinced of a belief, that is their life. It's almost as if there's no convincing them to see anything beyond it. We must realize this is the reason behind most of our suffering. It is our attachment.

To know how to let go, or understand the depths of possibility, is to understand how to become truly enlightened. It is why I've looked into Buddhism beyond religion. It is a concept of life that we all should follow. It's simply becoming self-aware of our own thoughts and how they are the cause of our pain.

I remember the first time I actually went to the book store with genuine hopes of learning. It was a time in my life when I was confused and hurt and needed direction. The more I think about how I created this book, the more I realize where it all started. For me to be able to elaborate on this subject it took years of studying. There were no rewards that would come from this except the peace I gained. No paper stating I've become a master of this subject was given to me. It was all desire and genuineness.

I now think about how clueless I was reading that first book. I was so unfamiliar with a lot of the terms and concepts that it was initially tough to read. There was never a moment when I thought I would eventually write my own book. It just hit me one day. Many people may go to school for more money or validation. It makes their intentions align with what they've prioritized. I've realized while in college, my heart was never in it.

I never learned the information from genuine interest so it never truly stuck with me. That's why most people may study for a test but forget all the information afterward. Follow and do the things that have your true interest at heart. That's the true essence of manifestation. That's the only way we will actually put time into it. The amount of work you put in doing something can seem effortless when you want to do it.

You'll pass many people who may try to do the same things but are doing it for the wrong reasons. I desired peace, and it made me search and read relentlessly until I understood what the cause of my suffering was. Many people may seek a therapist to help them deal with the trauma in their past. I became the therapist for myself. All therapists will try and do is help you gain new perspectives creating peace with the bad things you've experienced. We can all become better people if we sought the information that made us more aware. We can all become peaceful if it is that which we strive for.

The now

Jason was one of the coolest guys you'd ever meet. He was always well dressed, stayed out of trouble, and had great character. Many people in his school took note of this. He was well respected by most popular kids. He even related to kids who weren't as popular. Jason could hold an intellectual conversation with anybody from the principal to the nerd who was going on and on about astrophysics.

As perfect as he may have been perceived, Jason wasn't as perfect as they thought. He was extremely shy, but he played it off very well, mostly because of his self-consciousness. He often would worry about his future. If he wasn't worried about his future, he was always thinking about the past and what he could've done better.

This made him a lot of times completely out of tune with reality or the moment. He still would get anxiety about speaking in front of large crowds. He did this once in 8th grade and got choked up. Now the thought of doing it again made his stomach turn and heart race. Jason had all the qualities of a leader, but he was holding himself back in ways he didn't realize.

One day while walking home, he saw a man meditating in his yard. At first, Jason wanted to laugh, but the man seemed so peaceful, he stared a little longer. Eventually, he would keep walking home. Jason was a senior in high school now and the only problem he had was his inability to control his thoughts. Many people looked up to him, but he didn't see the qualities that they saw in him.

His junior year he was picked to give a speech for student council which wasn't the first time. He turned it down. He was on the debate team, and a lot of times, when he had an important point to make, he would back down. Even times during class when he had a funny joke to say he wouldn't simply because he didn't like the spotlight. I mean, what if he stuttered over his words?

As much as Jason wanted to reach his potential, he didn't want to go back since he knew people generally respected him throughout the school. There was something missing and Jason knew it. After another day of school, he was walking home as usual. Once again, he noticed a man meditating in his yard. Jason was curious as to what the man got out of sitting there with his eyes closed for so long.

All of a sudden the man's eyes shot open. He was looking right at Jason. Jason was about to run away, but the man smiled and waved him over. He hesitated but eventually walked over to him. "Welcome." The man said. "What are you doing?" Jason said. "That is a great question I'd thought you'd never ask son. See it as you've been staring at me every day for the past week." Jason embarrassingly grinned. "My name is Bhodi, and I am meditating."

Jason had heard of meditation before but he didn't know exactly what benefits the man gained from it. He finally asked, "Why?" Bhodi laughed as he knew the boy was soon to discover the possibilities of life and his mind. "Before I answer that, why does it capture your interest so much?" Bhodi said. Jason responded, "Well, you look so peaceful and, and I" Bhodi interrupted, "And you want to be peaceful?" ...." yea," Jason said. Bhodi didn't normally do this if he ever did, it would certainly cost. He was feeling friendly today and sensed how Jason was in need of some teachings. "Come in, and I will show you why I meditate."

He gave Jason a book. "Study this book every night, every night," Bhodi said. Jason shook his head. "Now! Relax, and I'll show you the strength of your mind." Jason made himself comfortable and began to prepare to meditate. Bhodi lit candles and played some soothing tunes which Jason assumed were things people did specifically to be romantic. He realized how calm he felt and that these were methods that actually eased his mind. After all, he had never met this man before and knew better to enter strangers' houses, but he felt right at home for some reason. "Sit still, close your eyes and breathe," Bhodi said.

The instructions were simple, but Jason was having a tough time actually doing this. Soon as he started, he begins thinking about school, what he was going to eat for dinner, and many other things. Bhodi could tell and smirked a bit. Jason was a little frustrated, but he continued. After about 10 minutes Jason had begun to doze off. It was as if he was awake but sleeping at the same time. He then begins to hear Bhodi speak to him, but he kept his eyes closed.

The more Bhodi spoke, the deeper meditative state Jason sunk to. Bhodi was helping Jason's subconscious mind reprogram how he felt about himself. At the same time, Jason was becoming more in tune with the moment. The now. After about an hour Bhodi told Jason to open his eyes. He slowly opened them and had this blissful feeling of serenity. He didn't speak or say anything immediately he was just at ease. "Come to me every day until you learn how to do this on your own and you will gain everlasting peace," Bhodi said.

Jason did this for weeks with Bhodi right after school and he noticed a big difference. At some point during the day Jason's anxiety would kick in but after meeting Bhodi, it never happened. He'd do the normal things he'd always did at school, but it wasn't to appear like the coolest guy or to go unnoticed at times.

One morning in class everyone was joking and playing, the teacher was having trouble settling everybody down. Without thinking, Jason stood up and said, "Hey! Everybody calm down Mr. Rodgers is trying to teach!" Everyone was shocked that he spoke out including Mr. Rodgers since this wasn't like him. Even Jason was a little surprised at this. And at that moment while everyone was looking at him he realized something. He was no longer nervous about speaking.

In fact, he may have never even started talking before meeting Bhodi because of how he usually would begin thinking about adverse outcomes. Jason was so in the moment that he just acted at the moment. At that moment Jason just spoke without worrying, he just let things be. "I'll give anyone 10 dollars if they can solve the problem on the board Mr. Rodgers was trying to teach." All of a sudden, there was silence, then there was an explosion of noise from the students wanting to be picked to show they could work out the problem.

Many may not have been paying attention, but they were willing to try, and Jason realized how he motivated them to learn in a way that he didn't even know he could. Eventually many of the students would try until someone got it right. The amazing thing after that is Mr. Rodgers had everyone's attention after. The students didn't want to be caught in a situation where they didn't know the answer, which would cost them money. Mr. Rodgers adopted this idea for future lessons and it helped him gain better control over his classes. Sometimes it was money, candy, and even entertaining items he would offer to those who could solve the problems.

Jason had done something he was always capable of doing, which is being a leader. He eventually would give student council speeches and ran for class president. He led the debate team all the way to the finals. Before he knew it, he had done so many things that he felt like he always could, but he was just distracted. The respect he had around the school went to another level. He wasn't even shy about talking to girls anymore. It's like his life went to another level, but why?

It had been 2 months since that day Bhodi called him over and showed him how to meditate. He knew how to do this on his own now and still studied the book Bhodi gave him. It was as if he saved his life. One day after school Jason couldn't wait to go to Bhodi and tell him about everything he had accomplished. When he got there Bhodi was gone. His house was for sale and Jason just stood there. A tear fell down his face and he wondered if he'd ever see Bhodi again.

He soon realized Bhodi had never left him. He would always be with him spiritually and will always be his teacher. Jason would grow older and become a great speaker. He would help others around the world tap into their potential to live the life they always dreamed of. He realized how powerful his thoughts were and where he'd be if he never met Bhodi. He would tell stories about him to others and reminisce about the life-changing moment when he called him over. He could probably never thank him enough.

One day after giving a very inspirational speech, Jason was shaking hands and talking to a few people as everybody was preparing to leave. All of a sudden someone behind him said, "What an amazing speech, where did you get the inspiration?" Jason was asked this question a lot and couldn't wait to tell the same story he had hundreds of times about how he first started meditating and who taught him. As Jason turned around, it was him.

Jason immediately started laughing and crying while hugging his mentor that he hadn't seen in a decade. "Thank you for everything Bhodi, I..I never got the chance to tell you everything I've done since meeting you, I. "I know I know son slow down. I've been watching you and I'm proud of you." Bhodi said. "I want to thank you." "You inspired me to open up a school back home to help young men and women like yourself." I left my home to become peaceful. Then I went back to show my people what I had discovered.

It was all because of how much you reminded me of myself and all the kids back home." Jason was so happy. "I always felt like you were still with me Bhodi all I had to do was meditate and I could feel you next to me. I could never thank you enough for what you did for me." Jason said. They hugged and talked for hours. They would go around the world, helping people, and teaching these simple methodologies. BHodi would grow old and one day passed away. His life was celebrated like no other.

Many people appreciated what he did on this earth and the lives he impacted. Jason would grow old as well and eventually retired in his own home. To honor Bhodi he would still meditate out in his front yard. With the sun beaming on his skin, the feeling of taking a deep breath, and the sounds of birds making him feel at one with nature, he had everything he could ever desire. With his eyes still closed, he heard footsteps. The footsteps stopped, and Jason's eyes shot open, initially startling the young boy who was staring, wondering what the hell he was doing. Jason grinned and waved the boy over.

CHAPTER 8

Fear and Failure

Keep going

I'm sure you've had times where you felt like you weren't going to make it. There may have even been times where you felt like it was impossible to reach certain goals. You may feel that way right now, which made you pick this book up and read it. Nobody ever just woke up and had everything they ever wanted. It took action and commitment. It took not getting it right but trying again and again.

Even in our lowest moments, our attitudes determine if we give up or fight for what we want. Life will do this to you. Life has done this to me. It's as if life will challenge you like it's saying, "How bad do you want it?" I've failed at things in the past because of my lack of commitment. You can say I didn't want it bad enough. The success or big break I needed may have been right there, but I stopped. Success may never find us because we never stick around long enough for it to happen. We all know this feeling, so I'm here to tell you, you're not alone.

Success isn't determined by money, fame, or even awards. Success is having a goal and reaching it period. I wanted to write a book and I'm doing it. When I finish this book that will be a success. If someone wanted to open a store, or become a teacher, or even start their own business and is committed to doing that, they are a success.

I'm forced to take my advice whenever things aren't going quite my way. It's a great reminder. I must take my own advice for once. If you're reading this, it is because I didn't stop. Even in these moments when I felt down because I'm not where I want to be in life, I kept going. I want to be an inspiration to others who are reading this, so you will know, all I did was keep everything I'm writing about in mind as I pursued my goal. The odds were stacked against me just like they may be in your case. If I did it, you can too. All you must do is start. We perceive failure as not being good enough, but our subconscious mind just hasn't acquired enough information to create the outcome you desire. You have to be patient with yourself.

It is said that your twenties are your prime years, but I think that's your "figure everything out" years. We'd all love to be successful in our careers by at least 22. If we're not, we feel the pressure from everyone else and ourselves to reach our goals. It can be depressing. If you can remember that it's just a part of the process then you're on the right track. I've also learned how to live my life without expecting things to happen when I want to. Things happen when we let go of when they should.

You could get your big break early in your life or later. A lot of books and videos that talk about success say you must show gratitude for the things you want as if you already have them. Well, I think I'm passing the test life is throwing at me because my head is held high. I'm happy as if I have this book in my hand, even though I don't know what will be the results after I'm finished. I have faith though. Notice all these things I'm saying are necessary for success. I won't let a bad perception keep me away from success this time.

A big reason success may never happen to us is because we get discouraged. Especially when others don't believe in us. I've told people about my desire to write a book, and there wasn't much enthusiasm from them. There wasn't much encouragement. Nobody is wrong for not motivating you. It should already be there within yourself. It is your vision, nobody else will see it the way you will. Don't get discouraged from others not being supportive or excited about something you want. Believe in yourself and keep going. Remember it is all perception.

There is no such thing as failure. It is impossible to fail. Failure only comes to those who stop pursuing a goal. Or to those who have never given themselves any definite purpose in life. If you're having trouble figuring your purpose out, think about what you would do if money didn't exist. Think about something that comes naturally to you, but you may have never paid much attention to it.

For me, it was always writing. Even when I was

younger and in college, the writing classes were always the easiest. I felt like others could easily write as well, but it came so naturally to me I never thought of becoming a writer. Now all I must do is stay committed. Even in moments when we don't succeed at our first attempts, it is a step toward success. Imagine if a salesman quit after the first person they attempted to convince to buy said no. Imagine if you just stopped trying the first time you fell off your bike. We must give our minds time to construct our new experiences enough to where we are familiarized and become masters. This is a natural process. Failure is perceived as not being capable when, in reality, it's only a representation of how unfamiliar we are with whatever we're doing.

If you keep going you notice how easier it becomes. Failure can easily make us want to stop and ask what's the point. Stop yourself immediately and realize that your thoughts are why most people fail. Stop yourself during a negative thought and tell yourself, I won't allow myself to vibrate at this low frequency. Whenever you face adversity, look at other people who failed but continued only to succeed eventually.

Thomas Edison failed at creating the light bulb. It took between 1000 to 10000 times to get it right. Not to mention his teacher told him he was, "too stupid to learn anything." Jim Carrey dropped out of school at age fifteen to get a job as a janitor to help his family financially. In his first stand-up comedy attempt, he was booed off the stage.

Jay-Z started his label, but that was only because of several attempts to be signed by a record label first.

They all declined. Bill Gates's first business Traf-O-Data, eventually flopped but led to the creation of Microsoft. Henry Ford failed countless times before he was successful at his automotive company. Even the people working for him may have thought he was crazy at one point when he asked them to design a motor that was at the time perceived as impossible. Eventually, it happened through persistence.

Colonel Sanders (inventor of KFC chicken) was 62 with a 105 dollar social security check in his hand trying to pitch his chicken recipe to restaurants. It is said over a thousand people told him he was crazy. Walt Disney was fired in 1919 form his Kansas City Star paper because he "lacked imagination and had no good ideas." His first go at the business even led to bankruptcy. We all know eventually his persistence led to generations of cartoons.

All they had was a dream that they never stopped chasing. There was a desire for something that created persistence. If you want something, you will be persistent in getting it. The list goes on and on. So don't think you're any different. It should get to the point where failure should excite you because you know that by continuing, you're separating yourself from most who would quit. I've always hated the thought of rejection. I'd avoid it at all costs. This is the main reason I'd never really accomplish anything. Rejection doesn't mean you aren't good enough or don't have a great idea.

In the same way, you will receive rejections, you will receive acceptance. You know yourself more than anybody else ever will. Never let someone tell you what makes you happy or what's worthy of high praise.

Trust the process

One way to look at failure is to look at it as a part of the process. We only see people and their success. We never really look at what they may have gone through to get there. I was reading an interesting book called, "Shoe Dog." Phil Knight in the book was describing his journey into making Nike one of the biggest brands we see today. It was truly a journey. You talk about a guy flying across the country twice to fight for rights to sell his shoes with no guarantee of how things would turn out. That's inspiring. On the plane, he had the same thoughts as you and I would. Thoughts of giving up, and questioning why he's even still trying. And at the end of the day, his desires overcame them. He did it anyway.

If you have a goal don't stop. Keep going. Nothing worth having comes easy. Instead of looking at this as if it's a struggle, why don't you just enjoy the process? Enjoy the journey chasing this dream is going to take you on. You don't know who you will meet, and what other opportunities will come your way. So much happens through action. We find ourselves in places and positions we never thought we'd be. Simply because we put ourselves out there. Never lose sight of this.

We wonder why we listen to motivational speeches and are filled with energy and are ready to act. It's because our thoughts are in a great vibrational state. Then we sink right back into the inconsistent reactionary negative thoughts that put us right back in the state of mind that gets us nowhere. No, not anymore. Repeat and remind yourself until your subconscious mind believes it and you don't have to fight these thoughts. Think if someone told you that your idea is golden and is worth millions, but you have to find the right person to invest in it. Your confidence would probably increase. You would act as if you know you have that million dollars, you just have to come across the right person.

The beauty in perspective is that nobody has the formula for what is good and what is bad. It is a matter of perspective. They could be judges, managers, agents, etc. Somebody will see value in your ideas, your goals, and aspirations. Especially when you come off as confident and willing to do what you must do to achieve it. You don't have to know how it is going to happen, leave that to your subconscious mind and the wonders of the universe. It has the power to bring to us anything we ask, we have to trust it. It has guided you to attracting everything you have in your life today. You have all those things because you wanted it.

Your deepest desires and goals are achievable as well, just enjoy the process, and know it is coming. Know that with each call, or whatever specific action we take, no matter how small, it is getting closer and closer to us. It is a law that we get what we put in. The universe gives us back whatever energy we give out. Remember that. Focus on what you want to do, and you will notice ways to make it come true. The same way if we focus on negative things, we'll notice them in our reality more. Take control of what you see so that you can see your way to success.

Writing a book isn't as easy as it first seemed to me. It takes consistent revising and expression that can sometimes be hard to put into words. I've noticed that I write more when I'm in a great mood. At the same time when I feel down, I become more expressive. It's been a true journey for me, as I thought it would. Recreating that positive attitude and changing my perception gives me that energy that made me start the book in the first place. Reminding myself all those people have gone through the same process as I have brought that inspiration back. Creating this book has been a long process, but getting it published can be even longer. I imagine J.K Rowling, the author of Harry Potter, and her initial struggles with getting her book published. It was denied over ten times. Imagine the faith, desire, and mental strength someone must have to continue to go on.

When you realize what it takes, and that there are people out there no different than you, it motivates you. Sometimes we get caught up thinking it is just us that seem to have bad luck. Or it is us that can't do it, but others can. Know that you're not the only one going through whatever you're going through. Everyone has been there.

The Jump

There I was standing outside my mom's new apartment after her and my dad had split helping her move in. I never could understand why until I got older, why things didn't work out for them. I never really knew how to handle that situation. I had always been under a two-parent household. I was 15 at the time, and life still had many lessons to teach me.

I was mature enough to understand that some things just don't work out. I'd consider that situation a reality check at an early age for me. Something that possibly stills rubs off on me in subtle ways I may have never acknowledged or even considered regarding my own love life. It, in a way, made me realize the illusion in marriage.

We have this idea of meeting someone and living happily ever after when it's rarely ever this simple. Sometimes people are only in your life for a particular time or are there to teach you something. Sometimes love doesn't even mean you both were meant to be together. It's made me appreciate it when I happen to find an authentic connection like that even if it doesn't last forever. It's also made me comfortable with being alone, knowing that sometimes we get lost in other people. We get so consumed in making them happy or giving them all our time and energy that we lose ourselves. This all comes from experience, and we all live and learn.

This all was the least of my concern at my age. I was going through my transition to a young man and marriage was the last thing on my mind, yet girls were becoming more of an interest to me naturally. My voice was getting deeper, and I was taking care of my appearance, getting waves, you know, trying to get the ladies.

The experiences I would gain during this summer would be more valuable than I could've ever predicted. As we got settled in, there were a few guys my age that I would hang around. We became pretty cool friends. One day we're all hanging out by the pool, and I had been bragging about being able to swim. My ego wouldn't allow me to admit I didn't know how. We were all standing around the pool, and I was pretending as if I was going to jump in when I really wouldn't dare. I wasn't stupid. I didn't know how to swim.

I'd eventually have to tell them, but it wasn't as embarrassing as it first seemed. Everyone doesn't know how to swim. It wasn't a big deal. At the same time, it was because that was one of the main activities kids in that city participated in during the summer. Smacking the pool was fun but only if you were able to dive in the deep end, it made you cool. This was my first time seeing the pool, and I was around the edge, looking down at how deep it was. It was about 8 feet. At this moment I hadn't been paying attention to G. He had snuck behind me, and before I knew it, he pushed me over the edge.

The amount of fear that came over my body was unlike anything I may have ever experienced. While I'm still in the air, it was if it happened in slow motion. I thought to myself, "Wow, I'm really about to drown. Why the hell did I pretend as if I could swim? What the hell am I gonna do now?" Before I knew it, I had hit the water, and my instincts kicked in. I knew that 5 feet wasn't that far away from where I landed and I knew how to stroke. I just didn't know how to stay afloat.

Immediately as I hit the water I started swimming to the shallow end. As I was doing this something came over me. It was as if I wanted to face this challenge of swimming. Instead of continuing to stroke to the smaller end, I rose in the deep end, attempting to swim. I immediately realized I had made a mistake. I wasn't staying afloat, in fact, I was drowning. If I had been calm, I'd realized how easy swimming was. Instead, I panicked.

I always thought to myself if I had ever been in a situation where I was drowning, I could keep coming up for air until someone saved me. This planned failed quickly because every time I would come up for air, I was splashing water in my nose and mouth. Not only that I quickly got tired. I didn't know if they had run or if I would live past that day. I still remember the last time I tried to come up and finally gave up.

I was sinking, and it appeared to be over. Before I knew it I was standing up in the five feet while still splashing. My eyes were of someone who was in shock about the whole thing. G had dived in to save me, and I hadn't even realized anybody was around. He pushed and punched me to the shallow end, which I wasn't too far from anyway before I decided to face my fears. There I was embarrassed sitting on the edge of the pool breathing in and out more thankful for air then I'd ever been in my life.

From that moment on, I would stay away from the

deep end. I would dog paddle for months in the shallow area of the pool. I had got pretty good at it without allowing my feet to touch the ground. One day my friends were at the pool, and they were all diving in, jumping over chairs, running around in a line having a blast. I had learned how to dive as well but only in the five feet. I finally had enough as my friends hyped me to jump in the deep end, and I stood there, I remember how I felt before I attempted the jump. I was uncertain and felt extremely uncomfortable, but there was this desire that I had to learn how to swim.

It made me realize I'd be willing to possibly drown again just to have the exhilarating feeling or rush, which holds the key to the most blissful feelings life has to offer. It was on the other side, but fear and potential failure were the only things keeping me from this experience. And if I drowned surely someone would save me again, hopefully. Before I knew it I did it.

I ran jumped off the edge headfirst into the deep in of the pool. I dove directly across and swam to the other side, grabbing on to the side, which was the smartest safest thing to do. Then, I let go and practiced the same techniques I used to stay afloat in the five feet and it worked. I was swimming, kinda. It was more dog paddling. Hahahahah I would get better and better and eventually I made it look easy.

While this story is very comical as I recall this moment now, I look at the lessons I can take from that experience that reveal a bigger message. First, I could've drowned. I recently saw a video of hundreds of kids at a pool party.

There was a kid who died because he drowned and nobody seemed to notice. There were phones out recording as if it were more important than a life. I saw this video after writing this, and it only made me realize why I wanted to share this story in the first place. It's because at that moment as I was drowning, I felt how close death can be.

I still remember it all so vividly. It makes me not want to take anything for granted. I've seen many videos of people having near-death experiences where if they were standing just one foot to the left, they may have gotten hit by that car or somehow dodged an object that could've killed them. At any given moment anything can happen. This life we have doesn't last forever.

Instead of us spending it thinking about all the things we don't have or being depressed, we should realize how many things there are to celebrate our very existence. Secondly, life is sacrifice. We all have to make them to receive the things we want and deserve. There are things that could potentially hurt us but if we overcome it we can experience the most blissful moments you could ever imagine. It's no different than the jump you take to start your business career, acting career, modeling career, etc.

Sure there are risks involved, and it could all potentially end very badly. If I could've avoided the anxiety tied to the bad things that could potentially happen before that jump, I would've, but at the end of the day, you have to do it.

I remember watching a video of Will Smith explaining how fearful he was when he first attempted to skydive. When you think about failing at this, it probably means it'll cost you your life. He went on to explain how it was one of the greatest moments of his life. Why is it that when we live on the edge like this, it creates the most amazing experiences? It's because there's no such thing as failure. Had I not been brave enough to jump in the deep end or write this book, I may feel as if I kept myself from falling when, in reality, not trying would be a more significant failure. You only fail at the things you never even attempt to do.

Think about a time where you had a near-death experience or were in a situation that could've ended badly for you. Think about how much your life would be changed. Now feel the gratification that comes with still being healthy and taking your next breath. Concentrate on how peaceful and appreciative you feel at this moment. This feeling you have now was all created by your own thoughts. Use this gift to create consistent blissful experiences in your life.

> *"The cave you fear to enter holds the treasure you seek" ~ Joseph Campbell*

The illusion

Fear is an illusion. Fear consistently holds us back from opportunities that hold the keys to our biggest dreams and desires. We may seem comfortable within these fears, but we are far from content. None of us want to be old thinking back on our life on the things that we should've done. Asking ourselves what if? Some of us already ask ourselves these questions. Are we going to do this our whole life?

At some point, we're going to have to face them. When you aren't doing what you genuinely love to do when you aren't chasing after a dream you want, eventually you'll become fed up. Don't become fed up when it's too late. Fear isn't real because the outcomes are going to happen regardless.

The anxiety we have doesn't change the outcome. Me spotting an aggressive dog and being fearful of its actions are pointless. Either the dog is going to attack me, or it isn't. The fear I have built up isn't going to help me. Be fearless. Successful people will tell you to do something that makes you scared every day. Why? Because that's when we experience the most blissful experiences in our life. That's when we look back and realize how far we've come.

I see fear as an adrenaline rush now. I know that means I'm really living. Fear may be a misconception. Our body in a fearful state may be excited. Sure, we may feel uncomfortable, but we aren't scared, we are uncertain. If you think about it, you never have anything to lose.

When you do something despite your fearful feelings, I guarantee you will learn something that takes you further than you would have had you not done anything at all. Of course, when we don't do anything we fail anyway by default. Sometimes we forget we don't have anything to lose. In every case, the fear we have can be entirely altered by our perception.

Whenever you are having doubtful or fearful thoughts, think about how you perceive the situation. Here's a funny movie scene that comes to mind when I think about fear. Adam Sandler starred in a movie called Waterboy. Toward the end of the movie, they were playing the final football game of the season. The head coach was extremely fearful of the opposing team's head coach. Adam Sandler told him to picture the coach as someone you're not afraid of. He then pictured the coach as a baby. It removed his fearful state and gave him the courage to call the right plays, bringing them to victory.

I don't know why this pops in my head, probably because of how funny it was to me. It still gives us a simple analogy of how it is all in our heads. We can overcome fearful states. Once we do it'll become a habit. All of this sounds simple, and you've probably heard this before. But why don't they stick with us? It's because we haven't changed our paradigm to where we actually overcome these fears. We haven't gained the awareness to counteract these thoughts quickly. That's all it takes. Being comfortable your whole life isn't going to get you what you want. Doing new things, trying different things, and taking new paths will.

If you are wondering why you haven't had success in your life, ask yourself what efforts have you made to make them come true. Your mind will naturally try and protect you from harm. It is how we gained a keen awareness of predators or anything dangerous. It can fool you into never doing things you're not familiar with.

Your mind will always tell you, "No that might not be

safe." "You sure you want to do that? You've never done that before." "It is safer if we do what we're more familiar with." But you're also an explorer with the ability to search and discover. You must tap into that side of your mind. If someone were to offer you 100 dollars to call 100 people and try to sell them an item, you'd be surprised at the ending result. Not in how many items you actually sell, but the confidence and habit you've gained. After those calls, it won't be hard at all to call someone. It never is as bad as is seems. How many times have we perceived certain things and then experienced them for ourselves and said, "Aw, that wasn't so bad." This has happened to all of us plenty of times.

Our perception of things painted a picture that we wanted no part of, but if we are brave enough to try, it rarely is as bad as it seems. In fact, we may want to do it again, and again. Keep this in mind when things appear to be scary, or you perceive something you think you wouldn't like. That feeling of overcoming fear is great.

One reason is that you realize you almost missed out on something that was an illusion created in your head. Sometimes you may laugh at the fact you were fearful. Accomplishing things makes us feel great. Even the smallest tasks.

Procrastination and fear seemed to be embedded. If we're not fearful, we put off tasks because we think that is a more fulfilling feeling than the accomplishment when we get it out the way. Just get it over with. The weight that leaves your chest when you're done is like no other. Think about the feeling you get after you've cleaned up your house, or finished that homework, overcame a fear, or mowed the lawn. It could be anything.

I must say I've procrastinated, and it honestly becomes a habit like anything else. Imagine if your first thought was that feeling of accomplishment whenever you're faced with a task or something you need to get done. The reward centers in your brain will feed off that thought instead of rewarding you for avoiding it. It is brain change we are attempting to do. The brain feeds off repetition. The more you fear out of habit, the more you will instinctively fear everything. The more you put off tasks, the more you will instinctively procrastinate.

It is the opposite when you change your habits and ways of thinking. The more we understand the way our mind works, the more accountability we can take for our actions. I myself may reread this chapter over because if there's any advice I can take from myself, this is it.

Talk to yourself positively 24/7. I now understand the deeper meaning behind why you should never say I can't. Never say you're afraid, or it's impossible. Say I'm brave, say I can, say I will. You will accept these statements and your subconscious mind will make them come true. You shall no longer program yourself to be a limited version of your potential. You have the choice, so believe in yourself, speak positively to yourself.

We often don't pay much mind to these statements as if they don't make a difference. I am here to tell you that they do. They change the activity in your brain. They turn your perception; they improve your life. If a kid growing up has heard repeatedly that he can't do something eventually his subconscious mind will accept this as true. Even if he initially begged to differ. It is the repetition involved that made this happen. It's the main reason we accept the world the way it is today without questioning anything. You've heard it so much, you've accepted what you've been told.

Water

This works the same way through experiments with the molecular structure of water. A man named Dr. Masaru Emoto discovered how the change in our thoughts and the words we speak change the expression. Our bodies are all made up of close to 70 percent water. To undermine this significant information is to completely ignore the physical manifestations of the very words you speak to others and yourself. The water molecules literally form different positions when they are presented with positive or negative emotions.

Interestingly, the fear we have when it comes to people who appear to have power over us is equally the same on the opposite end. Some of the most influential people in the world instill fear in people because they ironically fear you in the same sense. They know that fear is one of the most manipulative ways to control you. Fear strikes an emotion in us that makes us think illogically. We're more worried than focusing on realizing our strength.

We are thinking emotionally and it never makes our situation any better. Think about how 9/11 created a perception of another country that still lasts today. When our brain marks certain things as dangerous, it sticks with us forever. It can make us treat others wrong even when we consciously know we're being irrational. It can hold us back from showing fortitude in life's most critical moments. It paints a picture of the world that isn't real, only a film projected in our head.

Fear can hold you back from meeting a potential wife, taking a job across the country, giving a speech, asking questions, expressing yourself through music, poetry, art, and other forms. It can essentially keep you from success. That's all that fear does. It gives you a false feeling of comfort, but you are deep down fearful. Much of propaganda isn't based on desires, it is based on people's fears. They know fear can kill any desire you have for yourself and the potential success in your life. There are even marketing concepts that play on these fears. Kill these thoughts because they will only hold you back in this life.

Right now, think of whatever it is you want to do. We all have vivid visions of how our life should be. Usually, they never happen because there isn't much action that takes place after. We assume it's just an unrealistic dream that can't come true for us. We've already ruined our faith and trust in ourselves in making it come true. You're more than capable if you are willing to try consistently. It is all in your head.

If you can remember this in those moments where you feel fear or doubt, you can channel that energy into persistence and fortitude. Two things that will help you to achieve anything. It's so easy to think negatively. I don't why this is. I do know that this is the reason we never put enough effort into accomplishing things. Looking back on my life, I can recall many times where my attitude caused the failure in my life, if anything. Fear of rejection, fear of criticism, fear of not being accepted for who I am, fear of not being good enough, fear of failure. Once you conclude that the one thing that makes you stand out is you being yourself, you've discovered your gift.

Rich dad Poor Dad

As I was writing this chapter and looking back on everything I've written so far, I felt as if something was missing. I stumbled upon a book called Rich Dad Poor Dad written by Robert Kiyosaki in my closet. The timing of this is what was so amazing to me. The way we can feel like something is missing and somehow find it is incredible. It was initially because my phone game controller was charging, so I found myself sitting there looking for something to do. I finally sat up and realized I had time to read.

For some reason, I never took the time to read this book. As I looked in my closet, something guided me to finally take a look at it after all this time despite buying it months ago. It was clear that the goal of the author was to instill valuable insight on financial literacy. After carefully studying the information, I realized how this book and its lessons went beyond money. It taught me something that supported the things I've been trying to express throughout this book.

Earlier in chapter one, I explained why money doesn't equal happiness. Rich Dad Poor Dad only enhanced my awareness of how our perspective of money can cause us to get caught in an illusion. I've always been able to acknowledge it all being a game, money that is. I've never been able to identify why it was able to keep millions of people so trapped, though. Rich Dad Poor Dad identified something that is so strong, it supports why I found it so significant to write about perception in the first place. The book is merely a depiction of the choices we have in life. Sometimes our beliefs are so emotionally driven that we fool ourselves into believing we don't have a choice. We can become so misguided because we may have trouble identifying harmful emotions that alter our whole approach to life. We become slaves to our emotions. The main reason money can keep people working countless hours and paying taxes despite being paid the bare minimum is fear.

We have this fear-based emotion that drives us to work for money because we don't want to be without it. So we do what appears to be the logical thing which is getting a job. There are certain statements made by rich dad that stuck out to me. Just reading and genuinely thinking about money differently made me change how I see it all. As hard as it may be to grasp the concept of what he is saying, it is all because of how deeply misguided we are about money and the denial we are in regarding our true feelings. I'll try to make more sense out of some of these statements he makes.

The Rat Race

In the book, he says, "Most people have a price. And they have a price because of human emotions named fear and greed. First, the fear of being without money motivates us to work hard, and then once we get that paycheck, greed or desire starts us thinking about all the beautiful things money can buy. The pattern is then set. The pattern of get up, go to work, pay bills; get up go to work, pay bills. Two emotions, fear, and greed forever control people's lives. Offer them more money and they continue the cycle by increasing their spending, the rat race."

This statement makes me see how we can easily become a part of the trap. It truly is our emotions that guide our behavior rather than us truly thinking. He never appears to make people feel bad for having a regular job although the harsh truth makes it appear so. It's more of an eye-opener to what emotions can make us do. He points out how emotion is simply energy in motion. This is why we feel compelled to do things that are backed behind powerful feelings like fear, anger, or greed. It's all that we are, pure energy.

The speed in which we may vibrate based on feelings can be at such a high speed it appears motionless. It can also be vibrating so slow it appears motionless. A job from his perspective is something designed for the short term. Nobody wants to work 8 hours a day their whole life. Some people enjoy what they do for a living, but still may prefer to live a life that didn't require them to get up at some point continually.

When we truly think about what's making us do the things we do, we will realize how it can create an approach that gives us a feeling of doing the right thing. He talks about how the rich know how to make money work for them, not work for money. This will make you look at the world in ways you may never have when it comes to making money. Instead of your immediate emotional reactions, always directing you straight to a job application, you'll start looking around you for opportunities to make money work for you. He says when you do this once, you never miss an opportunity to make money work for you.

It's almost as if it directs you or helps you see opportunities for wealth that you never acknowledged because your idea of how to get money was limited. Many of us have had jobs that require us to convince customers to buy items. If we create something for ourselves sometimes, we may only need one or two sales to easily make what we'd make in a week working a 9-5. If we just think wealth or money is all about going to college and getting a high paying job we'd be misguided. It is the safest and most logical approach to people, and it can put us in situations that leave us with tons of debt. All because of how our emotions may guide us.

I don't think having a job is a bad thing or the message he's trying to send, especially if it's something you love to do. He's simply pointing out why this money game works in the first place. The more you understand this information, the more you will see money as something that no longer controls you. You will see how it is the attachment to money rather rich or poor that can be deeply embedded in fear.

Beyond the money is the control it has over you emotionally. We don't truly think rationally when we are in this state of mind. It all seems like the right things to do and appears as if we don't have a choice. Making money work for you and reaching that next level of wealth isn't easy to do. I realize how it's not meant for the average person to understand as well. The low tier jobs people have across the world are often the most important to society even though the pay doesn't truly represent that. Depending on how we may view the world and money, which is simply energy, will determine our approach to it all.

Fear of losing

This concept applies to everyone. The author continues to explain how the money game works and how it is intertwined with our emotional outlooks.

"Even rich people do this. The many reasons many rich people are rich isn't because of desire, but because of fear. They believe that money can eliminate the fear of being poor, so they amass tons of it, only to find the anxiety gets worse. Now they fear to lose the money. I have friends who keep working even though they have plenty. I know people who have millions who are more afraid now than when they were poor. They're terrified of losing it all."

The fears that drove them to get rich got worse. That weak and needy part of their soul is actually screaming louder. They don't want to lose the big houses, the cars, and the high life money has bought them. They worry about what their friends would say if they lost all their money. Many are emotionally desperate and neurotic, although they look rich and have more money. The kid then asked, "So is a poor man happier?" The man replied, "I don't think so; the avoidance of money is just as psychotic as being attached to money."

If our attitudes are always centered around money, whether we have a small amount of it or tons of it, it will create anxiety or unstable emotions. Money makes us move, it is what people desire and fear not having. His statement makes me realize how life's goals should steer more toward the balance of one's feelings. We want enough energy and feelings to strive and get money, but we don't want it to control us.

We also want to identify these emotions and think about how we can create a different approach to money or even our happiness, which can generate wealth without constant feelings of fear and greed. Those emotions will make us do things to get money irrationally in these mental states. That's why I've approached making money with something that I love to do and makes me feel happy. This will rid yourself of doing anything out of fear.

Instead, you're doing it out of love. Instead of receiving that money and spending it with a mindset full of greed, we share and help others, knowing it will only come back to us.

The money will forever come and go in life. If we can realize that and make the best with what we have in those moments when we have plenty, and times when we don't, we then have mastered our attitude towards money. You may now see why you can be miserable with or without money when you don't have an awareness of your emotions. Know that there's a bigger picture to this all. We think life and everything is centered around money when it is the power of our emotions that created it in the first place.

Money is an illusion

As I continued reading this book, the author pointed out something else significant about money to me.

"The rich know that money is an illusion, truly like the carrot for the donkey. It's only out of fear and greed that the illusion of money is held together by billions of people who believe that money is real. It's not. Money is really made up. It is only because of the illusion of confidence and the ignorance of the masses that this house of cards stands."

As much as I read this book thinking it would give me the answers to how to become wealthy. It helped me realize the illusion within it all. Think about how free you feel once you come to the realization that all of this is made up. Think to yourself what life would be like if money didn't exist. The money game is still a part of life. Many play this game simply because, as a collective, we always give it our energy. If only we had enough awareness to understand things don't have to be this way.

Even within this system, if we understood the real power we have as a collective, we'd make it work for us. Think about how much money is generated for people who need donations for some tragic occurrence. The feeling you get makes you emotional enough to want to help. Think about if we came together and made money work for us as a people.

There's enough money in the world to end world hunger and many other things. Why hasn't it changed? Greed. As much as we want for ourselves when we look at the bigger picture we see how it only hurts others and the world. The greed will eventually catch up to us and hurt us as well. Greed makes people feel no responsibility to take care of the oceans. We regularly throw garbage in or the air that's continuously being polluted.

Everyone prioritizes money over everything. It makes people do immoral things for a profit. The earth, our bodies, spirit, and character all come second to money. It's almost as if it's a disease. What are we doing to each other? Our approach to happiness is off and it shows how selfish we are. We don't see how being helpful and freeing ourselves from greed will ultimately make us happy.

It is only when we show greed that we slowly destroy the world and ourselves. We think we are doing the right thing when we're showing the exact reason why the world is in the frenzy it's in today. Money is only used as a concept to make us appear better than other people. It gives us this feeling of being different or superior. When you genuinely think about it, we're all beyond it. The moment we start seeing the world in more enlightening ways, the more you'll see how your soul, your spirit, your mind was here before these concepts.

Familiarity

When you think of any person who may be successful now, they always have a story of the things they did when they first began their careers. A music artist may have sold CDs out the trunk of their car for a long time before getting enough exposure to ascend to the next level. A writer may have written dozens of books before the next one takes off on another level. Then people go and appreciate the older work more.

In some cases, the author doesn't live to see the praise his creations received. The most interesting thing about success is that you have to start somewhere. As we begin the road to our dreams the motivation alone will put us in situations that the lack of motivation won't. The key and unconscious thing going on here are the things we become familiar with, and the people who become familiar with us.

Once something enters our subconscious mind, whether that be a learned behavior, a picture, a thing, a word, or any experience we have with the objective world, it is stored. It's why we can immediately know when we've seen something before and when we haven't. Even at times when we can't quite make out the exact name of what we're seeing or thinking, it can be on the tip of our tongue. It's usually the feeling of familiarity that brings about that big statement, "I've seen this before" or "Do I know you?" Even when we can't consciously recall, the feeling we get still in a sense directs us. As you put yourself out there, people will notice you whether they realize it or not. We can consciously ignore things, but we cannot block things from entering our subconscious mind. This means you could ignore a commercial, and it can still influence you without your realization.

In fact, besides Super Bowl commercials most people pay them no mind most times, but they still work. That's why marketing companies still spend millions doing it. Because despite whether you're paying attention doesn't change the extent to which it can influence you to buy the product, only through familiarity.

One of the most tricky ways it's done in the music industry is how you can hear a song a few times and don't like it. Say it's always on the radio or becomes a huge trend. Whether you wanted to learn the song consciously or not is now irrelevant. You may catch yourself singing this song even though at one point in time, you said you didn't like it. In reality, you're just familiar with the melodies, the hook, and other influences like your peers may even make you participate in dances as well.

There have been studies done in classrooms as

well. Women were asked in several studies about guys in their class and to what extent they were attractive. The interesting thing about all of the studies is how the men that were seen as most attractive were the guys who were in the class the most often. The guys who rarely appeared weren't as familiar as the guys who came more consistently, so subtly there was some sense of comfort and liking for those particularly familiar. This isn't always the case, and I don't know if this will make any guys in college go to class more, but never underestimate the power within these examples.

Him

It was another busy morning for Sandra. At least it was hump day, and no matter how busy a day was set out for her, she always made time to stop at Starbucks for coffee. We all have these particular habits that make our day right. Some people need their coffee. Some people have to meditate/yoga to start their day. Some people may read and others may sleep until the last minute they can before pushing being late. All of these types of things happen out of habit.

It can become so routine that we don't feel right if we haven't done things this way. It could throw our entire day off. The routines we go through give us this sense of comfort to go about doing things in the right mind frame. That's why Steph Curry has a pre-game workout he does, and many other athletes like Michael Phelps have strict routines.

Anyway, this morning was like any other morning until she noticed a man in front of her while standing in line. Sandra was always busy, rarely had time for a man, but when she saw someone appealing to her, she did not mind looking. But how did she know this man was appealing, she was staring at his back. The shape of his shoulders, the way he was standing, and the shape of his head made Sandra feel as if she knew him.

She began to become a bit anxious for him to turn around. As he finally ordered and took his coffee, he turned around, heading for the door. He passed her on the way out, and their eyes finally met. In less than a second Sandra had become star-struck, her pupils were dilated. Her body had been overcome with this feeling of joy as if she had found her long lost friend.

Her whole demeanor had shifted into this state of excitement and nervousness, and she didn't know exactly why. She couldn't pinpoint why she had been so excited. She saw attractive guys all the time, but this was different. There was something familiar about him, but she wasn't sure, so as he walked past her, she glanced away, avoiding any signs of coming off as interested. As he passed her his eyes got big as if he had seen his long lost friend too. He looked as if he was about to come and approach her.

Looking a bit amazed, he kept walking as if he was unsure exactly why he felt as if he knew her. Sandra got her coffee after having to think about what to order even though she orders the same thing every morning. She was just a little distracted and disappointed. She may never get to the source of why he looked so familiar. As she walked outside and headed for her car he was outside waiting. She could've left but seen he was walking over, so she pretended to be looking for something in her car to give him time to come. "Hi," he said. What's your name, you look so familiar.

At this point, she was overwhelmed with joy. She had forgotten how it felt to be so mesmerized by a male and out of nowhere at that. "I'm Sandra; I see you need your coffee this morning too, huh?" She gave a nervous chuckle. "Every morning!" He corrected her. "My name is Austin. I'm down here with my family that I visit every so often. Look I got to run, but I came over here because I couldn't help but introduce myself. I would love to continue this conversation, but I'm already a bit late for a meeting with a friend. Could I have your number and maybe we can continue to talk?"

Sandra gave a look as if this would be a tough decision despite the fact she had been waiting for him to ask. "Sure, I guess." She said. By this time, Sandra had examined this man down from his hair and cologne to his belt and shoes. She liked the fact he had to go; it made her feel as if his time was valuable. So any time he made for her would make her feel important. She didn't actually consciously acknowledge this, but those are the type of things women pick up on that can make a man even more attractive. "Maybe I can show you around. I'm from here." She said. "Ok, well hopefully I'll see you again". He said.

From that moment on she had been waiting for her phone to vibrate from him. Later that day he finally texted her. They eventually started talking more and more. He would text her good morning every day. They talked on the phone and laughed for hours. They eventually went on a date as well. In two weeks, her life had drastically changed. She thinks she may have caught feelings for a man she hadn't known a month ago.

Everything seemed to be happening so fast. Something had begun to make her feel differently. It was as if everything was too perfect. She had feelings of anxiety after entertaining the thought of this connection being too good to be true. I mean, after all, Austin was single, attractive to her, he had a great job and loved his family. Surely he had a woman back home. Or was something wrong with him that she hadn't found out? Her thoughts continued to race.

Meeting someone's family is a big step. She hadn't met them yet and was nervous about the fact he may ask her soon. Austin would be leaving back to his home which was in California in another week. He promised they would keep in touch, and he would fly her out and everything. "What if he doesn't, though? What if he forgets about me?"

Just the thought started making her doubt everything. Her confidence in herself and the future for them lowered. She wasn't feeling very optimistic about the future with him. Sandra had done this before. The last few good guys she had met, she pushed them away because of her fear of being hurt. She had always done this. Ever since her last relationship she always would begin to contemplate these adverse outcomes.

Sometimes when everything is going right, we panic,

thinking something terrible is going to happen. She had been causing her own problems by being too cautious. She had realized this pattern and why deep down she did want to fall in love again. "I won't let myself go down this road again." She said. It was kind of late, and despite the fact he might be sleep, she texted Austin. She remembered how she was supposed to show him around and decided to tell him to meet her at this particular location. She usually only went there by herself. He immediately texted back, "Be there!"

This secret spot was a path through the woods that eventually led to a beautiful, quiet, and peaceful beach. Sandra hadn't been there since her sophomore year of college during a spring break. It was the last time she recalled having the time of her life. She arrived first and Austin showed up soon after.

His face was so excited when he pulled up to the spot. "I can't believe this, he said. I haven't been here in years." He said. "Wait, you know where we're going?" Sandra said, surprised. "Yes, I came here with some buddies before and we had a ball. Word around town is not many people come out here or know about this spot." He said. Sandra jokingly replied, "Well apparently not, you know exactly where we are." They both laughed and walked through the woods following the path.

As they arrived the glare of the ocean as the sun was just going down caught both their eyes for a few seconds. "It's beautiful, isn't it?" He said. "Yes, I usually come out here to just get away you know?" She said. "Yea, I remember being out here with my friends. They all had girlfriends and I was single. Haha. I did see one girl that I wanted to meet, but I never got the chance. It's crazy how I'm back here again except this time I have that chance."

Sandra wanted to ask what he meant by that, but before she could ask he continued. "I remember everything going great. Then chaos broke out. She was right over on the other side of the bonfire. The cops were on their way and all I remember was looking at her eyes for a split second. It was the only time she had looked back at me. My friends were rushing me and pulling me to the car and all I could do was look in her eyes amongst everything that was happening. It was like I didn't care. I just wanted to meet her. I never did." He said.

All of a sudden, Sandra started to remember that night of her spring break and what happened that night. She started recalling how drunk she was. She then started remembering this moment of staring at this guy over the fire while her friends were panicking and running around. "I was just standing there." She said. "Then my friends grabbed me, and we left immediately."

Sandra stood up immediately. "It's you! That's where I know you from! I knew when I saw you in Starbucks, I knew you from somewhere, I just, I just. "I know," Austin said. "The moment I saw you at Starbucks, I knew who you were. Your eyes, I could never forget the feeling they gave me. It was the same feeling when I saw you that morning. I never brought it up to you because I had planned to take you here and explain. I didn't think you'd possibly remember."

Sandra was speechless. As quickly as she'd fall into

this negative way of thinking where she felt like things were too good to be true, it only got worse. How did she end up here? How did this happen? This wasn't the movies, things like this only happened in movies. Well, this was reality, she was still awake, and Austin was still standing there looking nervous. "I want you to come back to LA with me." He said. Sandra began to get lightheaded, so they sat down.

I know all of this is overwhelming, but I can't let you out of my life again. Not twice. I never stopped thinking about that night." Sandra knew at this moment she had a big decision to make. Sure she could easily sway herself to say no. I mean her job, her apartment, her friends were all here. She couldn't just up and leave. Then again, she knew at some point she had to do something that she was afraid to do. She had to face her fears. Her fears of leaving the town she always loved, her fears of falling in love, her fears of stepping outside of her comfort zone all hit at once.

Then Sandra got this feeling that she never had before. She was no longer afraid. She felt ready for whatever life had to offer. She didn't focus on what could go wrong. She focused on the many beautiful experiences she could look forward to. She slowly started smiling as she was glancing at the last few minutes of the sun above the ocean. "I'll go!" They stood there and kissed as the sun went down.

We all at some point have opportunities that we either take or shy away from. It can be opportunities for a promotion, starting a business, or even approaching a guy/girl. When we are in the right frame of mind, we are ready for these opportunities. When we entertain feelings of doubt, we make excuses for why we didn't want to do it when really we're afraid. We are sometimes afraid of failure, but what about success?

Many people who have naturally gifted talents don't pursue their dreams full force because they're not ready for their life to change. You have to be ready to handle big changes in your life. It's all required to vibrate in a way that'll attract people to our work. You have to know and be at a point where you no longer even question your purpose and what you're doing.

When you are faced with those opportunities, take them, ready or not. Many people wish they could go back in the past to make different decisions because surely their life would have turned out perfect if they could change a few things. This is false. We will always have some regret for the decisions that we make, even if we could go back and redo.

The more important thing to realize is those experiences are where the real value lies. Whether a bad experience or a good one, there's something beneficial you can take from it. This is the art of embracing life and its possibilities. There's no one way to be successful or do anything. There's an abundant amount of ways to live happily. Just like Sandra, there comes a time in our life where we have to make a decision, one we've never been confident enough to. We have to see what's on that other side.

Marketing book

CHAPTER 9

Self Confidence/Self Perception

You're worthy

In chapter 1 I talked about the truth we have to face while looking in the mirror. Take a look in that mirror again. What do you see? You should see someone worthy of wealth, good health, and happiness. Our self-perception can make us feel unworthy of things we are truly worthy of. We may see others that have things we don't and perceive them as more worthy. We may even see them as better than us. This is a horrible way to go about thinking. It causes you to live the life of someone who will never receive the things you deserve.

Throughout this book, I've discussed emotions and how they're simply a result of our perceptions, which makes us act accordingly. You can see how the perception of ourselves can determine what we receive in life. The next time you look in the mirror or think about yourself, think of yourself as a genius. You may think a genius is a scholar or has a high I.Q. No, a genius is someone who sees the value of themselves within.

When we change the way we see ourselves and our potential, our confidence changes as well. We model our behavior after someone sure of what they want. People will notice this in the way you talk, walk, and the way you carry yourself. Assurance makes others confident in what you say. It makes you come off as someone persuasive. Nobody will ever be convinced you know what you are talking about if they sense someone who isn't too sure or confident in what they're saying. Even if you are speaking the truth.

People notice your energy, desire, and passion in the things you do and say. It makes them want to be a part of it or stay away. Another thing that makes confidence increase is repetition. The more you practice, the more it'll be easy to perform under pressure. Kobe Bryant once spoke on pressure and how he's able to overcome the pressure of the moment. He said that he had taken a million shots the same way. What's one more shot? Practice and prepare for whatever you are doing and you'll be more comfortable in any situation.

Earlier in this book, I gave examples of how repetition causes any specific action to sink into a deeper area of the brain. Many people describe this as top-down and bottom down. When this happens, we can perform actions without thinking. Yea, like the way you text while driving even though it is dangerous. We are really trusting our subconscious mind to drive for us while we consciously pay attention to something else. Use this to your advantage when preparing for anything in life.

Imagine trying to text and drive for the first time. You're able to do it now because the repetition has sunk to a deeper part of the brain. It never seems easy after the first try, but it naturally gets easier and easier. It becomes more and more familiar. This is why we must trust ourselves and have faith in what we do. Naturally, our mind is designed to work this way. Once you've worked at whatever it is you're doing you can become a master of your craft. People will look at you as if you are the most gifted person in the world when really you have just done it repeatedly. You've built up the neuron connections that allow you to perform it better than someone who hasn't done it repetitively. Confidence increases when you know that you've done it so many times, you'll find comfort doing it anywhere.

Nobody else in this world is any different than you. We all have the same potential. It is the self-confidence, and high self-esteem others have that makes the difference. It is your perception of them being better. If you are seeing yourself not good enough or not worthy enough, that makes the difference in your life and theirs. Stop holding yourself back. This very book may have been written and completed a lot earlier, had I not had my own doubts about myself.

I took notice at times when I would read my writings and feel as if the words were amazingly articulated. Other times that I would read it, I would feel as if maybe they weren't as great as I thought. I took notice in my shifting perspectives and realized it only supported the very conclusions of this book.

My different moods and thoughts changed the way I was perceiving it. If I were hungry or sleepy while trying to work on the book it didn't seem as good, but really my present mood was simply changing my attitude. At the end of the day, confidence in yourself is critical. It's better to use perception in a positive way rather than a detrimental one. I mean we do have a choice.

Symbolic Acceptance

There have been studies conducted where people were given a white jacket and posed as a doctor. People would see this symbolic jacket and would trust that whatever they would tell them was accurate. They never thought even critically to think about what they were doing. Their perception of him made it appear everything he said was right.

Anything he may have demanded out of them would've been done because of the authority and perception of them being smarter. There was a study done called the Milgram experiment that showed how powerful this could be. It can even cause us to overlook people when those symbolic things aren't available.

There was a famous trumpet player who makes tons of money performing around the world. He once sat at a busy train station and played. Time and time again, people walked past him without even noticing him or the music. Their perception of him was some homeless guy playing tunes. Little did they know they were walking past a professional who was playing for free without anybody caring.

There are homeless people that you may think are dumb, but are some of the smartest people in the world. Their habits, bad luck, and lack of belief in themselves may have put them in an unwanted situation. It's almost as if relying strictly on our perception of things isn't too reliable, no matter how accurate or logical we think we perceive things. Since there's no way to be sure of everything we perceive, always construct your perceptions in a way that allows you to see the beauty in it all.

As you become more aware of this you'll find beauty in yourself and others off instinct. We all can achieve things. We must instill the belief in ourselves, though. Beyond the breaks that I took to experience life, the minute I thought of somebody criticizing the book was when I felt discouraged to complete it.

It wasn't until I realized that the same way negative thoughts discouraged me, the positive ones uplifted me. Ironically, the knowledge of this was already there, which showed in the introduction of this book. The deep belief in myself wasn't though. You can have the knowledge of something, but if deep down you still feel indifferent, you'll get the same results. I knew when my mind started to accept the consistent positive thoughts when the positive affirmations were overriding my negative thoughts.

At times, I would become frustrated because as many law of attraction videos as I would watch, as many books as I would read, as many times I would meditate, I would wonder why things never manifested into my physical reality. It was because the negative beliefs were still affecting me deep down. Now, I believe. Now I see myself no different than the wealthiest man in the world.

Every book, video, and positive affirmation is only trying to do one thing. And that changes the way you perceive yourself, your circumstance, and the world. It makes the difference. You can hear quotes, motivational speeches, read books, or watch as many videos as you'd like. It won't make any difference until you wholeheartedly believe it. This can take time, know your subconscious mind is always taking things in that you're not aware of. Feed your subconscious mind, compelling content, and experiences consistently. If not, we may not strengthen or restructure ourselves enough to change.

We may feel motivated for a moment and then sink right back into the same negative thoughts that keep us from being committed to our goals. Some people naturally have this confident mindset and may not even understand why they are more successful than others. When you look at the bigger picture, we know they're no different than you, it is the mindset.

I always thought I understood this. Then I'd instinctively, or subconsciously blame the world for my lack of success. I'd say to myself yea, it's the economy, or they may have been born rich and I wasn't. I would hear, "You can do anything you put your mind to" or, "Believe in yourself." And I would always think I was doing these things. In reality, deep down there was some doubt there.

When we talk about self-confidence or even self-esteem, I have a comparable state of mind that is essential to have despite the humor behind it.

In the movie, Dumb and Dumber there was a scene towards the end that always made me laugh. One of my favorite actors Jim Carrey, had traveled to Aspen to deliver a suitcase to a woman he deep down admired and wanted. He finally arrived and stated his feelings about her. He asked what were the chances of a guy like him being with a guy like her. She said, "Not good." Then he says, "Like one in a thousand?" And she said, "No, more like one in a million." Then he paused, the look on his face was of obvious disappointment. Then suddenly he looks up and says, "So you're telling me there's a chance?"

As funny as I always thought this scene was, Jim Carrey in this movie doesn't seem as crazy or dumb as I thought. Self-confidence and self-esteem won't allow you to settle for not being good enough. Self-confident people interpret feedback the way they want to. It creates the level of persistence needed to accomplish or have anything you desire. There's a line to be drawn in regards to how unrealistic certain situations are, and I'm not saying those guys were smart in that movie. Yet, the things they experienced and possibilities they ran into, (at the end) happened from simply being in the presence of possibility. As dumb as they were supposed to be in that movie, they did end up spending a lot of money and having a lot of fun. People may have thought they were crazy, but opportunities and success never present themselves to the people who are stagnant or hesitant.

Subjective Interpretations

You don't have to be the wisest person in the world to become wealthy or successful. You must be willing to do things the average person isn't confident enough to do. I once listened to a guy giving a speech about self-confidence. He spoke on how his son wasn't that good at sports. When he would ask his son how he did in his hockey game, he would respond saying he did all these wonderful things from assists to goals. The dad paused as he looked in the crowd and said, "I didn't see my son touch the puck." The crowd had burst into laughter.

One thing he loved though was his son's self-confidence. That's something he would never take away from him. That's more valuable than any goal or assist in a game. He went on to talk about when he asked his wife out the first time, she said no. He asked again thinking she must not have seen him in the right light, or it must've been his shirt. Without his persistence, I'm sure she wouldn't be his wife today.

In fact, his persistence may have made her look at him differently to the point where she gave him a chance. I'm not saying you shouldn't take no for an answer, or become some stalker whenever a girl or guy turns you down, I'm saying you should choose how you interpret responses that don't ruin your confidence.

Think about this quote. "Do just once what others say you can't do, and you will never pay attention to their limitations again." Imagine if Muhammed Ali told himself, "I'm a failure" instead of "I'm the greatest." When we talk about grades, diplomas, credit scores, religions, science, etc... It is all created. We as people have consumed this information and have followed the conventional ways of thought provided by people no different than us.

We measure our intelligence and worth based on these creations when they have no real definitive way to measure your abilities. It is only our belief that they do that makes us feel unintelligent or smart. Our perception of ourselves is based upon how we measure up to these scores or guidelines as if they weren't invented at all. As if life came with a specific manual that gave humans a good measure of what is intelligence and what isn't.

The only people who are intelligent are the people who are inspired to use their mind power to make any vision they desire come true. We were given the gift of life to create whatever we'd like. Whatever it is that makes us happy, we have the tools to bring it to reality. While experiencing this beautiful creation, called earth. This is accurate information. The more you believe in yourself, and rid your mind of the false descriptions, the quicker you will embrace everything.

Ms. Sullivan

Ms. Sullivan was a really straightforward teacher. She would joke around, but more often than not, she was about her business. She was serious about her students as well. She paid attention to her students and expected most of them to comply with her lessons. She had a new class coming, and this was always an opportunity to set the record straight.

A lot of kids know which teachers to take seriously and which ones they could take advantage of. Ms. Sullivan wasn't to be played with. As long as you stayed on her good side, she was fun. Upon meeting her new classmates, she recognized a young man that was related to another young man she taught who already graduated. She loved that student. He did great things in her class and excelled at all his work. He made everything she taught seem simple and easy, for that she never could forget him.

Seeing someone who was closely related to him excited her. There was only one problem, Jason wasn't like his cousin Tim. He didn't have the best grades. They were average. He wasn't Tim, but Ms. Sullivan had expectations as if he were. Jason recognized this quickly and knew it wouldn't be long before he disappointed her. It wasn't that he couldn't perform better in school. It was his self-perception and lack of inspiration that made him average.

Over the course of the school year, Ms. Sullivan would constantly call on him and make him solve problems on the board in front of everybody. It was irritating at first, but he knew what type of expectations Ms. Sullivan had for him so he'd always try his best. When he'd get the answer right it boosted his confidence. He would think to himself, "Maybe I am smart." One day she was teaching one of the toughest lessons of the year.

This was a lesson that everyone struggled with, even some of her smartest students. The way she treated Jason was different. She downplayed the information as if to Jason, it should be easy. Jason felt more pressure than ever to grasp the concept of her lesson but was a little intimidated.

Later that week as she continued to help students with the work, she would look at Jason at times when he seemed to be struggling. "Oh, Jason, stop acting as if you don't understand, stop playing around. I need you to help tutor some of the other students in our class." Jason was flattered. Why was Ms. Sullivan so convinced he was intelligent? Sure Tim was his cousin but that doesn't mean he was capable of the same things.

She expected him to tutor other students and didn't quite understand himself. From that moment on, Jason's attitude and demeanor begin to change. He began to adjust his behavior in a way that fulfilled the expectations Ms. Sullivan had for him. He would provide answers to problems on the board and would surprise himself at how he was able to work out the complicated problems.

It wasn't long before he was helping other students in the class. It felt so good to have somebody believe in him, even when he didn't quite believe in himself. It gave him a reason to believe. Whenever he would sink to his old ways, or downplay his intelligence, Ms. Sullivan would say, "You know better Jason" or "You're so smart stop playing around and get serious."

This did something to him he didn't realize until years later. The expectations and belief she had in him caused him to align his character and work in ways that aligned with her expectations. It was all on the basis of what she expected from him. Jason would end up making an A in the class. He had realized he was smart. He realized that if she had not believed in him, his attitude toward the work wouldn't be good. He would never forget Ms. Sullivan for helping him change his own perception of himself. Had he viewed himself as smarter and expected to be the guy in class who always helped others, he'd have more success.

From that moment on he would never doubt himself or have an attitude that would cause him to underachieve. She taught him how to believe in himself. Many times other people who we respect that have high expectations for us can cause us to perform in ways we wouldn't without that support. You can see how supporting other people or only having expectations can cause them not to want to disappoint. Having expectations for people a lot of times can cause disappointment simply because we have such high hopes for them. In this case, it did wonders for him because he used her motivation to transform his attitude. Some people fail to do this despite being motivated by others which means they simply haven't realized how to use energy to their advantage.

Are you ready to receive?

Many times we find ourselves lusting over particular things that make us feel like our life would be perfect if we had it. Yet, if we aren't truly ready to receive these things then we won't ever see it in our reality. This can be because of our lack of confidence or fear. Why do we say we want things only to turn down those opportunities when they present themselves?

It could be that man that will treat you right or that job opening you've been wanting, or maybe it's that opportunity to speak in front of an audience to promote your ideas. It's as if the universe does its job by bringing you these opportunities, but you won't follow through because you second guess yourself.

You'd be surprised how many people turn down fame, or chances to make money all because they don't want what comes with it. It'll make you question what you really want and at what expense. Some things may not be worth your peace of mind, but if you dedicate your life to something, many will die for it. Regardless of how far you're willing to take it, it is critical to assure you are ready to receive it because it is then when it comes.

CHAPTER 10

Belief

Belief is the only thing that makes anything true. It is said that psychics have a great feel for the energy and the ability to tap into different dimensions. It gives them the ability to see in the future or past. We as humans have powers that we never tap into because of our inability to protect our thoughts, meditate, and keep the body from toxic chemicals.

If you went to see a psychic, you would potentially be inclined to accept whatever fate they foresee upon you. A part of the reason why many of the things they say or predict come true is because of our acceptance of what they've told us. From the moment you leave there, the thought of your future consumes your mind. To the point where eventually it becomes your reality. The belief in those words or predictions made them happen.

I firmly believe in cosmic energy and how we can tap into it for wisdom. I also understand how the mind makes any concept of words come true for you. With that being said, that psychic could be a phony, but if your belief in what they say is strong enough, it will inevitably still come true. People who do hypnosis can program the same reality of others as well. They ask them to close their eyes and begin to speak to their subconscious mind. They could tell them to act a certain way, or make them feel a certain way. Then with a snap of a finger, they may immediately react as if this is true.

It may not be as simple as that, but to give some simple, vivid description, you're in a trans-state, which means you're open to suggestions. When you watch tv, you're somewhat in a trans-state as well, this happens more often then you may think. The point of this is to tap into something deeper than what you're consciously aware of. Like when you bite your nails or when for some reason you are craving a soda, it was really because sublimely an hour ago you saw a commercial showing a soda with bubbles.

It is said that throughout the day we are operating 95% subconsciously and 5% consciously. Which means we are reacting to everything due to formulated habits and learned behavior. I'll put it this way, anything that you don't have to think about doing has entered a deeper part of the brain. It initially was consciously learned, like riding a bike or driving a car.

Your brain picks up on repetition and eventually, you don't have to think about how to do it anymore. That's why we can engage in behaviors without being consciously aware sometimes. It is a gift and a curse being that it allows us to master our craft and focus on other things. When we are doing something for the first time, the brain activity in our head is going crazy. It is picking up on so many subtle things and taking notes on the dopamine that is released when we succeed.

It's almost as if it is downloading this information. When it is fully downloaded, it is your subconscious mind that now reacts in splits of seconds based on cues. Your brain needs about 20% of the body's oxygen. All cells in the body need oxygen, including neurons. You have billions of neurons, so even though the brain weighs only 3 pounds, it uses a lot of energy creating electrical impulses to communicate. It works the same way in regards to our deep inner belief systems.

You can notice a face, a shirt, a smell, or anything and immediately connect it to danger, or a blissful experience based on that stored information. This can be the reason why we may not like someone and can't quite figure out why. We just know we have a bad feeling. That's why intuition is a strong indication of what you should really do. It has some connection to good or bad results, which is the art of human evolution and why we survive in this world.

We store this information subjectively so even if the outcome may be irrational on our end, it is irrelevant to our subconscious mind. That's why belief is ultimately what it comes down to. The amount of studies that have been conducted on two different groups of people dealing with placebos has incredible results. One group is given the real pill that is designed to heal people, and another group is assigned a fake medicine.

Remarkably, a lot of times many of the placebo group participants are healed. This has happened with surgeries as well. Our minds can heal itself through belief, which is connected directly to gene activations. We as humans don't know the genetic codes it takes to heal parts of our body only your genes. When we talk about the law of attraction, it uses the same concepts as prayer. Faith and belief are well known to be enough to work miracles in your life. When we say things to ourselves, whether they be good or bad, it is an indication of what we truly believe about ourselves and what is possible. So it is only right that it comes true. Our subconscious mind doesn't know the difference between these things. It is only marking and storing information based upon how you believe them to be. Throughout history, people have stated many things to be impossible. Then it happened.

Nobody thought it would be possible for people to communicate around the world without any wired connections. Nobody thought anybody could run a mile in under 4 minutes. The list goes on and on. Impossible is only an illusion we deem on ourselves. If our minds can see it, it can be created. If our minds can believe it, the power we truly possess comes forward to make it a physical reality.

This very day, no man can tell you the potential of what your mind can do. The things you are capable of go beyond his very understanding. Look around you. Look at the world and how beautiful it is. Look at how the seasons intelligently interchange based upon universal laws. Look at how nature created you to be a witness of it all. If you understand these laws work the same way in relation to your thoughts and things we attract in our lives, you've become a genius. I am a genius, you are a genius. That isn't even a question at this point. The real question is, do you even believe it?

If someone were to tell you there is no such thing as white or black people, you may think they were crazy. They aren't as crazy as you'd think. We often are quick to call people crazy because we think what we see is real. We think what we see is what everyone sees. This is where we all go wrong. This is where we begin to understand that people are living in different worlds based on how they interpret their surroundings.

Are we oppressed or do we believe we arc oppressed? Surely if you believe this then yes, yes you are. Yea, some people have agendas set out to do things based on their desires and dreams. It could be power, it could be money, it could be anything. We have that same power. Imagine if everybody believed that. There wouldn't be any control over you. The only control someone has over you is to the extent to which you believe in their control.

Don't allow your perception to become a deception. We live our life based on the belief that tyranny exists, or school is the only way to succeed, or certain things aren't possible to happen to us for whatever reason. We don't even question why we believe these things anymore. We just accept it.

I've never looked at perception and how it holds you back like I do now. After years of repetitive information telling me the truth of who we are, my subconscious mind has finally accepted these things as true. I don't question it anymore. If you can't unlearn and relearn information, then you'll never gain the awareness or perception of people who accomplish things and go far in life. This reprogramming of the mind doesn't happen overnight.

We must learn and study this information. It's the most important and life-changing thing you could possibly do. Why do you think none of it is taught in school? Because control is giving you something to believe in, instead of allowing you to create.

The countless examples I portrayed in this book hopefully help you see something you never have seen before, and that's possibility. Take a look at what you believe deep down. Isn't that everything you see in your reality. Isn't that why when someone says something that doesn't match up to that deep belief, you call them crazy or engage in typical arguments? What do you see? That's the beginning of everything.

The beginning of what you create, what you perceive, what you attract, what you fear, your health, your productivity, your doubts, etc... All of these thoughts determine our vibrations. Everything is vibrating, everything is energy. Whatever it is that you want to do, go for it. Remember that possibility lies within the real art of perception.

Millennials

From generation to generation we see the different types of perceptions that formed different styles and trends in particular eras. The 70s, 80s, 90s, and 2000s have all been different in sports, fashion, music, technology, and many other things. It's why we all love talking about how we grew up and what the hottest trends were during that time. It's like that generation's perception of the world will never be truly understood by the ones before or after it. With these new generations come opportunities to change the world in whichever ways they choose.

This power goes beyond hereditary inheritance. Many wish to preserve or keep specific family knowledge and wealth among the few, but the real power always lies with the next generation. To think the people who were before us were faced with the decisions of how this world should work, or who's land is theirs to claim, only shows how power is an illusion. That next generation will grow older and look at the things previous generations dedicated their lives to and may not understand why, or they may question the whole approach to life as we may know it.

They see the world as the potential to be something that generations before them could never quite reach spiritually. They see opportunities to do things that can change the world for the better instead of living passively through the ignorant ways of the ones before them. They think in terms of a bigger picture to life and the inevitability attached to it. Instead of forcing our perception of how the world should operate, we embrace the fact that one day this world will be left for the generations after us.

It reminded me of the great Dalai Lama. He said something interesting on his social media account that created mixed feelings for me. He said, "The young people of this 21st century represent our planet now. They have the ability to bring about change. Even as climate change increases in intensity, they can work together in the spirit of brotherhood and sisterhood to find and share solutions. They are our real hope."

It was as if he'd lost hope in baby boomers and their ways. Now he looks to millennials to save the world from ignorance since we indeed may be our only real hope. It angered me that we now are the only hope. You'd think humans would truly invest in the children, build them up and prepare them in the most dignified ways. Yet, it appears we've only been taken advantage of mentally and financially.

Our ideas and proposals have been shut down continuously because of bigotry. Misunderstood are millennials for not doing what the generations before us have normalized. It's foolish to believe those traditional concepts will always be the best way of life. We have the opportunity to take advantage of technology and change the world. We must not allow ourselves to be held down when all it takes is our desire to make a difference.

All of these words I've written have only made me realize who I am. These words have only been created as a reminder to myself about the nature of who we all are. It reminds me to never forget what I'm capable of. I will always read this book and work on my mental attitude. Finally, I shall take my own advice. I shall look in the mirror. This wasn't a book that was created to inspire others, it was created to inspire myself. Because I genuinely believe if we all decided to do this, we'd immediately see the difference in the world. The way we see and treat people is a reflection of who we are if anything. Before I look to form any judgments, opinions, and beliefs about the world, I must build the highest amount of love for myself.

In the introduction, I mentioned how I didn't know what my full motive for writing this book was. I said how it'd be a journey for the both of us. Well, it certainly was for me. It taught me things about myself. It taught me about my inner thoughts and pure motives. I begin writing this book when I decided that it was what I wanted to do. It was that simple. I left it to my mind to make it come true. Each chapter brought different emotions out of me. Now that I'm here at the end, I think of when I first started and how far I've come. Similarly to life, when we look back we see beauty in the process of growing.

SELECTED BIBLIOGRAPHY

Greene, Robert. The Laws of Human Nature. New York: Penguin, 2018.

Carnegie, Dale. How to Win Friends and Influence People. United Sates: Gallery Books, 2011.

Paine, Thomas. Common Sense, Rights of Man, and other Essential Writings of Thomas Paine. New York: New American Library, 2003.

Zander, Rosamund., and Zander, Benjamin. The Art of Possibility: Transforming Professional and Personal Life. Boston: Harvard Business School Press, 2000.

Brooks, David. The Social Animal: The Hidden Sources of Love, Character, and Achievement. New York: The Random House Publishing Group, 2011.

Goleman, Daniel. Focus: The Hidden Driver of Excellence. New York: HarperCollins Publishers, 2013.

Kiyosaki, Robert. Rich Dad Poor Dad. Arizona: Plata Publishing, LLC, 2017.

Hill, Napoleon. Think And Grow Rich. New York: Penguin Random House LLC, 2016.

Rhoden, William. Forty Million Dollar Slaves: The Rise, Fall, and Redemption of the Black Athlete. New York: Three Rivers Press, 2006.

Dennett, Daniel. Consciousness Explained. New York: Back Bay Books, 1991.

Duhigg, Charles. Smarter Faster Better: The secrets of Productivity in Life and Business. New York: Random House, 2016.

Haycs, Nicky. Understand Psychology: Teach Yourself. Ohio.The McGraw-Hills Companies Inc, 2010.

Printed in the United States
By Bookmasters